ROUTLEDGE LIBRARY EDITIONS: COLONIALISM AND IMPERIALISM

Volume 48

WEST AFRICA

WEST AFRICA

Quest for God and Gold, 1454–1578:
A Survey of the First Century of White Enterprise in West Africa, with Particular Reference to the Achievement of the Portuguese and their Rivalries with other European Powers

JOHN W. BLAKE

LONDON AND NEW YORK

Originally published in 1937 under the title European Beginnings in West Africa 1454–1578

This edition first published in 2023
by Routledge
4 Park Square, Milton Park, Abingdon, Oxon OX14 4RN

and by Routledge
605 Third Avenue, New York, NY 10158

Routledge is an imprint of the Taylor & Francis Group, an informa business

This second edition, revised, enlarged and retitled published in 1977 by Curzon Press Ltd

© 1977 John W. Blake

All rights reserved. No part of this book may be reprinted or reproduced or utilised in any form or by any electronic, mechanical, or other means, now known or hereafter invented, including photocopying and recording, or in any information storage or retrieval system, without permission in writing from the publishers.

Trademark notice: Product or corporate names may be trademarks or registered trademarks, and are used only for identification and explanation without intent to infringe.

British Library Cataloguing in Publication Data
A catalogue record for this book is available from the British Library

ISBN: 978-1-032-41054-8 (Set)
ISBN: 978-1-032-42495-8 (Volume 48) (hbk)
ISBN: 978-1-032-42497-2 (Volume 48) (pbk)
ISBN: 978-1-003-36304-0 (Volume 48) (ebk)

DOI: 10.4324/9781003363040

Publisher's Note
The publisher has gone to great lengths to ensure the quality of this reprint but points out that some imperfections in the original copies may be apparent.

Disclaimer
The publisher has made every effort to trace copyright holders and would welcome correspondence from those they have been unable to trace.

WEST AFRICA
QUEST FOR GOD AND GOLD
1454 - 1578

A survey of the first century of white enterprise in West Africa, with particular reference to the achievement of the Portuguese and their rivalries with other European Powers

JOHN W. BLAKE

CURZON PRESS : LONDON
ROWMAN AND LITTLEFIELD : TOTOWA

Originally published in 1937 under the title
European Beginnings in West Africa 1454–1578

Second edition, revised and enlarged, retitled
West Africa: Quest for God and Gold 1454–1578

1977

Curzon Press Ltd : London and Dublin
and
Rowman and Littlefield : Totowa, NJ, USA

© 1977 John W. Blake

UK 0 7007 0098 6
US 0 87471 965 8

Printed in Great Britain by A. Wheaton & Company, Exeter

To my Wife

CONTENTS

	LIST OF ABBREVIATIONS	ix
	PREFACE	xi
	INTRODUCTION	1
I.	CASTILO-PORTUGUESE RIVALRY IN SENEGAMBIA, 1454–56	16
II.	PORTUGUESE PROGRESS, ESPECIALLY AFTER THE GRANT TO FERNAO GOMES, 1456–75	26
III.	THE CHALLENGE OF CASTILE, 1475–80	41
IV.	THE CONSOLIDATION OF THE PORTUGUESE MONOPOLY, 1480–1530	57
V.	TRADE AND FORTIFICATION IN WEST AFRICA, 1480–1578	79
VI.	FRENCH INTERVENTION IN WEST AFRICA, 1530–53	106
VII.	TRIPLE RIVALRY IN WEST AFRICA, 1553–59	138
VIII.	MONOPOLY ON THE WANE, 1559–78	161
	APPENDIX	193
	BIBLIOGRAPHY	225
	INDEX	238

LIST OF MAPS

I. Part of the Cantino Map, which was sent by Alberto Cantino from Lisbon to Hercule d'Este, Duke of Ferrara, before 19 November 1502. The original may be found in the Biblioteca Estense at Modena . . *facing page* 36
(*By permission of the Trustees of the British Museum*)

II. Section of the undated Map of Luis Teixeira (*c.* 1602?). Copy in the British Library, Maps, 64990 (9). See also A. Z. Cortesão and A. T. da Mota, *Portugaliae Monumenta Cartographia*, iii (1962), 67–9, plate 362, from which this has been reproduced . *facing page* 72

III. Guinea of Cape Verde and the Malagueta Coast. This Map, based on contemporary (late-15th and 16th-century) records, was kindly drawn by Mrs. Shirley Tinkler of the New University of Ulster . . *facing page* 110

IV. The Ivory Coast and the Mina Coast. This Map, based on contemporary (late-15th and 16th-century) records, was kindly drawn by Mrs. Shirley Tinkler of the New University of Ulster . . . . . *facing page* 144

V. The Slave Coast and the Niger Delta. This Map, based on contemporary (late-15th and 16th-century) records, was kindly drawn by Mrs. Shirley Tinkler of the New University of Ulster . . . . . *facing page* 180

ABBREVIATIONS USED IN REFERENCES

A.H.R.	*American Historical Review*, The.
Barros, I. iii. 8	Barros, J. de, *Da Asia*, dec. 1, pt. iii, bk. 8.
Alguns Documentos	Coelho, J. Ramos, *Alguns Documentos do Archivo Nacional da Torre do Tombo acerca das Navegações e Conquistas Portuguezas*.
Davenport	Davenport, F. G., *European treaties bearing on the history of the United States and its Dependencies*.
E.H.R.	*English Historical Review*, The.
Hakluyt	Hakluyt, R., *The Principal Navigations, Voyages, Trafficques and Discoveries of the English Nation*.
Ensaios, II. ii. 3–4	Lopes de Lima, J. J., *Ensaios sobre a statistica das possessões Portuguezes na Africa Occidental e Oriental*, bk. II, pt. ii, pp. 3–4.
Roncière	Roncière, C. B. de la, *Histoire de la marine française*.
Quadro Elementar	Santarem, (Viscount) Barros e Sousa, *Quadro Elementar das relacões politicas e diplomaticas de Portugal com as diversas potencias do mundo*.
Barcellos	Senna Barcellos, C. J. de, *Subsidios para a historia de Cabo Verde e Guiné*.
Viterbo	Sousa Viterbo, F. M. de, *Trabalhos nauticos dos Portuguezes nos seculos XVI e XVII*.

ADDITIONAL ABBREVIATIONS

Ajayi	Ajayi, J. F. A. and Crowder, M. (eds.) *History of West Africa*.
Blake	Blake, John W., *Europeans in West Africa*.
Daaku	Daaku, K. Y., *Trade and politics on the Gold Coast, 1600–1720*.
JAH,ix.4(1968).501–4	*Journal of African History*, vol. ix, no. 4 (London, 1968), pp. 501–4.
JHSN,v.4(1971).406–7	*Journal of the Historical Society of Nigeria*, vol. v, no. 4 (Ibadan, 1971), pp. 406–7.
Rodney	Rodney, W., *History of the Upper Guinea Coast, 1545–1800*.
Ryder	Ryder, A. F. C., *Benin and the Europeans, 1485–1897*.
THSG,ii.2(1956).61–4	*Transactions of the Historical Society of Ghana* (formerly, the Gold Coast and Togoland Historical Society), vol. ii, part 2 (Achimota, or Legon, 1956), pp. 61–4.

PREFACE TO THE SECOND EDITION

'Formerly the Portuguese served for Setting-Dogs to spring the Game, which as soon as they had done, was seiz'd by others'. (*William Bosman*, 1705).

I BEGAN work on the first edition of this book, then titled *European Beginnings in West Africa*, some forty years ago, to be exact, in the autumn of 1933. The book was published in 1937 at a time when nearly all Africa was ruled by European powers. In that imperial age, now fast receding into the forgotten past, if some—a tiny few— were beginning to question the foundations of the colonial era, most Europeans accepted the existing order, uncritically endorsed the view that Africa had benefitted from 'civilisation' and 'christianity', and anticipated no great changes in the foreseeable future. Indeed, the attention of liberal-minded Europeans was not much focussed on Africa, but rather on the growing menace of Adolf Hitler's racist Third Reich. Despite the implications of self-government for India, colonial officials, French and British, Belgian and Portuguese, were largely left alone in Africa to proceed quietly with the numerous tasks before them in the vast territories over which they presided. In 1939, as war clouds gathered over Europe, they "were still congratulating themselves on the completeness of the conquest of Africa, and looked forward to many generations of quiet administration and evolutionary development" (Ajayi, ii.514). This book, then, when written, naturally reflected many of the assumptions of that imperial age when the tide of European rule in Africa still flowed strongly forward. But abruptly, within the span of not much more than one generation, the tide was reversed, and many of the comfortable premises of colonial rule—and of the book—were exposed. Partly as a result of World War II and the relative weakening of

Europe, most of Africa, by now strongly nationalist, rejecting alien ways and alien rule, and proud of its own indigenous culture, recovered its independence. The sixth decade of the twentieth century—the era of the 'wind of change'—was, in this respect, a momentous and memorable one, and a vital part of the dawn of the new age for Africa was the accompanying revolution in African historiography. Already in the late 'forties, a few scholars could begin to sense the shape of things to come. For my part, I remember very well the astonished but delighted reaction of a young Nigerian scholar, Dr. Kenneth A. Dike, to an appeal which I made in March 1949 "for the study of African history mainly through African eyes . . . in language which by its sympathy and emphasis will have meaning, reality and appeal for the African peoples themselves".[1] In such circumstances, it became clear that my book, if it was to have any validity in the post-war world, would need to be revised.

Looking back over the past forty years and having the advantage of hindsight, I think it doubtful whether the book would have been written at all, had I been able to envisage in the middle 'thirties the remarkable progress destined to be made after the war in the study of African history in general and of West African history in particular. Indeed, the 'new view' of the history of the peoples of Africa was partly pioneered in West Africa, notably in the graduate school of history founded and fostered in Ibadan University by that same Dr. Dike to whom I have already referred. Specialised studies about the African past proliferated so fast and on such a scale as to render a comprehensive account of an entire region, such as West Africa from the Senegal to Cape St. Catherine—the geographical limits set, rightly or wrongly, for this book—an almost impossible task. It has certainly now become a formidable and challenging task. One has but to consult, for example, the patient, exact and scholarly writings of Dr. P. E. H. Hair[2], or for that matter the works of many other scholars, to appreciate the very real and nice problems to be met with in the study of the subject. This is, I think, specially true for the scholar who seeks to reconstruct the story of what was happening among the very many different peoples who inhabited West Africa during the sixteenth century. Part of the general story is probably now lost beyond recovery; part can be recovered—and, indeed, is being recovered—by thorough and unrelenting analysis of the extant, written historical sources, fragile

PREFACE

(and often confusing) though they are, and by the collation of this type of evidence with the evidence of oral tradition, archaeological investigation, linguistic studies, etc.

Notwithstanding the implications of this fine new historiography, I think it reasonable to argue that this book was intended to be, and in this new version still is, primarily a survey of the first century of European enterprise—some might prefer the terms 'rivalry' or even 'exploitation'—in West Africa. In this respect, the essential outline of the book, with such modifying additions as are made here to the text in the form of an Appendix—some of these notes regrettably elaborate due to the complexities of current research—can stand. The Index has also been left in its original form. The book is really designed to summarise the achievements of the Portuguese in West Africa during the century following their exploration of its shores, and the successive attempts of rivals—mainly Castilians, Frenchmen and Englishmen—to dispute, if not to destroy, the commercial monopoly claimed by Portugal in West African waters. The book traces the story of how Portugal established her claim to monopoly, and then seeks to show that the challenge of her rivals was aimed at securing a share in the profits of the Guinea trade, profits thought to be enormous and known to be made by the exchange of cheap European (and Indian) goods, such as beads, metalware and cloth, for gold, slaves, ivory, pepper and other, less important, products such as wax and hides. Because this was the theme of the original work, a case can be made for a new and revised edition.

The book can also be justified as having intrinsic value, simply because the 'new view' of African history sees the European impact on Africa as essentially peripheral. The interest of the disciples of the 'new view' has focussed, not much on what the early European explorers, traders and missionaries did or did not do, but rather—and in my opinion rightly—on the story of African peoples and African societies, and on such themes as the rise and fall of the Sudanic empires or the African reaction to European penetration and European rule. The new historiography of Africa, then, has not added very much to our knowledge of the first century of white enterprise in West Africa, except in one important respect which is explained in the next paragraph. So my book, even in its original form, may still have some value.

In the light of the new perspectives on African history, however, the first edition suffered from at least one major defect. This was its failure to deal adequately with the local African societies contacted by the Portuguese, the effects of European activities on these societies, and the reaction of Africans, individually and collectively, to the arrival on the Guinea coast of white explorers, traders, officials and missionaries. Such were the assumptions of the age of colonial rule that this particular weakness in the book, which was rightly criticised on certain other grounds, occasioned no comment from reviewers. As far as I can remember, I was not myself sensitive to this defect, nor were any of the distinguished scholars who taught me and generally advised and guided me in my work. This was at that time less surprising than many of the present generation of Africanists, trained in the new historiography, might imagine. It can be explained, in fact, in terms of the premise, widely accepted and scarcely questioned in Europe on the eve of World War II, that Africa had no history prior to the coming of the Europeans. What is more, even had I possessed the foresight and imagination necessary to enable me to realise and repair what can now be clearly seen as a defect in the book, the source materials then available to me were limited and they had not been subjected to detailed, rigorous and critical scrutiny. The notes in the Appendix to this edition of the book are designed to some degree to remedy this weakness.

It is very different today. The old assumptions have almost gone. The archives of the world in general and of West Africa in particular have been pretty thoroughly combed and screened, and quite a lot of new historical evidence has come to light. The long-known source materials have been critically examined and analysed again and again, so that almost every scrap of relevant evidence has been extracted and interpreted. Beyond that, historians have been able to supplement the written records at their disposal by drawing extensively on the findings of other scholars working in allied fields, such as anthropology, archaeology, oral traditions and linguistics. With old tools sharpened, and applied in new ways and with discreet caution, with new perspectives inspiring new interpretations, and with literally scores of scholars across the world now dedicated to the task of unfolding the past of Africa—in my youth, you could count them almost on the fingers of one hand—the discipline of West African studies prospers and flourishes. However, one result of this is that the study of the Portuguese achievement in Guinea during the fifteenth and sixteenth centuries has become a highly-specialised and very complex function. This being so, the attempt here to bring this book up to date has proved to be a more difficult undertaking than I had expected.

There are in the original version of the book at least three matters of substance, apart from points of detail, which, being in need of revision, merit emphasis here.

Firstly, should any reader care to scrutinise the available record fragments, both those known forty years ago and those found since, he is likely to gain the distinct impression, as I do, that the Portuguese knew more than they disclosed and much more than the records literally suggest. It is a fair guess that the Portuguese were very knowledgeable about conditions in sixteenth-century West Africa, especially about the peoples on the coast and the several branches of trade. It is also a fair guess that they must have been as deeply and continuously involved in complex and delicate negotiations with dozens of African state rulers as we know their Dutch successors were a century later. Year by year, the Portuguese could not have avoided building up and maintaining regular African contacts, frequently sending agents and emissaries along the coasts and into the interior, and cultivating good relations where they could with all those African chiefs, their subjects and the merchants who in one way or another exercised control over the various trades and trade routes. Admittedly, this is no more than a general inference, but it can be substantiated from a growing collection of records, some discovered very recently. Most of the original records—governors' reports, narratives, financial accounts, general correspondence, etc.—have long since disappeared. Much of what is known today, though by no means all, comes to us at second-hand through the accounts of the Portuguese chroniclers, which for various reasons and in varying degrees are somewhat suspect. But here and there among the precious original dcouments that have survived, such as governor Affonso Caldeira's letter from the fortress of São Jorge da Mina to King Manuel of Portugal, written in January 1513 just before he died (Blake, i.112–14), we get a revealing hint of the unknown story which lies behind the ruin of the records.

Part of the new source-material now available to the scholar has been incorporated in the volumes of *Monumenta Missionaria Africana—Africa Ocidental*, edited by Father Antonio Brasio.

These new documents, together with many others found—and still being located—in the archives of Portugal, particularly by Commander A. Teixeira da Mota and his colleagues, are mostly fragments and await rigorous study, analysis and interpretation. Three striking examples of the new evidence may be mentioned here, all found since this book was first written. Thus, we now have the mutilated day-ledger of trade transactions kept by Gonçalo de Campos, the factor of the fortress of São Jorge, which covers the years 1529-31: it was discovered in 1971 by Dr. John Vogt of the University of Georgia, who summarised its contents in the *THSG*, xiv.1 (1973). 93-103. This document is, he writes, apparently the " sole surviving day ledger for São Jorge da Mina during the period of the Portuguese occupation and must be accorded a major find ". Next, there is the exciting and suggestive ' Enquiry ' made in 1499 at the fortress of São Jorge, first listed by Dr. Alan Ryder in the volume of *Materials for West African history in Portuguese archives* (1965), and afterwards analysed by Dr. Vogt in the *THSG*,xv.1(1974,103-10: this concerns the salaries, emoluments and trade privileges of the officers and residents of the fortress, and can be usefully collated with the *regimento* of 1529, which was designed to regulate the conduct and organisation of affairs at São Jorge and was presumably an elaborate revision of earlier instructions.[3] In certain respects, however, possibly the most exciting of all finds relating to the Portuguese achievement in West Africa is the chart of Guinea made by Luis Teixeira and printed in 1602: it contains much interesting material about the Mina coast, derived apparently from a Portuguese mission into the interior of *c.* 1573 (see Cortesão and da Mota, *Portugaliae monumenta geographica*, iii[1962], plate 362). Its location of identifiable African states in the interior behind Mina and its fairly accurate delineation of the course of the Upper Volta river are alike remarkable. The reader may well ask why a journey so far into the interior was made. What a vista of possibilities it opens! But we may never know the full answer, nor precisely where this mission fitted into the calculations of the Portuguese: the full story of their achievement, particularly on the Mina coast, has been largely lost. Indeed, because of the disappearance of the bulk of the day-to-day records of their doings, and despite all the dedicated scholarship which has been given to the study of the Portuguese in sixteenth-century Guinea, we are still very largely only able to draw general but often unproven inferences.[4]

Secondly, as a result of the progress of research, notably the work of such scholars as Dr. P. E. H. Hair and Commander A. Teixeira da Mota, the claim can be made that we now know rather more about the coastal peoples with whom the Portuguese made contact and a little more about some of the peoples of the interior. The names given to the different peoples of Guinea by such contemporary writers as Duarte Pacheco Pereira and Valentim Fernandes, have been rigorously scrutinised and in many instances these peoples or tribes have been successfully identified. This has been done, not just by the patient and systematic analysis of all available written evidence (chronicles, narratives, administrative records, maps, charts, etc., both printed and in manuscript), but also by checking the results with other types of evidence, notably the study of languages. This being so, the chapters in this edition of this book which deal more particularly with local conditions in West Africa (e.g., chapter V on ' Trade and Fortification ') will be found to contain rather more annotated revision than the parts concerned with international rivalry. Thus, a major amendment of this kind relates to the story of the invasion of Sierra Leone by the warring peoples called the Manes. New note 38 corrects and supersedes the account of this episode given in the first edition of the book. In this context, too, another important conclusion about the peoples of West Africa emerges from modern studies: it is that there has been much more continuity in the location of the coastal peoples of Guinea than was formerly supposed. Dr. Hair has put the point cautiously but decisively:

> If we ... compare the ethnolinguistic inventory of today with that of the period before 1700, we find a striking continuity. In the particulars compared, the ethnolinguistic units of the Guinea coast have remained very much the same for three, four or five centuries (the period depending on the date of the earliest documentation). This continuity is striking because it contrasts with the impression of wholesale disturbance, and hence discontinuity, given in the standard history texts ... or in the oral traditions (see P. E. H. Hair, ' Ethnolinguistic continuity on the Guinea coast ' in *JAH*, viii.2[1967].247).

Thirdly, it is now clear that African resistance to European penetration in Guinea was strong, persistent and relatively successful. The reluctance of Caramansa, local ruler of Fetu, to agree to the request of Diogo d'Azambuja in 1482 to build a Portuguese fortress at Mina, if an outstanding example of the African reaction to white pressure, is only one of many. Despite the technological superiority of the Portuguese, they were generally unable to impose their rule firmly over the Africans on the Guinea coast, even along the Mina coast which, as the main source of the gold they wanted, was so important to them. Except within and around their forts and strong points, they did not succeed in substantiating their claim to conquest. Their regime was uncertain and vulnerable. It became more so, when it was challenged in the middle years of the sixteenth century by other white peoples (French and English). There developed a fluid and changing situation everywhere along the coast, which the shrewd Africans exploited to the full; and this circumstance allowed them to re-assert themselves, to drive harder bargains with the Europeans, and to preserve intact their independence. It was not that they did not welcome the arrival of European traders, first the Portuguese and then the white rivals of the Portuguese; on the contrary, the strangers from the sea were encouraged to come because they brought many goods which were useful. But they disliked the use of force by the whites; many of them, particularly in the earlier decades of contact, strongly objected to slave raiding, though the Oba of Benin and the Dyula merchants on the Mina coast at the turn of the fifteenth century were clearly not embarrassed, the one to sell and the others to buy slaves, always provided this limited slave trade was properly regulated; they seem to have resented initial Portuguese attempts to wrest from them the local, coastal, carrying trade; they successfully resisted all efforts by the white traders to secure a share in the profits of trade along the routes into the interior, save for the limited activities of white and half-caste *lançados* in Upper Guinea; they persistently and entirely excluded white men from the gold-bearing regions of Ashanti, the middle Black Volta, Bambuk and Bure; and, with the exception of the Mina Blacks, they always opposed all forms of European domination. Thus, along the Gold Coast, an area where antagonisms were sharp, the Fantyn peoples remained sovereign in nearly all their towns and villages, in spite of ruthless efforts by the Portuguese to subdue them. Indeed, it is argued by some scholars that one of the effects of the escalation of trade, consequent upon the arrival of the whites, was to stimulate urbanisation along the Mina coast, to add to the wealth of Fantyn rulers (for the chiefs seem to have kept the profits of the trade in their own hands), and thereby to augment the resources at their disposal to resist subjugation. Caramansa put the African point of view nicely in 1482:

'... [If d'Azambuja built a fortress in Mina], quarrels and passions might arise between them all; he asked him, therefore, to be pleased to depart, and to allow the ships to come in the future as they had in the past, so that there would always be peace and concord between them. Friends who met occasionally remained better friends than if they were neighbours, on account of the nature of the human heart—for it resembled the waves of the sea, which, breaking upon a rock barring their path, were tossed up to the sky, so that a double mischief was done, the sea being churned to fury, and the rock, its neighbour, being damaged. He did not speak thus to disobey the commands of the King of Portugal, but for the benefit of peace and the trade he desired to have with those who might come to that port ' (Barros, *Da Asia*, dec.i, bk.3, ch.1).

His warning was disregarded.

One additional and general point may be made. In view of the failure of the Portuguese to occupy and effectively dominate and control the lands they had discovered, it may appear remarkable that they somehow held on to their monopoly of the Guinea trade for so long. Despite the hammering which they experienced in the mid-sixteenth century, particularly on the Gold Coast, from the French and the English, they seem to have repaired their fortunes, at least in part; and thereafter for most of another fifty years their special position of ascendancy, not least in the gold trade of Mina, was not seriously challenged by envious white rivals, that is, not until the onslaught of the Dutch. It is clear from the records that they strongly reinforced the naval defences off the Mina coast in the middle 'sixties; and it would seem that the principal reason why their most dangerous rivals, the English, abandoned the Mina gold trade after 1566 was because it had become too hazardous and therefore not profitable. In other words, if Portuguese diplomatic pressure from Lisbon on London (and also Paris) proved relatively ineffectual, superior firepower in West African waters temporarily restored to Portugal her former ascendancy. It would seem, too, that the Spanish conquest of Portugal in 1580, traditionally linked with the weakening of Portuguese power in West Africa, did not have this result. On the contrary, King Philip II of Spain gave full support to Portuguese efforts to maintain their position on the Gold Coast (see new note 54); and it is surely significant that the Dutch were not able to capture the fortress of São Jorge until 1637.

The reader will observe that, in this edition of the book, the device of additional notes has been used in the attempt to adjust perspectives and to show where recent research has advanced our knowledge of the subject. Otherwise, the original text of the book has been allowed to stand except that minor errors throughout have been corrected in the page. On many pages, however, the reader will come across numerals (1, or 22, etc.) placed on the outside margins. These are numbered references to the new set of notes which are given at the end under 'Appendix to the Second Edition'. As indicated above, they are designed, where it seemed desirable or appropriate, to correct errors in the first edition, to draw attention to recent or current research, and to guide the reader to the book, periodical or record from which the new material is derived. I do not think it an exaggeration, however, to warn that the current output of historical scholarship in this field is so great that not more than a bare summary of what is now known can be contained within the compass of a single volume. The method used here for this edition of my book was thought to be a possible solution to an almost intractable problem. In addition, new—and, I hope, more accurate—maps have been included. Beyond that, a few of the more useful books which have appeared since the first edition have also been added to the bibliography. It is a highly selective list and no more. Lastly, allow me to say that errors in the new edition are entirely my responsibility.

JOHN W. BLAKE.

Limavady, N.I.
1977

NOTES

[1] See John W. Blake, 'The study of African history' in *Transactions of the Royal Historical Society*, 4th ser., vol. xxxii (1950), pp. 49–69.

[2] Dr. P. E. H. Hair, in a series of articles, has examined nearly all, if not all, of the known written records of the Guinea coast, with a view primarily to the sixteenth-century identification of the various peoples on the coast, their locations and their movements. His main conclusion confirms what I have long suspected, namely, that there has been more continuity in the tribal locations along the Guinea coast than oral traditions about past migrations suggest. Among his many scholarly contributions to the study of the subject, the more important include: 'Ethnolinguistic continuity on the Guinea coast' in *JAH*, viii.2(1967),247–68; 'An ethnolinguistic inventory of the Upper Guinea coast before 1700' in *African Languages Review*, vi(1967), 32–70; and 'An ethnolinguistic inventory of the Lower Guinea coast before 1700' in *Ibid.*, part I in vii(1968),47–73, and part II in viii(1969),225–56.

[3] This *regimento* was printed in full by Dr. Jorge Faro in three articles in the *Boletim Cultural da Guiné Portuguesa*, xii(1957),386–442, and xiii(1958), 75–108, 305–63.

[4] Here it is fitting to report that Commander A. Teixeira da Mota has been engaged since 1963 in a thorough search of the Portuguese archives with the object of listing all records relating to the region from Arguin to São Thomé of the period from the mid-fifteenth to the mid-seventeenth century. It is evident from samples of his finds, which he has kindly allowed me to see, that valuable new insights on the Portuguese achievement in Guinea will be possible when these records are published, as is planned, under the title *Os Portugueses na Guiné*. Scholars will look forward to the completion of this monumental task.

INTRODUCTION

WE may trace the roots of white enterprise in West Africa to the Iberian political situation in the early middle fifteenth century. At that time, the peninsula presented a curious spectacle. There were four christian states, Portugal, Castile, Aragon and Navarre, each of which, though it might cherish the crusading ideal, was unwilling to sacrifice its hard-earned independence upon the altar of unity. After nearly seven centuries of war against the Moors, the inhabitants of these states had developed at least a strong sense of provincial patriotism and by 1450, they had managed to pen back their muslim enemies in the single province of Granada. A long siege began of this last refuge of Islam in western Europe. Granada was already surrounded on land. It remained to complete the encirclement by sea, to interrupt supplies sent by the Moors of North Africa to their friends in Spain and to clear the Moroccan ports of those heathen pirates, who troubled christian shipping. These objects could best be realised by the occupation of the African mainland. It was a natural step, then, for one of the christian powers to transfer the campaign to Africa.

Portugal, in fact, played that rôle when, in 1415, she occupied Ceuta. In view of her situation this was a remarkable achievement. Her population of scarcely one and a half millions was comparatively poor ; her manufactures were negligible ; she was exhausted by war against Castile in defence of her frontiers ; her unity was endangered by the power of the feudal grandees ; and, geographically, she was partially cut off from the main stream of European development. Recently, however, her dignity and prestige had been enormously enhanced, not only by the glorious victory of Aljubarrota which had saved her from bondage to Castile, but also by the accession to her throne of the dynasty of Aviz (1385). This House ruled Portugal for well-nigh two centuries—the greatest period in the history of that country. Its first member was King John I and, among his lasting bequests to his people, was the policy of expansion in northern Africa. It was he who inspired the capture of Ceuta.

The other three christian states did not take so keen an interest in the African coast. Navarre regarded the Pyrenees and southern France as her natural field for expansion. Aragon and Castile were sea-powers: of this the maritime activities of the Catalans and the Andalusians provided ample testimony; but circumstances decreed that neither should anticipate Portugal in Africa. It so happened that the gaze of Aragon was fixed mainly upon Naples and Sicily, while Castile, for her part, was hardly likely to operate in Africa on a large scale as long as Moors remained on Spanish soil in Granada. Not that Castile lacked the will to overseas expansion; the merchants and seamen of Palos, Seville and Cadiz were fully alive to the commercial prospects of such lands as might be discovered. When, subsequently, they heard of the Portuguese trade with Guinea, they did not hesitate to brave the elements of the " Ocean Sea " beyond the Straits of Gibraltar, and some of the bolder spirits among them actually made their way south as far as the river Senegal. But their rulers did not encourage such efforts. The House of Trastamara projected no ' Greater Castile ' like Prince Henry's conception of a ' Greater Portugal '. Indeed, the court of Valladolid did not give a lead in colonial matters until the dynastic union of the kingdoms of Castile and Aragon. When, with the marriage of Ferdinand and Isabella, this was consummated, a new phase began in Castilian maritime enterprise. Hitherto the court had practically ignored the feeble efforts of the Andalusians; yet afterwards, in the war between Portugal and Castile, the catholic sovereigns advanced public and national claims to Guinea, and Portugal found her position in the newly discovered lands seriously threatened by a powerful rival.

Before passing to the Portuguese voyages, a word may be said about a disputed French claim to the honour of prior discovery in Guinea. The nature of the French claim, as expounded by Nicholas Villaut in 1669, was briefly as follows: two French ships sailed from Dieppe to the Rio Fresco, just south of Cape Verde, and thence to the Rio dos Sestos, as early as the winter of 1364-5. The success of this venture led to other

INTRODUCTION

voyages, in which the merchants of Rouen as well as those of Dieppe were interested. Trade was opened up with the modern Grain and Gold Coasts and, in 1382, a fort was built on the site of the later castle of São Jorge da Mina. Various key trading points around the coast received French names, like the Rio Fresco, which was called the Bay of France, and the Rio dos Sestos which was termed Petite Dieppe. Unfortunately, civil war in France withdrew attention from this lucrative traffic so that, after 1410, it was abandoned.[1]

Although many later French writers accepted this story, modern opinion regards it as a fabrication. An erudite and scholarly Portuguese historian, the second Viscount de Santarem, challenged and really shattered the French assertion a century ago, but the controversy dragged on until M. Charles Bourel de la Roncière finally disposed of it.[2] Criticism of the claim has been directed mainly to the absence of contemporary evidence. Admittedly, as the French claimed, the bombardment of Dieppe in 1694 may have destroyed valuable records. But, if that be so, why do Portuguese and Castilian chronicles contain no references to the alleged voyages, and why do all other contemporary manuscript records reveal no trace of them ? Why, too, did Jean Barbot, soon after the claim was first advanced, question its validity ?[3] And, finally, why was it that no maps or charts of the Guinea Coast were available to assist the Portuguese explorers when they first began the work of discovery ? There are other questions like these which, if the French claim be accepted, do not offer easy solution.[4] Nowadays therefore, the view generally taken is that the French government, after the accession of Louis XIV, desiring to provide an historical justification for its territorial claims in West Africa, invented the whole story.

Setting aside the French claim, then, we may return to the Portuguese occupation of Ceuta, for this success led directly to the attempt to find Guinea. Prince Henry, third son of John I, was present at the siege and, while there, he heard allur-

[1] N. Villaut, *Relation des costes d'Afrique*, pp. 409–30.
[2] Santarem, *Recherches sur la priorité de la découverte . . au delà du Cap Bojador, passim* ; C. de la Roncière, *La Découverte de l'Afrique au Moyen Age*.
[3] J. Barbot, *Description of Guinea*, pp. 9–10.
[4] e.g. The nomenclature of sixteenth-century French maps of West Africa is, without exception, copied from Portuguese maps.

ing tales from the Arabs about the gold of Timbuktu beyond the Sahara Desert.[1] In the Middle Ages there was no direct commerce between Europe and West Africa, but Arab intermediaries were responsible for a flourishing trade. The domination of the entire north coast of Africa by the Moors completely cut off Europe from Guinea. Even so, occasional rumours filtered through the Moroccan ports regarding the land of 'Bilad Ghana'. It was said that beyond the Sahara was a mighty river, the Western Nile, and on the south side of this dwelt a black race of people. The Arabs bought gold from these people, transported it by caravan across the desert and sold it for distribution in Europe to Jewish merchants of the island of Majorca.[2] Stories which trickled into Europe, about the land of the black people, were extremely vague and inaccurate, and little could be done to clarify them by consulting contemporary works of geography. Three of the most celebrated Arab geographers, Albirouni, Edrisi and Ibn Said, while they furnished a full catalogue of all the places north of the great river, knew nothing of the region beyond, and made no distinction between the Senegal, the Niger and the Nile.[3] This vagueness, however, inspired rather than killed interest in the subject, so that Prince Henry's contact with the Moors at Ceuta led directly to the era of Portuguese expansion.

It is not easy to determine Henry's chief reason for seeking the land of which he had heard. Many believe that the crusading motive was uppermost in his mind : the prince, crusader rather than navigator, hoped to evangelise the negroes, to effect a union with the fabled christian prince, Prester John, and with his aid, to assault the Infidels of North Africa simultaneously in front and rear.[4] Others hold that the prince was interested primarily in geographical discovery for its own sake, while some go so far as to maintain that his ultimate aim was to open the sea-route to the East Indies. But the view, which is now gaining ground, makes commercial enterprise the chief

---

[1] C. R. Beazley and E. Prestage, *The Chronicle of the Discovery and Conquest of Guinea* (Hakluyt Society, 1899), ii, iv.
[2] Roncière, *La Découverte de l'Afrique au Moyen Age*, i. 71–108, *passim* ; *Cambridge Modern History*, i. ch. i.
[3] Roncière, *op. cit.*, i. 129.
[4] C. R. Beazley, " Prince Henry of Portugal and the African Crusade of the Fifteenth Century " (*A.H.R.*, xvi. 11–23).

INTRODUCTION

factor : Henry was spurred on by the desire to reach the gold mart of Timbuktu.[1]

One of the difficulties with which the champions of this view have to contend is the poverty of confirmatory evidence. Thus, Azurara, who has left us the most complete chronicle of the discovery of Guinea, in a chapter devoted solely to Prince Henry's motives, makes no mention whatsoever of gold.[2] Yet, elsewhere, there are two references to the prince's desire to promote trade with Guinea. Diogo Gomes, who took part in the discoveries under the inspiration of the prince, relates that when Henry heard of the gold, for which the Carthaginians had once bartered at Timbuktu and Cantor, " he bade [Gonçalo Velho] seek those lands by sea in order to traffic with them ".[3] Duarte Pacheco Pereira, the celebrated Portuguese captain who lived a generation later, records how " the prince was informed . . . that in those lands much gold and other merchandise were to be found ".[4] This evidence, scanty though it be, is probably more valuable, and presents a truer picture, than that of papal bulls and contemporary chronicles. Papal bulls naturally referred to the work of evangelisation, while contemporary chronicles, being laudatory in character, credited the prince with nobler motives than the desire for trade. It is probably true that all the motives set out above, with the exception of the wish to find a sea-route to the East Indies, influenced Henry the Navigator. We may conclude, however, that his chief object was to bring gold back by the direct sea passage from Guinea to Portugal.

Once Ceuta was occupied, he did all in his power to foster exploration. His seamen advanced very slowly, and nineteen years passed before Gil Eannes rounded the dreaded Cape Bojador. In 1441 Antam Gonçalves brought back to Lisbon the first cargo of slaves and gold. This was an event of considerable importance because many, with whom the work of discovery had hitherto been unpopular, now saw a chance of making profits. So more voyages were undertaken and swifter progress

---

[1] J. Bensaude, *Lacunes et Surprises de l'Histoire des Découvertes Maritimes*, pt. i, pp. 256–70 ; Hedwig M. A. Fitzler, " Portuguiesische Handelsgesellschaften des 15 und beginnenden 16. Jahrhunderts " (*Viertel jahrschrift für Sozial-und Wirtschaftsgeschichte*, xxv. 229).

[2] G. E. Azurara, *Chronica de Guiné*, ch. vii.

[3] Diogo Gomes, *De prima inventione Guineae* (ed. by Dr. Schmeller), p. 19.

[4] Pacheco, I. xxii.

made, with the result that, before the prince died, the Cape Verde Islands and the coast of all Guinea as far as Sierra Leone had been found. In the island of Arguin, where the Lagos company established a factory and built a fort, a flourishing trade in gold, slaves, ostrich feathers, amber and gum was opened up, and profits soon began to flow into the coffers of Portugal. Both government and people tried to conceal from the rest of Europe the news of their commercial enterprises but in vain, for widespread attention was aroused. Andalusian seamen were the first to try to probe the Portuguese secrets, and the result was half a century of colonial rivalry between Portugal and Castile. If we care to go back to that fifteenth-century struggle, we shall find associated with it the earliest features of European enterprise in West Africa.

When the bold sailors of Lisbon and Lagos gazed wonderingly upon the land of Guinea, they must have experienced many a rude shock. Their forefathers had thought of ancient ' Ghana ' as a vague inland kingdom centred about the western branch of the Nile, with the rich mysterious city of Timbuktu as its great commercial emporium. " Called by our merchants ' Gheneoa '," wrote the Moor, Leo Africanus, " . . . this kingdom extends on the river Niger about 250 leagues."[1] But now, as their caravels ran forward before the wind, following the sinuous coast of West Africa, though they found numberless small and hostile tribes, Timbuktu remained as elusive as ever. Accordingly, they broke away from the medieval tradition and gave the name of ' Guinea ' to the whole littoral from the river Senegal to the kingdom of Manicongo north of modern Angola. In Portuguese writings this new connotation for ' Guinea ' was preserved, but the word was sometimes used with a different meaning. After 1466 the Cape Verde islanders were granted the privilege to trade with the mainland from Senegal to Sierra Leone, and the custom sprang up of referring to this strip of coast as simply ' Guinea of Cape Verde ', or ' Guinea '. Thus, we find the name used to distinguish this more restricted region from other parts, like Malagueta, Mina and São Thomé, whose significance we shall later explain. Yet again, as if to add another complication, Duarte Pacheco Pereira thought of ' Guinea '

---

[1] Roncière, *La Découverte de l'Afrique au Moyen Age*, i. 135.

INTRODUCTION

as the whole region from the Senegal to the Cape of Good Hope ! It seems, then, that the Lusitanians used this name in both a special and a general sense.

We shall try to avoid confusion by accepting as our geographical limits the coast from the Senegal river to Cape St. Catherine. Although a few bold Portuguese penetrated inland, European enterprise scarcely affected the interior until long after the sixteenth century. Therefore, the story of the inland plateau will not interest us. On the other hand, the history of the many islands around the West African coast is closely bound up with that of the mainland. Of these, the most important were the Cape Verde group and the four largest islands in the heart of the Gulf of Guinea, São Thomé, O Principe, Annobon and Fernando Po. The nature of white enterprise on land was largely controlled by maritime factors and this, naturally, enhanced the importance of the islands. Moreover, in a commercial sense, the island of São Thomé and the coastal region beyond the modern Gold Coast were inseparable, as were the Cape Verde Islands and the mainland opposite them. The Portuguese discoverers colonised the larger islands and used them as bases for enterprise on the mainland.

It is not easy, so scanty are the records, to reconstruct West Africa as the Portuguese found it. They soon learned that, though the natives and the geographical environment varied very much, the same kinds of merchandise could be obtained along the entire coast from Senegal to Sierra Leone. Some of them settled in Santiago Island and traded along the mainland. They came, thus, to discern a unity in ' Guinea of Cape Verde ' or, as we shall sometimes call it, Upper Guinea. Sailing forward, they first looked upon the land of Senegambia, bounded on the north by the river Senegal and on the south by the river Gambia. An Arab people, the dark Azenegues, inhabited the region north of the Senegal, but to the south was the first true negro kingdom where lived the Jalofos, whose black skin distinguished them sharply from the tawny Arabs of the Barbary Coast.[1] The white discoverers learned, too, that away in the interior dwelt a mighty king named Mandimansa,[2] who

---

[1] Barros, I. iii. 8 ; Pacheco, I. xxvii.
[2] Barros, I. iii. 12.

may have been the ruler of the empire of Melli.¹ Many of the coast tribes were his subjects, but little was known about him. Occasionally the Portuguese attempted to get in touch with him, but no permanent contact was ever organised.² The kingdom of Jalofo, however, was quite well known to the Portuguese. It does not seem to have been a political unit. There were a large number of small potentates, each the lord of a tribe, like the subjects of King Boudomel, and like the Barbacini and the Serreri, who were perpetually at war one with another.³ Nor were the Jalofos a very rich people. Yet they gave the Portuguese a fair welcome, so that treaties were made and a flourishing trade developed between blacks and whites.⁴

The Mandiguas lived south of the Gambia, a powerful people and less easy to deal with because of native wars. They seem to have controlled the navigation of the upper reaches of the river Gambia where, at Setuku in the land of Cantor, they held a great fair once a year, and the smaller tribes, who lived in the river valleys further south, acknowledged their suzerainty. These subject tribes, the Beafares and the Guoguoliis, inhabited the land around the valley of the Rio Grande and as far south as the Cabo da Verga. The Portuguese found that they could trade with them as they did with the Naluns, the Teymenes, who resided beyond the Cabo da Verga, and the Bouloees of Sierra Leone.⁵

All these tribes, from the Senegal southwards, were apparently confined to the coast. In the interior dwelt others about whom the Portuguese heard and wrote little. Pacheco and Alvise Cadamosto, the Venetian traveller who visited Guinea in 1455–7, collected a few scraps of information about Jenni, Melli and Timbuktu, and their records may be correlated with that of Leo Africanus. But they have handed down a meagre portion. Perhaps, by way of illustration, we may be permitted to quote from the *Esmeraldo de Situ Orbis*, compiled by Pacheco:

"We know that the [Senegal] flows out of a mighty lake of the river Nile, thirty leagues long and ten wide, ... and at the

---

¹ " Navigatione di M. Alvise da Cadamosto " (G. B. Ramusio, *Navigationi et Viaggi*, i. 104–18).
² Barros, I. iii. 12 ; Viterbo, i. 305.
³ Ramusio, *op. cit.*, i. 114 ; Pacheco, I. xxvii.
⁴ Barros, I. iii. 1; I. iii. 12.
⁵ Pacheco, I. xxix–xxxiii. I have preserved Pacheco's spelling 'Mandiguas' for 'Mandingas.'

INTRODUCTION

head of the lake there is a kingdom which is called Tabucutu, which has a great city of the same name joined with the same lake. The city of Jany is that way, peopled by negroes, a city which is encircled by a wall of mud, and there are very rich stores of gold in it. Copper, tin, salt and red and blue cloths are very highly valued there, and all are sold by weight except the cloths. Furthermore, clove pepper, yellow pepper, fine silks and sugar are also valued highly, and the trade of that land is very great. . . ."[1]

It is plain that Pacheco, relying upon second-hand information, believed in the existence of a great interior lake from which flowed two mighty rivers, the Nile eastwards and the Senegal westwards. He and his contemporaries were even vaguer about the other inland kingdoms. The empires of Timbuktu, Jenni and Melli fascinated them because of the reports of their wealth, but the smaller kingdoms did not interest them much. It would seem that behind the Guoguoliis lived a tribe called the Jaalunguas and behind the Bouloees, the Souzos.[2]

The Portuguese found a large number of petty negro kingdoms along the coast beyond Sierra Leone just as in Upper Guinea. But the regional names, which they applied, were derived from the names of the most plentiful articles of trade, gold, ivory, malagueta pepper and slaves.

The Malagueta coast acquired its name early. Eustache de la Fosse, a Fleming, refers to the ' Manigette Coast ' which he had navigated in 1480 ;[3] the *Journal* of Columbus mentions ' la costa de la manegueta ' which the famous Genoese explorer visited ;[4] while the term ' Malagueta ' is frequently used by Pacheco to describe the district where a species of pepper of the same name was gathered in abundance. All through the reign of King John III of Portugal, Portuguese and French writers continued to use the same word to designate the stretch of shore from Sierra Leone to Cape Palmas. In the middle of the sixteenth century, however, English corsairs began to refer to malagueta pepper as Guinea grains, and so the fashion arose of describing Malagueta as the Grain Coast. The Portuguese did not abandon their term, but most seventeenth-

[1] *Ibid.*, I. xxvii.
[2] *Ibid.*, I. xxxii–xxxiii.
[3] Eustache de la Fosse, " Voyage " (*Revue hispanique*, 1897, pp. 174-201).
[4] H. Vignaud, *Histoire Critique de la Grande Entreprise de Christophe Colomb*, i. 52.

century writers generally used the later name. The native tribes of this region were, apparently, less approachable than those of Senegambia, for the Lusitanians never had any intercourse with them beyond the bare necessities of trade. The Bouloees, to whom Pacheco alludes, inhabited the coast as far east as the Cape of Saint Anna, but they were less civilised than their tribal relations of Sierra Leone.[1] Probably these negroes were wilder because of the geographical fact that no good harbours, few rivers and a dangerous foreshore rendered impossible a very close contact between whites and blacks.

The modern Ivory Coast, running from Cape Palmas almost to Cape Threepoints, was as difficult to approach as Malagueta. Here the natives, like the Beiçudos, were treacherous and wild, yet they offered an abundance of elephants' tusks to the Portuguese traders. This commodity gave its name to the region, but not until the second half of the sixteenth century, when French interlopers began to refer to it as the Tooth Coast (*Coste des Dents*).[2] It would seem, so far as records tell, that the Portuguese did not often distinguish between the modern Grain and Ivory Coasts. They generally used only one word, Malagueta, for both regions. This was not always the case, for Pacheco states categorically that the Malagueta coast ended at Cape Palmas.[3] Still, during their frequent negotiations with foreign powers, the Portuguese always referred to Malagueta as though it included the Ivory Coast.

Ten years after discovering Sierra Leone, the Portuguese reached the Gold Coast. At first they called it " the trade of gold "[4] or " the mine of gold,"[5] but later they generally spoke of ' the Mine ' or ' Mina '. Mina included the whole region where gold could be bartered for in great quantities : it consisted of a littoral belt, about 160 miles in length, mainly on the east side of Cape Threepoints but extending as far west as Axem. Soon after its discovery, the white traders built on this gold-bearing coast a great castle which they called *São Jorge da Mina*, or ' Saint George of the Mine '. They had not, in fact, found a gold mine, though they had tried for half a

---

[1] Pacheco, II. i.
[2] P. D. Marees, *Bescryvinge van het Gout-custe*, p. 15.
[3] Pacheco, II. iii.
[4] " *O resgate do ouro.*"
[5] " *A mina do ouro.*"

INTRODUCTION

century. The wish was father to the thought when they named the new land, but the much greater abundance of gold did suggest that they were very near to its ultimate source.

The Portuguese do not tell us much about the tribes whom they found living along this coast. However, a comparison of contemporary records with later descriptions of the Gold Coast suggests that, during the intervening period, the political situation did not change much. Duarte Pacheco Pereira, in his *Esmeraldo*, mentions four negro villages, which Jean Barbot long afterwards described: Samma, Great Fante, Little Fante and Little Sabou.[1] Moreover, at least two of the tribes, which dwelt behind the castle of São Jorge in the seventeenth century, the Fetu and the Comani, were living there in 1503.[2] The first discoverers, like the white traders who came after them, noted the business acumen of the negroes, their treachery, their proneness to war and the fact that most of them lived by fishing off the coast in their *almadias*, or canoes.[3] They also knew that the merchants, who sold the gold, brought it to the coast from the interior and sometimes found it difficult to persuade the coast tribes to give them through passage down to the shore. These examples indicate that conditions, like those existing when Barbot wrote, prevailed in the fifteenth century. He found a large number of small, warring tribes upon the Gold Coast at the end of the seventeenth century. We may conclude, then, that a similar situation obtained, when the Portuguese first visited Mina.

The Portuguese used no special term for the modern Slave Coast beyond Mina. It is true that one of the rivers of this part of Guinea was known as the Rio dos Escravos (River of the Slaves), and that, during the early sixteenth century, the Portuguese pursued a considerable traffic in slaves there. But, when speaking of this region, they were wont to refer to individual native kingdoms, like Benin, or to " the five rivers beyond the castle of São Jorge da Mina ".[4] They were familiar with the coastal navigation, but they knew practically nothing

---

[1] Pacheco, II. vi ; J. Barbot, *Description of Guinea*, bk. III, chs. iii, ix, *passim*.
[2] Bosman, *A new and accurate description of the Coast of Guinea*, p. 46 ; *Alguns Documentos*, pp. 133-4.
[3] Pacheco, *passim* ; Ruy de Pina, *Chronica del Rey d. Joao II*, ch. xl.
[4] *Ensaios*, II. ii. 3-4.

of the interior, not realising, for example, that the rivers which flowed into the Bight of Benin were distributaries of the Niger. Some of them visited the capital city of the kingdom of Benin. Thus, Pacheco records that he was in that city four times,[1] and tells us of its port, Gató. He, like others, heard also of a mighty interior empire whose sovereign, the Ogané, wielded an extensive hegemony and, furthermore, he supposed the Ogané might be Prester John. The coast tribes, all of whom the Portuguese called Jos, were semi-cannibals and always at war, especially those who lived in a big village at the mouth of the Rio Real —one of the " five rivers "—and who possessed the largest *almadias*, some of which would hold as many as eighty warriors.[2] The Jos negroes also inhabited the coast around the Bight of Biafra and were found as far south as Cape St. Catherine. With this region, however, the Portuguese had contact only as traders. There was commerce to be had at both Gabun and the Rio dos Camarões, but the Lusitanians, finding the negroes very treacherous, had ventured to neither place up to the time when Pacheco wrote his great book.[3] Generally speaking, then, the whites were very ignorant of this last section of Guinea.

The unusual physical and climatic conditions of Guinea amazed the Portuguese as much as the habits, customs and tribal organisation of the negroes and the commercial prospects of that coast. They found that certain geographical peculiarities of the country seriously restricted the nature of their activities. Firstly, white penetration into the interior was exceedingly difficult. A belt of dense tropical forest hindered land journeys up-country. This belt, which ran almost parallel to the coast, sometimes touching it, as at Benin, and sometimes stretching inland sixty miles and more, was terminated on its north and north-eastern side by a high plateau. The rivers were no easier to negotiate. Few of them, as the *Esmeraldo* shows, were navigable at the mouth, while further up-stream most were impassable by reason of swift currents and cataracts where they fell from the level of the interior plateau to that of the low-lying forest belt.

[1] Pacheco, II. vii.
[2] *Ibid.*, II. viii–ix.
[3] *Ibid.*, II. x.

Secondly, experience taught the whites that they could trade only during the so-called Guinea season. Traffic in West Africa was practically confined to the northern winter because heavy tropical rains, a humid atmosphere and terrific heat, from May or June to September, made life, let alone the pursuit of trade, barely possible for white men during those months. Consequently, ships, which engaged in the traffic, made the out-journey generally between September and January, and the return journey before or in May. The Portuguese soon learned these vital facts, doubtless by dire experience. Their annual fleets to Malagueta and Mina, therefore, sailed regularly from Portugal in the autumn: indeed, as we shall see, their ships were later forbidden to go to Guinea or São Thomé except between August and March.[1] Nor were their sixteenth-century rivals, French, English and Netherlanders, slow to discover the rules: their illegal voyages were made nearly always in the winter. The result was that the later struggles in Guinea between the Portuguese and the interlopers generally took place also in the winter. The northern summer was a time of little or no trade and of peace between the rival powers.

In the third place, the Portuguese had to contend with peculiar navigational difficulties both on the ocean voyage and on the Guinea Coast itself. A gentle current, flowing from southern Portugal to the Canary Islands and so to Cape Verde, together with the prevailing north-east trade winds, helped their caravels on the first part of the out-journey. Then, after taking in fresh water at the port of Beziguiche, just south of the Cape, they would push on to Sierra Leone and Malagueta, where they would meet the Guinea current. This current, which ran steadily eastwards, attaining its maximum velocity of three and a half miles an hour between Cape Palmas and Cape Threepoints, would serve to carry them forward to Mina. Thus, provided they experienced neither the tornadoes nor the calms, which are frequent in the doldrums, they might hope to reach the castle of São Jorge in less than two months. While in Guinea, great skill, exhausting toil and unceasing vigilance were required of them in avoiding numerous shallows and hidden rocks at river mouths, and in sheltering from sudden storms and variable daily winds. The most serious difficulty, however, lay

[1] *Leys e Provisões del Rei D. Sebastião*, Law of 3 November 1571, art. xvi.

in the homeward journey. If, as so often happened, they wished on the return voyage to trade on the Malagueta coast, they had to sail against the Guinea current. Moreover, the prevailing wind in Lower Guinea was south-westerly, except for a few weeks between December and February when the dry Harmattan blew off the land, and this south-west wind did not aid the returning caravels. The less difficult route from Mina to Portugal was to bear to the south until the Equator was reached and, there, to pick up the equatorial current which ran parallel but in the opposite direction to the Guinea current. In this way, by making a wide sweep, ships might more easily get back to Cape Verde, but, even so, the remaining part of the voyage to Portugal had to be made in face of adverse winds and currents. It follows, then, that it took much longer to come back from Guinea than to go there. Futhermore, as we have seen, ships were wont to return in the spring after trading during the winter. Accordingly, should they delay their departure from Guinea too long, as captain Wyndham did in 1554,[1] they might suffer untold harm. Their supplies of fresh water might give out and their biscuit might begin to perish. Moreover, the movement of the sun northwards after the end of March meant that they were more liable to be delayed still longer by the calms of the doldrums. Then it would often result that, for lack of proper food and by reason of the torrential monsoon rains of the summer months and the fierce heat of the sun's rays, many might succumb to fever and dysentery. Thus the rate of mortality on the return voyage was nearly always higher—sometimes far higher—than on the outward one.

In these circumstances, the achievement of the Portuguese was remarkable. Admittedly, their activities were confined to the coast and the bulk of their trade concentrated in the winter months. Yet, after a struggle with Castile, who claimed possession of Guinea (1454–80), they proceeded to build forts and factories, to found a number of civil settlements, especially in Senegambia and the larger islands, and to attempt the evangelisation of many of the negro tribes. For fifty years, holding a monopoly, they traded without hindrance (1480–1530). After 1530, however, their exclusive rights were questioned by other powers, first by France and, later, by England and Holland.

[1] Hakluyt, vi. 141–52.

Thus, the subsequent story was largely one of rivalry between Portugal and those other states which refused to recognise her unique position in Guinea. We shall try, in the following chapters, to trace the origin and development of the monopoly and to outline the story of the efforts of Castile, France and England to destroy it before the tragic death of King Sebastian in 1578.

CHAPTER 1

CASTILO–PORTUGUESE RIVALRY IN SENEGAMBIA, 1454–56

LONG before all Guinea had been explored, certain Portuguese merchants began to trade along its shores. They sent their men in caravels, mostly from Lagos, to purchase slaves from the Arabs on the coast of Barbary and, further south, to load small sums of gold dust. Later, when Senegambia was reached, black-amoors were seized on land and brought home. Prince Henry, though he sometimes frowned on the use of force by the slave-traders, encouraged peaceful traffic and sanctioned, if he did not inspire, the association of a group of Lagos merchants in 1444 for the more effective pursuit of trade. The members of the Lagos company, whose charter seems to have been renewed after three years, built a factory on Arguin Island (1448). Protected by a fort, Arguin served them as a base for trade on the opposite mainland. Prince Henry would not allow them to engross all the trade of Guinea, but helped individual merchants by providing them with ships for the voyage. The Lagos company, at first, operated chiefly on the modern Barbary coast. But, as time went on, a greater percentage of business was transacted with the negro merchants of Guinea, for trading caravels followed closely behind the explorers. So it was that by 1456, even the Rio Grande had been brought within the ambit of the company's activities.[1]

The merchants reaped huge profits, especially from their cargoes of gold and slaves. It has been estimated that their returns were hardly ever less than 50 per cent and sometimes as high as 800 per cent.[2] Azurara, the chronicler of this early

[1] " Navigatione di M. Alvise da Cadamosto " (G. B. Ramusio, *Navigationi et Viaggi*, i. 104–18).
[2] Hedwig M. A. Fitzler, " Portuguiesische Handelsgesellschaften des 15 und beginnenden 16 Jahrhunderts " (*Viertcl jahrschrift für Sozial-und Wirtschaftsgeschichte*, xxv. 239).

Barbary and Guinea traffic, records that, by 1448, nearly one thousand slaves had been transported to Portugal.[1] Moreover, small profits were made in civet, hides, wax, gum, ambergris, salt, fish, ostrich eggs and goats, while a little revenue was derived from fishing tolls which the Azenegues of Arguin had to pay their white rulers. Prince Henry must also have gathered a handsome reward, for one-fifth of all merchandise, carried from Guinea to Portugal, accrued to him and, should he have lent a merchant one of his ships, that merchant was obliged to pay him no less than half of the profits. The highest returns were registered between 1450 and 1458. Ten to twelve ships were sent annually to Guinea during those years and the traffic yielded from five to seven times the invested capital.[2]

The Portuguese tried to keep their good fortune secret, but such a lucrative trade could not be concealed permanently. Somehow the Andalusians of Seville, Cadiz, Palos and San Lucar in southern Castile came to hear of it. The news probably travelled through various channels. Possibly some of the Guinea slaves, whom the merchants of Lagos sold in Castile, were interrogated about the land from which they came. Perhaps Andalusian merchants who, at the time in question, were buying slaves in Morocco opposite Andalusia, heard from the Moors about the kingdoms of Guinea, Melli and Timbuktu.[3] Again, many Genoese sailed with the Portuguese to West Africa like Antonio da Noli, who is generally credited with having shared in the discovery of the Cape Verde Islands, and Antoniotto Usodimare, whom Cadamosto met near Cape Verde in 1455.[4] It may be that some of them brought reports of the trade in gold to Andalusia. A Genoese merchant actually sailed in the first Andalusian fleet, which went to Guinea in 1454, and, when captured, suffered greater harm, his hands being cut off, than the Castilians who were also arrested. The evidence points to his having merited special punishment from the Portuguese. Perhaps like several other foreigners, he had been privileged by Prince Henry to visit Guinea and, afterwards, leaving Portugal, had sold his knowledge to the Andalusians.[5] Another

[1] G. E. Azurara, *Chronica de Guiné*, ch. xcvii.
[2] Fitzler, *op. cit.*, pp. 237, 240.
[3] Azurara, *op. cit.*, ch. xciii.
[4] E. Prestage, *The Portuguese Pioneers*, pp. 115, 141, *et seq.*
[5] Las Casas, *Historia de las Indias*, bk. I, ch. xviii.

explanation of the leakage of tales about Guinea is suggested by the existence of a trade in ursella with the Canary Islands. As early as 1455 Castilian merchants were importing quantities of ursella, a kind of moss used in the process of dyeing cloth, from the Canaries to Cadiz and Seville.[1] Fourteen years later, two Castilians who had previously been engaged in the ursella trade with the Canary Islands, were empowered to import ursella from Santiago Island, near Cape Verde, to Seville.[2] Is it not possible that the expansion of this commerce took place before 1469 as the result of some earlier connection between Guinea and the Canary Islands? If so, the Castilian merchants, who discovered ursella in Santiago, may at the same time have learnt secrets about the Portuguese in Senegambia. Perhaps, again, the news spread, because Portuguese renegades were already betraying the secrets of their country. Lastly, the activities of Andalusian pirates may have been responsible. One or more Portuguese caravels, on their way back from Senegambia, may have been attacked near Lagos, the maps and charts on board confiscated by the pirates, and the crews forced to report on their adventures.

However, whatever their source of information, the Andalusians heard of the great profits being made by Portugal. Accordingly, certain merchants of Seville and Cadiz equipped a fleet of caravels to go to the " land which they call Guinea ". These ships set out not later than the early months of 1454 and traded successfully on the Guinea Coast. But on their return, when only a league from Cadiz, they were attacked by a Portuguese armada under captain Palenço, who already enjoyed a high reputation among his countrymen, for his earlier assault upon Castilian settlements in the Canary Islands. It would seem that part of the fleet got back safely into Cadiz harbour, but one of the caravels, together with crew and cargo, was captured and taken to Portugal.[3]

One cannot suppose that these ships journeyed southward very far. No word, other than ' Guinea ', was used in the resulting negotiations between Castile and Portugal to indicate where the Andalusians trafficked. Yet it is unlikely that they sailed

[1] Ramusio, *op. cit.*, i. 106.
[2] Barcellos, pp. 33–6.
[3] Las Casas, *op. cit.*, bk. I, ch. xviii.

much beyond the Senegal river. Portugal, for her part, had not discovered all Upper Guinea when this rival fleet weighed anchor. The records, indeed, give the impression that the government of Castile, when it took up the cause of the unfortunate merchants of Seville and Cadiz, knew very little about the configuration of the Guinea Coast. But this does not detract from the importance of this voyage. It marked the first appearance of a rival power in Guinea and thus introduced a new feature to white enterprise there. Until 1454, exploration and trade had been monopolised by the Portuguese. Now, actuated by the desire for commercial profit, the subjects of a rival state, Castile, appeared in northern Guinea and threatened to divert to Andalusian ports a percentage of the trade flowing to Lisbon and Lagos. Commercial competition was complicating the position on the coast.

Portugal and Castile, at the moment when captain Palenço attacked the Cadiz fleet, were struggling for the possession of northern Africa and the Canary Islands. The tone of their relations, then, was not conducive to a peaceful settlement of the new subject of dispute. King John II of Castile, indolent though he was, interfered personally on the behalf of his subjects. In a letter of 10 April 1454, he described Palenço's seizure of a Castilian caravel and charged King Alfonso V of Portugal with having given orders for its confiscation.[1] At the same time, envoys were sent to Portugal to protest against Portuguese voyages to Guinea. John II claimed for the crown of Castile " the ancient and exclusive right of sailing in the seas of Guinea " and instructed his ambassadors, Juan de Guzman and Dr. Fernandez Lopez de Burgos, to threaten a war, should Alfonso V refuse to abandon the Guinea traffic.[2]

The claim of Castile was groundless. It was neither the " ancient " nor the " exclusive " right of her crown to sail in the seas of Guinea. But contemporary evidence suggests that her exclusion from the traffic would have meant a loss to her royal treasury. Thus, Alonso de Palencia, the chronicler of the reign of King Henry IV of Castile, records that the Portuguese, in " cruelly preventing all others from cruising off those coasts "

[1] *Ibid.*
[2] Nunes de Liam, *Chronica e Vida Del Rey D. Affonso V*, p. 221 ; Alonso de Palencia, *Crónica de Enrique IV*, iv. 127–8.

of Guinea, were ruining the crown.[1] Palencia, as a patriotic Castilian, very probably exaggerated, but the phrasing of a later decree lends colour to what he wrote. This decree, issued by King Ferdinand and Queen Isabella from Valladolid in 1475, asserted that the rulers of Spain always possessed the conquest of Africa and Guinea and collected the 'fifth' of whatever articles were brought from those countries.[2] Ortiz de Zúñiga's *Annals*, a third source of information, substantiate what might be concluded from the above evidence. " For years, frequent voyages had been made to the coasts of Africa and Guinea from the ports of Andalusia," they run, ". . . and the royal exchequer was reaping considerable profits from the 'fifths'". Ortiz proceeds to explain how, unfortunately, towards the end of the reign of Henry IV, the Portuguese interfered, and the words, which he uses, imply that the profits ceased.[3] The value of these *Annals*, in this connection, is only secondary, for Ortiz wrote two centuries after the event. Yet he used contemporary chronicles and documents which he cites. His statement, if based upon the decree of 1475, cannot be regarded as additional evidence. If, on the other hand, it were drawn from an independent source, now lost, then it would seem to prove that the motive behind John II's claim was a financial one, even though the claim to monopoly had no real foundation.

King Alfonso V does not appear to have been very embarrassed by John II's threat of war. He replied firmly that the 'conquest' of Guinea indubitably pertained to himself and not to the crown of Castile. Nevertheless, he urged that peace should prevail between the two states until an investigation into their respective claims to Africa and Guinea should have been completed. The King of Portugal could await such an enquiry with confidence, for his country had justice on its side in so far as the principle of prior discovery was concerned. Moreover, both João de Barros and Ruy de Pina mention an early grant to Prince Henry by Pope Martin V, who held office between 1417 and 1431, of all the land which might be discovered from Cape Bojador to the Indies.[4] The papal bull which, presum-

[1] *Ibid.*
[2] Navarrete, *Colección de Viages*, iii. 465-8.
[3] Ortiz de Zúñiga, *Annales de Sevilla*, bk. XII, p. 373.
[4] Barros, I. i. 7 ; Ruy de Pina, *Chronica del Rey D. Affonso V*, ch. cxliv.

ably, included this grant is not known and perhaps never existed. If, however, the statements of de Barros and Pina be accepted, then Portugal had also a legal claim to Guinea, for the right of the pope to make such a grant would not, at that time, have been denied by Castile. This papal bull could not have been promulgated later than 1431, when Martin V died, so that one may not associate it with the subsequent patent of 22 October 1443, by which King Alfonso gave Prince Henry a monopoly of trade and discovery beyond Cape Bojador.[1] The text of this patent, indeed, contains no reference to the alleged earlier grant of the pope, but it does show that the crown of Portugal regarded as unquestionable its possession of the lands beyond Cape Bojador. Those who drafted the patent for their king did not, apparently, consider it necessary to explain how King Alfonso V had come by the lands, but accepted the fact of his ownership without question. The preamble describes how the prince had devoted great energy to the task of sending ships to discover the lands beyond the Cape " since up to this time no member of Christendom had known about these parts." It adds that Prince Henry had petitioned for the right to control personally all traffic to Guinea. Accordingly, all men were forbidden, on pain of confiscation of their goods, to sail beyond Cape Bojador except by the mandate or licence of the prince, while to him was given a ' fifth ' and a ' tenth ' of such commodities as might be brought from those regions.

Now the Andalusian fleet which sailed to Guinea in 1454 ignored the conditions of this grant. Always provided that Guinea was Alfonso V's to give away, the prince was, therefore, acting strictly within his rights when he ordered captain Palenço to arrest one of the interloping caravels on its return. His interest and those of his immediate friends were endangered by the enterprise and we may, therefore, assume that he was behind the rather curt reply of the King of Portugal to the ambassadors of Castile. There can be little doubt, then, of the superiority of the Portuguese case : Alfonso V had only to wait upon events for success.

Nevertheless, it seems that he determined to take advantage of the dispute to confirm his monopoly. The ambiguous grant of Martin V evidently did not satisfy him. This bull, even if

[1] *Alguns Documentos*, pp. 8-9.

it had existed, had been promulgated before the discovery of the land called Guinea and, on this account, might be questioned by the new claimants to the territories beyond Cape Bojador. The Portuguese king, therefore, having gained time by arguing that peace should be kept between the two adjacent kingdoms, appears to have petitioned the pope for an exclusive grant of all Guinea to Portugal. In the event, however, swift action was not necessary because of the death of John II of Castile in 1455. The latter's claim was abruptly dropped and the dispute remained dormant for twenty years, though, as will be seen below, an occasional interloper from Andalusia may still have stolen down the Guinea Coast.

This sudden change of circumstances did not shake Alfonso from his purpose. No evidence has been found to prove that ambassadors were sent to Rome soon after the complaints of Castile. But the fact that Pope Nicholas V issued the bull *Romanus Pontifex* on 8 January 1455, less than a year after John II's protest, seems to indicate that pressure was exerted, in some way, upon the papal court. The phrasing of the bull, like the close chronological sequence of the two events, suggests the work of Portuguese envoys. In the preamble, reference was made to the possible presumption of aliens who, out of envy, might penetrate to Guinea, and the suggestion was repudiated that the bull had been promulgated at the instance of King Alfonso or Prince Henry or " on the petition of any other offered on their behalf ". The " aliens ", to which the grant referred, were doubtless Andalusians, and the official denial of pressure exerted upon the papacy surely indicates that the voyage of Portuguese ambassadors to Rome had kindled Castilian suspicions ! Proceeding, the bull granted to the king, his heirs and successors and those of the prince, all such " provinces, islands, harbours, places and seas whatsoever . . . which have already been acquired and which shall hereafter come to be acquired, and the right of conquest also, from the Capes of Bojador and Nam ".[1]

In the following year, a second bull, *Inter Caetera*, published by Pope Calixtus III on 13 March, defined more exactly the nature of the grant. To the Portuguese Order of Christ was bequeathed " ecclesiastical and ordinary jurisdiction in the

[1] Davenport, i. 13–26.

islands, villages, harbours, lands and places, acquired or to be acquired from Capes Bojador and Nam as far as and through all Guinea, and past that southern shore all the way to the Indies."[1] Thus Prince Henry, as the grandmaster of the order, received the jurisdiction over the whole of the new-found lands beyond the capes.

The tone of the two grants points to the conclusion that they were an indirect result of the Castilo-Portuguese dispute. Unfortunate, indeed, in its consequences had been the protest of the late King John II. Instead of weakening the Portuguese position in Guinea and instead of securing recognition of the claim of Castile, John II's letter had served enormously to strengthen the developing monopoly of his rival. The pope had now fully sanctioned the Portuguese claim.

We may linger with advantage, for a moment, over the second bull. It was, perhaps, natural for the new pope, Calixtus III, to confirm the concession of his predecessor. But was there not more behind it? Some ground exists for believing that the Portuguese feared a continuation of Andalusian interloping traffic and so tried to protect themselves by a renewal of the papal grant of 1455. The excerpt from Ortiz de Zúñiga, already quoted, suggests that one or two caravels from Seville, Cadiz or Palos may have trafficked to Guinea even after the death of John II. No clear evidence of this has been found, but it is known that, in 1460, an interloper named de Prado, who seems to have been an Andalusian, purchased a cargo of gold in Senegambia.

The extant version of the second voyage of Diogo Gomes, made to Guinea in 1460, relates that, when Gomes was buying negro slaves south of Cape Verde, certain caravels from Gambia reported the presence of a man called de Prado who was bringing back a richly laden caravel. Gomes immediately sent Gonçalo Ferreiro, with an armed ship, to Cape Verde to lie in wait for the intruder. De Prado's caravel, on board which the Portuguese found a lot of gold, was arrested, and the unfortunate captain was sent to Portugal in the company of his captor. He was put in irons for selling arms to the Moors in exchange for gold, and afterwards—significantly—burnt as a heretic.[2]

[1] Davenport, i. 28–32.
[2] Diogo Gomes, *De prima inventione Guineae* (ed. by Dr. J. Schmeller), *passim*.

Towards the end of Diogo Gomes's narrative, the captain referred once again to the interloper and, this time, did not call him " de Prado " but "ille de Prado ". This type of allusion suggests at once that the illicit trader was a native of Prado, a town in the province of Cadiz, Andalusia, the very centre of Castilian maritime activity and from which ships sailed to Guinea, not only in 1454 but also during the later Castilo-Portuguese War of Succession (1475–80). It is practically certain, therefore, that de Prado was an Andalusian interloper. Additional colour is given to this assertion because the charge of selling arms to the Moors, which years afterwards the Portuguese levelled against the English sea-dogs in Guinea, was made in this initial stage of commercial rivalry against de Prado.

The episode, when seen in perspective, throws light upon the bull *Inter Caetera*. Unquestionable evidence exists that a fleet of Andalusians went to Senegambia in 1454; it is equally certain that Andalusians frequented the trade of the whole of West Africa between 1475 and 1480. The story of de Prado makes it almost certain that a Castilian caravel was buying gold in the river Gambia in 1460. Bearing in mind that, for every captured interloper, at least one and probably more must have gone free—for this alone rendered such hazardous adventures worth while—may it not be deduced that, throughout the period from 1454 to 1475, Andalusians occasionally, though not frequently, visited Guinea ? If so, were voyages like that of de Prado partly responsible for the speedy confirmation of the bull *Romanus Pontifex*, and was the addition of the words " all the way to the Indies ", which appeared, in the second bull, the result of Portuguese alarm lest Andalusian interlopers should find their way beyond Sierra Leone and should claim for their country such lands as they might discover ? Possibly material may exist in the archives of Spain to verify these speculations. Present evidence conceals the answers.

What we have described in this chapter amounts to little more than a story of tentative beginnings. The traffic of the prosperous Lagos company and the explorations of Prince Henry's captains and pilots were suddenly disturbed in 1454 by Andalusian rivals. King John II of Castile, encouraging his subjects, demanded the withdrawal of the Portuguese from

Guinea and tried to expropriate their trade in that region. His untimely death temporarily ended the resulting tension between the two nations but, probably, his countrymen, unwilling to give up their claim, continued secretly to equip ships for an occasional voyage down the African coast towards Guinea. Portugal's claim, by virtue of prior discovery, was infinitely stronger, but Alfonso V, taught wisdom by experience, sought to ensure his new possessions against a repetition of the threat from Castile. Consequently, two bulls, whose promulgation was evidently a result of the Andalusian voyage of 1454, granted to Portugal all land, discovered or to be discovered, beyond the capes " as far as and through all Guinea ". Sure of the moral support of the papacy, for what it might be worth, the Portuguese could now proceed, in greater safety, to promote existing trades and, if possible, open up new ones.

CHAPTER II

PORTUGUESE PROGRESS, ESPECIALLY AFTER THE GRANT TO FERNÃO GOMES, 1456–1475

PRINCE HENRY died four years after the promulgation of the bull *Inter Caetera*. His servants continued their voyages of discovery while he lived, so that, by 1460, the whole coast of Upper Guinea had been mapped. The Lagos company, its traffic now unhindered by Andalusian competition, made a handsome profit in 1458 equal to five times the invested capital. It is certain, moreover, that some of the Cape Verde Islands were discovered during this time, because the prince granted the temporalities of five of them to the king on 18 September 1460.[1] However, after Henry's death, Portuguese progress came almost to a standstill. Apart from a voyage made by Pero de Cintra in 1462, admittedly no mean enterprise, for he seems to have sailed beyond Sierra Leone, and apart from the full discovery and first settlement of the Cape Verde Islands, it would seem that exploration was abandoned. This is not surprising, for the soul of the earlier movement had been the prince, the cost of farther exploration was prohibitive, and King Alfonso V was personally more interested in Castile and northern Africa than in the West African aims of his late uncle.

Nevertheless, after a few years, Alfonso's indifference led to an unexpected resurgence of interest in Guinea. The king was not unwilling to shift the responsibility for discovery on to other shoulders and so, when the opportunity occurred, he made a conditional grant of the privilege of sailing beyond Sierra Leone to one of his subjects. The fortunate recipient was a wealthy merchant of Lisbon named Fernão Gomes.

This grant proved to be so important that it will merit detailed attention. The original, unfortunately, has not been found: perhaps it was destroyed in the Lisbon earthquake of 1755. Still, some of its clauses are recorded by the historian, de Barros,[1] while additional light may be thrown upon it owing to the lucky existence of a manuscript copy of a second grant to Gomes which confirmed the first.[2] De Barros informs us that, in November 1469, the king leased the trade of Guinea beyond Sierra Leone to Fernão Gomes, subject to certain conditions, for a period of five years. Each year, Gomes was to pay 200 milreis in rent to the king, and to discover 100 leagues forward along the coast. Furthermore, he was forbidden to trade either at Arguin or on the coast opposite the Cape Verde Islands, and such ivory as he might obtain he was to sell only to Alfonso. However, he received the highly valued privilege of purchasing annually one civet-cat: the civet, extracted from the pouch of this animal, came to be valued in perfumery for blending scents. De Barros says no more, but the second grant made to the Lisbon financier in 1473 supplements the former's evidence. We learn from it that Gomes was given the exclusive right of gathering malagueta pepper in the lands he discovered on the payment of a further 100 milreis to the king, that he was allowed to buy out the rights of certain merchants who had been licensed by Alfonso V to trade to Guinea, and that, during his lease, no other person was to obtain any permission from the crown to traffic in his preserve. It would seem, then, that Gomes was awarded sole rights to send ships and to trade in the lands which his agents might discover.

The obligation to discover 100 leagues beyond Sierra Leone every year brought him unexpected good fortune. Within three years, a gold-bearing region, far more profitable than any yet found, was reached. Gomes himself did not go with the fleets which were equipped to fulfil the conditions of his grant. He adopted instead, apparently, the rôle of financier and organiser. His ships, sailing steadily forward close to the shore and helped by the Guinea current advanced very rapidly, though there are few recorded details of their adventures. The most important incident in their progress occurred in January 1472, when Samma, " the place where the gold could be purchased," was discovered by a fleet under captains João de Santarem and Pero de Escolar and piloted by Martim Fernandes and Alvaro

[1] Barros, I. ii. 2.
[2] Torre do Tombo, Chancellaria de D. Affonso V, Livro 33, f. 147 v.

Esteves. Gomes had other fleets also exploring the seas of Guinea during that year: Ruy de Sequeira found and named the Cape of St. Catherine; Soeiro da Costa reached the Rio de Soeiro in the neighbourhood of Axem; Fernão do Po lighted upon the island later called after him, but which he named Formosa; and the other three large islands of the Gulf of Guinea, São Thomé, Annobon and O Principe were also discovered. " Besides the above discoveries," wrote João de Barros, there were "other trades and islands, of which we do not speak in particular, because we do not know when, or by what captains, they were found."[1]

Fernão Gomes was amply compensated for the effort and expense he incurred in thus extending the limit of discovery. Before the renewal of his five-year contract for one further year in 1473, he was rewarded by a knighthood, his coat of arms consisting of a shield argent, embossed with the figures of three negro chiefs wearing gold rings and gold collars. Subsequently, after serving his king also in northern Africa, he was honoured with the title Da Mina, elevated to the royal council and the Lagos company having been dissolved and its rights in Arguin taken over by Prince John, son of Alfonso V, he received the trade of Arguin from that prince at a yearly rent of 100 milreis. These distinctions, however, can have been only secondary to the great reward of gold with which he was endowed by the discovery of the Mina region. Annual quantities of gold dust, equivalent in value to 170,000 dobras, were being brought from Mina to Portugal at the end of the century and of this, one-twentieth was regularly appropriated by the crown.

Fernão Gomes, then, in the years of his grant (1469–75), must have made huge profits from the gold traffic of Samma. It may be, of course, that Alfonso V claimed all the gold which was found, in accordance with some lost clause of Gomes's grant, but this is unlikely because, while de Barros mentions the regulation about ivory in that contract, no reference to gold occurs either in the *Da Asia* or in the second Gomes patent. The Lisbon merchant, presumably, did grow enormously rich, yet we lose sight of him after the outbreak of war between Portugal and Castile in 1475 when, as was perhaps inevitable,

---

[1] Barros, I. ii. 2; Pacheco, bk. II.; and, for an accurate account in English, *vide* E. Prestage, *The Portuguese Pioneers*, pp. 184–5.

Prince John took over his contract. It is just possible that he was the Fernão Gomes who served as captain of the island of Fogo from 1510 until his death in 1520.[1] His daughter, Urraca, married an official of the household of Queen Catherine, the wife of John III.[2] He may also have had a son, for another Fernão Gomes lived in the reign of King John III, and owned ships which traded with the East Indies.[3]

However, apart from these personal details, he had left a permanent memorial to himself not only in the cape which was named after him,[4] but also by the opening of the coast from Sierra Leone to Cape St. Catherine.

The King of Portugal now ruled over a new dominion which stretched for 2000 miles beyond Cape Bojador and in which commodities, prized highly in the markets of Europe, could be obtained at small cost. But, so far, trade with Guinea had been developed rather unsystematically. Its range had been extended piece-meal with the irregular and jerky advances of the explorers southwards and eastwards. There were obvious dangers in its unbridled exploitation. Free competition between white traders on the coast was likely to bring prices tumbling down and rapidly to reduce profits, because as the Portuguese soon found, the negro merchants were keen business men. Uncontrolled traffic would deprive the crown of much revenue which it might otherwise collect. The absence of a strict surveillance of all ships which sailed to Guinea might lead, in addition to smuggling, to a leakage of information about the gold of Mina and so to a repetition of the quarrel with Castile of 1454. Accordingly, simultaneously with the discovery of Lower Guinea, Alfonso V issued new regulations which not only subordinated the traffic entirely to himself but also provided for the exclusion of rivals.

The main purpose of the Portuguese crown was always to exploit the Guinea trades to the highest royal advantage, but its methods varied, for different schemes were tried, according to the particular preference of the reigning king. At the time of the first grant to Fernão Gomes, the organisation of the

---

[1] *Ensaios*, I. ii. 23.
[2] Barcellos, p. 37.
[3] J. D. M. Ford, *The Letters of John III*, pp. 66–7, 86, 95.
[4] Cape Fernão Gomes, situated just north of Cape St. Catherine in the Cantino Map of 1502.

Guinea traffic was still in the experimental stage, and it could not be foreseen what method might be most profitable. Even afterwards, few principles were followed consistently for the regulation of trade, and this was because the volume of trade with West Africa underwent first a rapid expansion and, after 1530, a slow decline. The crown followed a policy of shifting opportunism. Systems, which worked for the trade when prosperous, proved unsuitable during its subsequent decline and were abandoned.[1] Nevertheless, through all the superficial fluctuations of economic policy, we may discern a constant effort to make profit by the creation of monopolies. Variety occurred, not in the underlying purpose of the crown, but in the types of monopoly.

There was little uniformity even before the captains of Fernão Gomes achieved their triumph on the coasts of Mina and Malagueta. King Alfonso V, realising that governmental con trol must follow upon the heels of discovery, if he wished to exclude unwanted traders, had previously issued certain regulations and created a few monopolies. The traffic of Arguin Island, as we have seen, was engrossed by a company of Lagos merchants from 1444. This company, despite its great profits, seems to have been liquidated shortly after the death of Henry the Navigator, and its privileges passed into the hands of Prince John, son of Alfonso V, who sold licences to such merchants as desired them.[2] Arguin, it is true, lay north of Guinea, but it exemplifies one type of monopoly, which had been created a generation before the discovery of Lower Guinea.

It would seem, moreover, that Diogo Gomes was given a kind of superiority over a part of the Senegambia coast in 1460. He relates that Alfonso V, besides granting him authority over " the shores of that sea ", commissioned him to seize all ships engaged in illegal trade there, and bade him send reports thereof to Portugal. In this way it came about that de Prado's caravel was arrested.[3] But, since his evidence is vague, we do not know whether Diogo exercised merely supervisory duties or had sole rights of trade in a particular area. Were he granted such rights, he probably had to pay a rent for them to King Alfonso V,

---

[1] L'Abbé Douais, *Dépêches de M. de Fourquevaux*, p. 301.
[2] Barros, I. ii. 2.
[3] *Vide supra*, p. 23.

in the same way as Fernão Gomes subsequently leased the Arguin trade for 100 milreis per year.

All Upper Guinea, as we saw in the first chapter, formerly appertained to Prince Henry in accordance with the letter patent of 22 October 1443.[1] No merchant or captain had been allowed to sail beyond Cape Bojador without a licence from the prince. When he died, his monopoly reverted in a normal way to King Alfonso. Diogo Gomes, then, must have received his privileges, whatever their nature, from the king. However, a complication was introduced after the discovery of the Cape Verde Islands. These islands were granted to the king's brother, Prince Fernando, by a letter patent, dated 19 September 1462.[2] Santiago, the largest of the group, was peopled at once and, possibly, S. Philip too.[3] But, in order to encourage the young settlements, King Alfonso V, upon the petition of his brother, allowed the colonists to trade with the mainland. The inhabitants of Santiago, in the words of the chronicler Damião de Goes, were " privileged to treat and to trade in Guinea."[4]

This concession, of which the full terms throw light upon the organisation of the traffic of Upper Guinea, was made on 12 June 1466.[5] Alfonso V empowered the islanders to go with ships to all " our contracts of the parts of Guinea " except Arguin, since it was his pleasure that this " contract " should remain a royal monopoly. Following one of the strictest rules of medieval Christendom, he forbade them to sell arms, iron, ships or naval equipment to the heathens. The crown would impose a duty of one-fourth on all imports from Guinea, but exports were to be exempted from the customary ' tenth '. Each ship, which might engage in trade, was to carry a royal official, a clerk, whose function would be to draw up a list of the cargo, while royal magistrates, resident in Santiago Island, would collect the ' fourths ' on the cargo in accordance with information supplied by the clerk. Finally, should the king in future come to farm out any of the contracts of Guinea, the privileges granted to the Santiagians would be duly respected.

[1] *Vide supra*, p. 21.
[2] *Alguns Documentos*, pp. 31-2.
[3] *Ensaios*, I. ii. 1-31
[4] Goes, *Chronica do Principe D. João II*, ch. xvii.
[5] The full text of this grant is printed in Barcellos, pp. 21-3.

The net result of these concessions was to give the islanders a general and continual permit for the traffic of Guinea. Their trade would be encouraged not only by exemption from the 'tenths,' but also because they would no longer have to apply for a separate licence before each voyage to the mainland. Alfonso, however, had not sacrificed any of his fundamental rights over West Africa. The theory behind the charter was that Upper Guinea belonged to the Portuguese crown and that all privileges sprang from royal grace, a fact which no trader could forget, because he had to pay duties on the articles, which he imported from the mainland of Guinea, and, on his ship, sailed the royal official who counted his cargo and prevented him from smuggling. Moreover, the king retained the power, not only to license individuals to make voyages and to farm out the Guinea traffic provided that, in such a lease, the privileges granted to the Santiagians were not superseded, but even to revoke the entire grant of 1466.

Soon after, Alfonso V did, in fact, issue at least eight separate Guinea licences. Fernão Gomes was allowed to purchase them from the interested merchants in 1469. He still held them four years later and, when the second grant was made to him, he was warned that, should he not use them before the end of his contract, they would thereafter be invalid.[1] These licences must have been granted in the usual way to certain merchants of Portugal. The latter can scarcely have desired to seek out new lands, for, had this been so, they would surely have demanded a more valuable concession than the mere right to send one or more ships to trade. It would rather seem that they intended to direct their caravels to land already discovered, that is, to Upper Guinea, where the traffic was now the special privilege of the islanders of Santiago. The grant of 1466, then, clearly did not exclude other merchants from continuing to trade in that region provided the requisite licence were obtained.

But Alfonso V did not exercise his further prerogative of leasing the trade of Upper Guinea to an individual or a company. Fernão Gomes was not allowed to trade there, as de Barros relates, "for that was the right of the inhabitants of those islands [of Cape Verde] ".[2] As we have seen, the privilege of

---

[1] Torre do Tombo, Chancellaria de D. Affonso V, Livro 33, f. 147v.
[2] Barros, i. ii. 2.

the islanders was not exclusive, but Alfonso V did not wish, apparently, to interfere with, or to impede the growth of trade between the mainland and the islands. The white colonists who lived in Santiago, thus came to assume most of the traffic of Upper Guinea for themselves, and continued to do so during the sixteenth century. The researches of Sr. J J. Lopes de Lima have substantiated this: " the land from Senegal to Sierra Leone remained for long a dependency of the Cape Verde Islands," he concludes, " and an exclusive centre for trade for the inhabitants of the islands."[1] This is why contemporaries began to speak of ' Guinea of Cape Verde ' when they referred to the region between the river Senegal and Sierra Leone.

A new type of grant was devised when Fernão Gomes undertook further exploration. The lost letter patent of 1469 evidently gave him complete rights for five years over navigation in the seas beyond Sierra Leone. By the second patent, which the Lisbon merchant received on 1 June 1473, Alfonso V promised that, provided Gomes fulfiled his obligations no other person would be licensed to trade in Guinea. Probably, the earlier grant contained a similar clause. · Presumably, then, only ships belonging to the fortunate Gomes could sail beyond Sierra Leone, and so this monopoly differed from the grant to the Santiagians. It differed too, of course, in that, while the patent of 1466 gave privileges to an unknown number of persons, the one of 1469 was given to a single individual. Also it differed in the terms of the contract. While the grant to the islanders was to continue as long as the royal favour might be extended to them, a definite limit of five years was set to the Gomes patent: issued in November 1469, it would normally have expired in October 1474, but, as we saw, it was renewed for a sixth year. The rent which Gomes had to pay King Alfonso V for his concessions further differentiated them from the grant of 1466: the Guinea contract cost him 200 milreis per year, the Arguin contract 100 milreis and the sole privilege of buying malagueta pepper another 100 milreis.

Gomes thus paid at least 400 milreis annually to the crown during the period of his lease. In addition to this revenue, King Alfonso also made a profit from such ivory as the ships of Gomes brought to Portugal. The merchant, according to his

[1] *Ensaios*, I. i. xv.

contract, had to sell all ivory direct to the king at 1500 reis per quintal. Alfonso then resold it, at a higher price, to Martim Annes Boviage, for " by another contract, made before this," all ivory from Guinea was to be sold to this man.[1] Lastly, Alfonso probably appropriated one-twentieth of the gold which came from Mina. It is thus clear that the contract of Lower Guinea must have proved as profitable to the crown as the concession of privileges to the Santiagians. Each grant brought in revenue which the government could not afford to ignore.

After Fernão Gomes's discoveries, Alfonso V began to issue general decrees for the better regulation of the traffic of Guinea. Already, a letter patent of 19 October 1470 had absolutely forbidden the purchase of civet-cats, malagueta pepper, unicorns, every kind of spice, precious stones, dyes and gums by any merchant or town holding privileges to trade in Guinea.[2] All these commodities were reserved for the king himself, although Gomes was given a monopoly of the malagueta and the right to import one civet-cat per year. A more important edict was issued on 31 August 1474. This law stated that Alfonso V had "made a gift of the said contracts" of Guinea to Prince John, and it prohibited, except by royal licence, all contracts, wars, trade and the seizing of Moors, in Guinea, on pain of death and the forfeiture of all wordly wealth. Acts of piracy there were to be visited with the same punishments, and any captain or clerk, of any of the ships which made the voyage from Portugal to Guinea, who deliberately deceived the officers of the contract respecting the value of a cargo, was also to be punished according to the measure of his crime.[3] The significance of the decree would seem to have been that Alfonso V, never very actively interested in West Africa, thus bequeathed its administration to his son and empowered him to use force, and even the death penalty, in order to exclude interlopers.

A second law, published ten days later, supplemented that of 31 August. The preamble emphasized the need of keeping a strict watch on maritime preparations at all the seaports, so that official registration might be made of every ship which was

[1] Barros, I. ii. 2.
[2] *Alguns Documentos*, p. 33.
[3] Torre do Tombo, maço I de Leis, no. 178 (printed in J. Bensaude. *L'Astronomie nautique au Portugal à l'époque des Grandes Découvertes*, pp. 273-4).

equipped for Guinea. A good deal of piracy had resulted from slack work on the part of the officials. Accordingly, Alfonso V now ordered that every person who wished to arm a ship for the African voyage should enter recognizance for his ship. No ship was to be sent to Guinea except the fact should first be made known to the king, a royal licence obtained for it and also a certificate from the officers of the city, town or place where the ship might be prepared, showing why the licence should be granted. This law added that such certificates of safe-conduct for ships, going to Guinea, would be given henceforth to the subjects of friendly states as well as to those of Castile (10 September 1474).[1] It is plain that the motive underlying the law was to hinder the activities of pirates and interlopers. No ship could now leave Portugal without the knowledge of the government and any craft, encountered in Guinea, whose captain could not produce either a licence or letter of safe-conduct, would presumably be arrested by the armed ships of Prince John.

Why were the regulations thus gradually tightened? Probably the answer is that the increasing prosperity of the trade was attracting newcomers, some of whom paid little or no attention to law. The problem of scanty evidence, which all will meet who care to delve among the early records of Portuguese exploration, confronts us, when we seek to show the condition of the Guinea trade after the discoveries of Fernão Gomes. There are certain passages in the chronicles, which suggest that valuable profits were being made in the traffic of Senegambia. Both Azurara and Diogo Gomes give attractive accounts of the trade before 1460, and de Barros relates how well matters were prospering in Senegambia in 1469. At first, the natives were timid and sometimes even attacked the white traders, but, after a time, they grew bolder and, whenever they heard of the arrival of a Portuguese caravel, they would throng the shore to offer their wares in exchange for horses, basins, trinkets, beads and other articles of personal adornment.[2] The traffic grew in volume between the mainland and Santiago Island, where a small white settlement throve at Ribeira Grande. Caravels from Senegambia, privileged to trade by the grant to the islanders of 1466, would return to the harbour of Ribeira

---

[1] Bensaude, *op. cit.*, pp. 275-6.   [2] Barros, I. ii. 2.

Grande with their cargoes of hides, meal, wax, gum and ostrich eggs. In the town a church was built before the end of 1470 where were held the first regular services in Guinea.[1] Prince Fernando, who owned the Cape Verde Islands, encouraged the trade in ursella by allowing two merchants of Castile, João and Pedro de Lugo, the right to bring it from Santiago to Europe, though he insisted that clerks, representing himself, were to sail in the ships of the two brothers for the purpose of adding up and assessing the cargoes and making provision for the payment of the proper dues (30 September 1469).[2] Here are only a few glimpses of the traffic of Upper Guinea, but they give an impression of prosperity.

The discovery of the gold-bearing region of Mina undoubtedly brought quick wealth to those who trafficked beyond Sierra Leone. Yet, if this be so, only one or two indications have been found of the value of that commerce. Probably, the fortunate few took steps to suppress the true facts about Mina, but they could not hide from the public eye the decrees of 1474. The laws of 31 August and 10 September were passed, we believe, to prevent others, and especially Castilians, from tasting of the new fruits of discovery. Reports of lucrative trades had aroused great interest in Portugal. Keen business men seem to have wanted to participate in them. This state of affairs would appear to have been reflected by a letter patent of 24 October 1474, which granted to Antonio Fernandes das Povoas a fixed share in the contract of elephants' teeth brought from Guinea.[3] Presumably, a number of ships were now annually trading on the modern Ivory Coast, which had recently been discovered by the captains of Fernão Gomes, and this development had led to a sudden increase in the quantity of ivory obtainable in Guinea. Consequently, the king farmed out the right to buy all of it, and das Povoas became part-holder of the contract.

An episode in the history of the Portuguese Cortes throws light upon the gold traffic of Mina. Among the complaints of the Cortes in 1473 was a protest against the renewal of the contract to Fernão Gomes on the double ground that the crown

---

[1] Barcellos, pp. 29–31.
[2] Barcellos, p. 33.
[3] *Alguns Documentos*, p. 40.

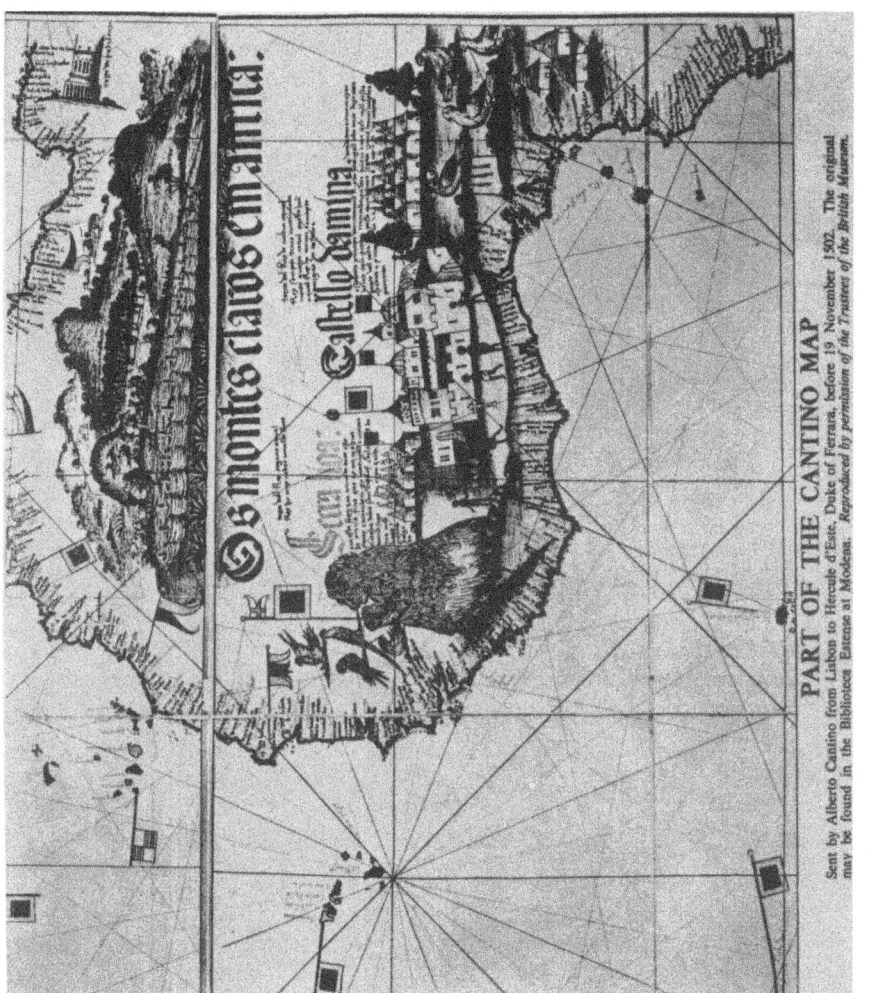

PART OF THE CANTINO MAP

Sent by Alberto Cantino from Lisbon to Hercule d'Este, Duke of Ferrara, before 19 November 1502. The original may be found in the Biblioteca Estense at Modena. *Reproduced by permission of the Trustees of the British Museum.*

I

could, with ease and justice, obtain an extra 100 milreis, and that the trade ought, in any case, to be free.[1] Two conclusions may be drawn from a consideration of this vain protest. Why, firstly, did the Cortes believe that 100 milreis could easily and fairly be obtained? It is surely very probable that the value of Gomes's contract had so increased that he could well afford to pay the extra sum. In itself, therefore, this fragment supplies indirect evidence of the rise in the prosperity of Lower Guinea, a rise mainly due to the discovery of big quantities of gold dust. But, secondly, it is notable that the Cortes proposed free commerce. A probable motive of those members who supported the petition, may have been the desire to share in the trade and, presumably, especially in the gold traffic. Such a desire can have been voiced only because rumour whispered of huge profits. Thus, if it be admitted that Fernão Gomes was interested chiefly in the gold of Mina, this protest of 1473 does confirm that he had been enriched. It was a reliable trade too, for now a fleet was " annually despatched " to bring back the Guinea gold.[2] We may turn, for more exact information, to the pages of the *Esmeraldo de Situ Orbis*, where Pacheco relates how a Flemish ship went to Mina in 1475 and loaded from five to six thousand dobras of gold.[3]

Indeed, prospects in Guinea were now so bright that several unlicensed adventures were undertaken. Pacheco records the presence of a Genoese navigator off the Malagueta coast in 1471, but his reference is very exiguous : he does not say whether this man's ship was also Genoese or even whether it was licensed.[4] But he tells with more detail the interesting story of the Flemish vessel to which we have already drawn attention. This ship, equipped in Flanders, employed a pilot of Castile, and so sailed to traffic beyond Cape Threepoints. After purchasing a cargo of gold, the ship turned homewards, but was cast upon the rocks of the Malagueta coast, the gold lost and all the crew drowned. Such an end was thoroughly deserved, writes Pacheco, for the Flemings had trafficked without a licence.[5]

[1] Santarem, *Memorias para a historia das Cortes Geraes*, pt. ii, p. 38 ; Azevedo, *Epocas Económico*, p. 173.
[2] Alonso de Palencia, *Crónica de Enrique IV*, iv. 205.
[3] Pacheco, II. iii.
[4] *Ibid.*
[5] *Ibid.*

One might assume plausibly that ignorance of the Guinea navigation was the cause of their undoing. Instead of sailing southwards from the Mina coast until they should run into the west-flowing equatorial current, they had struggled straight back, close to the coast, against the Guinea current and the prevailing wind and, having been caught in a storm, were wrecked off the shallow rocky coast of Malagueta. Against this view, however, it may be suggested that they wished to buy malagueta pepper on the return journey, and that even Portuguese caravels were often lost on this part of the coast, for the seas, sweeping up to the land, would sometimes hurl the small craft of those early voyagers upon the beach. Moreover, the Flemish ship carried a Castilian pilot who would have been familiar with the navigation of those parts.[1] More probably, therefore, neither the wrath of God—Pacheco's theory—nor ignorance of the navigation, but the mischance of a storm upon a dangerous foreshore caused the destruction of this interloper.

This story shows that certain Andalusian merchants, from whom, since the Portuguese pursued a national policy of secrecy, the Flemings must have drawn their information, were still interested in Guinea. The link between Castile and Guinea dated back, as we saw in the first chapter, at least to 1454. There can be little doubt about sporadic Castilian voyages between 1454 and 1475. Mention has been made before of the de Prado expedition (1460). One or two phrases in the grant of 1469 to João and Pedro de Lugo suggest that some voyages, of which no more tangible record appears to remain, were made from Andalusia—specifically named in the patent—to Senegambia or the Cape Verde Islands. Alfonso V, when sanctioning Prince Fernando's concession of the ursella contract to the brothers, referred vaguely to " certain injuries and damages," inflicted by the Castilians upon his own people, and only favoured the de Lugos with a safe-conduct to Santiago because they were not guilty of Andalusian reprisals and, therefore, would have to be protected by the crown from attack or arrest by the vindictive islanders. The Santiagians, apparently, angered by unrecorded insults from Andalusian pirates, were apt to be merciless in their treatment of those whom they managed to catch.[2]

[1] Alonso de Palencia, *Crónica de Enrique IV*, iv. 214. [2] Barcellos, p. 33.

Subsequently, we do not hear of the Castilians again until 1474. The letter patent of 10 September of that year, quoted above, refers to the spread of piracy. Many ships had been and were being equipped to make the Guinea voyage without offering recognizances of good behaviour. As soon as the port officials asked for the submission of these bonds, ships had been wont to steal out of harbour. Alfonso V, therefore, determined to enforce the giving of recognizances, and this was to apply to Castilians equally with Portuguese. Those who failed to do so in future would be liable, if caught, to forfeit not only their ships but also all their possessions. A question had been raised as to whether Castilians could enter bond to receive letters of safe-conduct. The law removed uncertainty by specially extending the opportunity to them. It would appear, therefore, that Andalusian interlopers had formerly been among the pirates and, if we collate this piece of evidence with the vague reference to reprisals in the de Lugo grant (1469), we may conclude that they had also perpetrated considerable damage in Santiago. One drawback was that the regulation of 1474 could not be enforced outside Portugal. Andalusians might still go to Guinea from their own ports. Some of their pilots, like the one who directed the Flemish voyage of 1475, already knew a good deal about the Guinea navigation. Indeed, this particular pilot must have made at least one earlier expedition to Mina, or else it is difficult to understand why the Flemings should have employed him. It looks as though several voyages may have been undertaken to Mina in the winters of 1473–4 and 1474–5. This leads to a further conclusion. Perhaps we may even presume that, news of the discovery of the gold source having spread quickly to Castile, the number of illegal Andalusian voyages began to increase.

The records are regrettably obscure about these interloping expeditions. They are also incomplete. More voyages than are here described were probably made by foreigners to West Africa in this period of Portuguese progress. We must, then, regard our evidence as directive rather than narrative; it shows not so much the sequence of events as the tendency, whereby news of the expansion of trade with Upper Guinea and rumours about the discovery of the mine of gold spread slowly across Europe, and ships were rigged, manned and sent out into the comparatively unknown Ocean Sea to bring back treasure. The voyages themselves were in another sense directive, because they were the forerunners of a long series of interloping expeditions during the following century : they reveal what was to be one of the salient features of commercial rivalry in West Africa. Private merchants, the subjects of sovereigns who have no legal claim to Guinea, will equip ships to make the traffic in spite of papal prohibitions, Portuguese protests and threats, and the lurking dangers of the ocean. Seen in this light, the Castilian, Flemish and, perhaps, Genoese expeditions of this period acquire additional significance.

The most important event between 1456 and 1475 was the discovery of the gold-bearing region of Mina. In Upper Guinea the whites made some progress. A few discoveries, including the full mapping of the archipelago of Cape Verde, graced the last years of the great Prince Henry, and the earliest scheme of white settlement was undertaken in Santiago. But the prospects of trade dimmed because of rather reckless exploitation. After 1460 the profits of the Lagos company began to fall, though the patent of 1466, issued in order to help the struggling settlers of Santiago, did lead to an expansion of traffic between the island and the opposite mainland. However, now that Prince Henry was dead, a more magnetic stimulus was needed to sustain interest in Guinea, and this was provided by the remarkable explorations of 1469–72. The richest part of West Africa was thus revealed : the Malagueta coast with its pepper, the gold-bearing region of Mina and, later, the slave marts which dotted the shores of Benin and Gabun. Admittedly these findings did not bring unmixed blessings to the Portuguese. Foreign merchants, attracted by tales of untold wealth, ignored Portuguese rights and sent their ships into the prohibited seas. Alfonso V responded by tightening the regulations in regard to Guinea voyages. In doing so, he prepared the ground for a monopoly in West Africa. We shall see, in our next chapter, how Castile was the first foreign power seriously to challenge these foundations.

CHAPTER III

THE CHALLENGE OF CASTILE, 1475-1480

WE have now reached the point when the alarums and rumours of war in Guinea between Portuguese and Castilians came to a head. Since the middle of the century, the latter had looked with desiring eyes upon the riches, which the merchants of Lisbon and Lagos, and the royal house of Portugal, were amassing from the traffic. They regarded Alfonso V's claims with suspicion and envy. They had ignored them, when they dared, but only at grave risk to their ships and to themselves. Now a quarrel, mainly of Alfonso's seeking, led to war and gave them a unique chance to make good their counter-claim. A vigorous monarch, Ferdinand of Spain, deliberately supported them, even assembling a royal fleet in Seville harbour to drive the Portuguese from Guinea. This challenge, as we shall see, failed, but the Portuguese were so extended in the struggle that, while securing recognition of their monopoly in Guinea, they admitted Castile's right to possess the Canaries.

Before describing the history of this conflict, we may be permitted to say something of the evidence. Surprising as it may sound, it is a fact that, until quite recently, the reality of these Castilian voyages was questioned! Most seventeenth century writers of West African history either ignored or disbelieved the statement of Faria y Sousa, a Portuguese annalist of the early years of that same century, that in 1478 a fleet of thirty-five caravels left Seville for the mine of gold and that another such fleet sailed in 1481.[1] Thus, for example, Jean Barbot, an employee of the French West African Company, who produced a *Description of Guinea* in the early eighteenth century, absolutely denied these " romantick relations ".[2] The

---

[1] Faria y Sousa, *The History of Portugal*, p. 297.
[2] Barbot, *Description of Guinea*, bk. III, ch. vi.

fact was that the French writers of those times were engaged in proving the priority of their own countrymen in the traffic of Guinea. This foolish controversy[1] tended for a long while to obscure the truth concerning the early history of West Africa. The question of Castilian participation was scarcely raised. But, with the advent of the nineteenth century, men began to study the history of the age of discovery with more science and less political prejudice. The Viscount de Santarem, after effectively disposing of the French claim to have traded in the ports of Guinea in the fourteenth century, proceeded to support the statement of Faria y Sousa.[2] He called attention in the first place to a manuscript in the Spanish archives, which was cited in Navarrete's *Colección de Viages*, and in the second place to a statement in the *Annales de Sevilla* of Ortiz de Zúñiga. Both the manuscript and the Annals referred to the activities of Castilians in Guinea. Castilian participation was thus indubitably established.

However, an analysis of Navarrete's *Colección de Viages* and of the annals of both Spanish and Portuguese chroniclers has thrown further light upon the nature of Andalusian enterprise in the seas of Guinea. It has shown not only that frequent voyages were undertaken, but also that the catholic sovereigns gave official sanction to the expeditions. They set the trade upon a monopolistic basis and collected a ' fifth ' from all merchandise imported to Castile from Guinea. Of the Portuguese chroniclers contemporary with these events, only Ruy de Pina and Damião de Goes refer to the Portuguese attempts to exclude the spirited Andalusian sailors ;[3] it is rather surprising that the travel-stained Duarte Pacheco Pereira makes no mention of Castilian enterprises in his *Esmeraldo de Situ Orbis*. As might be expected, the Castilian records are fuller. Three chroniclers, Alonso de Palencia, Hernando del Pulgar and Andrés Bernáldez allude to the Guinea voyages of their compatriots.

Admittedly the reliability of the Spanish chroniclers is very questionable. The fact that they were writing in an age of

---

[1] *Vide supra*, pp. 2-3.
[2] Santarem, *Recherches sur la priorité de la découverte . . . au dela du Cap Bojador, passim*.
[3] Ruy de Pina, *Chronica del Rey D. Affonso V*, ch. ccviii ; Goes, *Chronica do Principe D. João II*, ch. cciii.

THE CHALLENGE OF CASTILE   43

growing national patriotism made them the more biassed. For the most part, besides, they had special interests to serve. Alonso de Palencia and Hernando del Pulgar were both employees of the Castilian crown; the first became royal historiographer to Queen Isabella and the second held that office after the year 1482. It was, therefore, politic for both of them to praise—and to exaggerate—the exploits of their own countrymen. Andrés Bernáldez entered the Church and became curate of Los Palacios, a town in Andalusia. He was credulous and patriotic, so that one is not surprised to find him enlarging without scruple upon the exploits of the Andalusians among whom he lived. Nevertheless, the evidence of voyages from southern Castile to Guinea between 1454 and 1475, set out in chapters I and II, and the references of Goes and Pina confirm the statements of the Castilian chroniclers; while furthermore, the archivist records, printed in Navarrete, prove that these writers were not deliberately disguising the entire facts of the situation. Therefore, the skeleton of what they say may be accepted, though the details which they add are less reliable.

Accordingly, let us now attempt to reconstruct the true story of this challenge of Castile (1475-80). Keen rivalry, embracing the possession of the Canary Islands, North Africa and Guinea, marked the relationship between Portugal and Castile in 1475. Moreover, King Alfonso V, ambitious for power, had claimed the throne of Castile upon the death of Henry the Impotent (11 December 1474). He was affianced to the Princess Joanna, who disputed her aunt, Isabella's right of succession, and he invaded Castilian territory in May 1475.[1] The resulting war in the Iberian peninsular dragged on until the end of the year 1478, and then negotiations began for the settlement of the points in dispute.

The outbreak of this war was interpreted by many seamen and merchants of Andalusia as a signal for a new attempt to wrest the Guinea traffic from the Portuguese. Probably, they believed that Ferdinand and Isabella, joint rulers of the newly united Castile and Aragon, welcoming any means of exhausting the resources of King Alfonso, would give them diplomatic and, perhaps, practical support in their search for profit. The omens, on the whole, were more favourable than in 1454. War between

[1] Prescott, *Ferdinand and Isabella*, i. 259 *et seq.*

the rival states increased the chances of a successful issue to the Andalusian challenge. Accordingly, ships were made ready in the ports to sail to the Guinea Coast.

No estimate can be made of the number of vessels sent to West Africa by the Andalusians in these years. Many ships undoubtedly sailed to Senegambia to seize slaves. A contemporary chronicler, Alonso de Palencia, has described the activities of traders and especially of the fishermen of Palos. The men of Palos, apparently, were more familiar with the navigation of the West African coast than their compatriots of Seville and Cadiz. Some fishermen, before the outbreak of war, appear to have fitted out two caravels which loaded 120 Azenegues on the Barbary coast. Now, in 1475, perhaps with the encouragement of King Ferdinand, three caravels were equipped in the port and taken to the river Gambia, where the crew began to traffic with the local king. Slaves were bartered for brass rings, small leather shields and baskets of different colours. The negro prince, under the impression that the white traders were Portuguese, accepted an invitation to go with his relatives on board one of the ships but, having done so, found himself a prisoner in their hands. Some of the crew then armed, went on shore and captured 140 more of the natives. The caravels, thus loaded, returned to Palos. Later, when King Ferdinand heard of these happenings, he ordered the governor of the fortress of Palos, Gonzalo de Estuñiga, to see that the captive king was taken back to Guinea. After a few months, this was done, but the relatives of the unhappy prince were sold as slaves in Andalusia.[1]

This expedition may be regarded as typical of others which have not been recorded. We know that more trading voyages were made to Senegambia because Palencia says that, after the return of the King of Gambia to his own country, he avenged himself by seizing some of his " treacherous attackers, despite the caution with which they sailed ". Moreover, a triangular traffic in shells would seem to have been inaugurated by these sharp Castilian merchants. Quantities of sea-shells, gathered in the Canary Islands, were transported to Seville, where they were re-sold and carried to Guinea. Shells, being used for coins

---

[1] Alonso de Palencia, *Crónica de Enriqueiv*, iv. 129.

by the black merchants, were valued highly, and so the Castilians were able to get gold and slaves for them.[1]

A few trading voyages were also made to Mina. We have emphasized already that the Castilian pilot, who accompanied the Flemish expedition of 1475, must have made at least one earlier voyage to Mina. Hernando del Pulgar, whose evidence albeit is very unreliable, chronicles three voyages to the " mine of gold ". He declares that the first Andalusian voyage to this region was accidental : one of their ships having been carried forward by the current—quite a likely event—a country was found, where the natives would sell great quantities of gold. The fortunate crew then returned and spread the news in the ports of Andalusia. Their gold was tested and found pure. Accordingly, a second caravel was equipped and sent out. This adventure was equally successful, and so other men also took part and, in a third voyage, 10,000 pesos of gold, each peso being worth two Aragonese florins, were brought back. Those caravels which went to Mina took cargoes of shells, beads, old clothes, copper basins, brass manillas and other articles of small value.[2]

Hernando's evidence cannot be taken too literally but, if we collate it with the phrasing of a royal decree of 1480, which referred to " gold and other wares, acquired in the Mine " and brought to Castile, we may see clearly that the Andalusians tried hard to secure a share in the profits of Mina.[3] Senegambia and Mina were, in fact, their chief objectives. Presumably, they left the rest of the coast alone, concentrating only upon the more lucrative parts of Guinea.

Meantime, the war in the peninsular had led to important new developments respecting the struggle in Guinea. On the one hand, the catholic sovereigns, taking advantage of the occasion to revive the policy of King John II, had proclaimed their ancient right to possess North Africa, the Canary Islands and "the discovery of Guinea". On the other hand, certain of the Castilian grandees had discerned an opportunity to make private capital out of the rivalry of Alfonso V and Ferdinand : they offered their swords to King Alfonso in return for concess-

---

[1] Pulgar, *Chronica de los Reyes Católicos*, pt. II, ch. lxii.
[2] *Ibid.*
[3] Navarrete, *Colección de Viages*, i. xxxix.

ions in Guinea. Thus, the new conflict provided a unique occasion for the gratification of political ambitions and personal selfishness.

In 1475 the catholic sovereigns took certain steps which were calculated to encourage the bold efforts of their adventurous subjects. They began by renewing their claim to the coast of Guinea. The preamble of a royal edict, issued from Valladolid on 19 August 1475, recited the fact that the progenitors of Queen Isabella "always owned the parts of Africa and Guinea", described how the enemy, Portugal, had intervened, and how Henry the Impotent had submitted to the collection by the Portuguese of a duty of one-fifth on all merchandise imported from Guinea, and pointed out that the revenues of Castile had thus suffered great loss. Now, however, the government had decided to take Guinea from the Portuguese and to reduce it to obedience. Accordingly, the order forbade any voyage, henceforth to that country except by licence from Queen Isabella, and all those who might secure a permit were to pay the ' fifth ' to the receivers of the crown. Dr. Anton Rodriguez de Lillo and Gonçalo Coronado were appointed the official receivers in Seville, and an attempt was made to induce honest traders to seize interlopers by a promise of one-third of all such prizes.[1] Ferdinand and Isabella then proceeded to order the preparation of an armada of thirty ships in Seville. This fleet, under the command of Carlos de Valera, was to go to Guinea to expel the Portuguese.[2]

In thus raising the whole question of Portugal's right to Guinea, they did not act blindly. Some might suppose that the invasion of the Portuguese having reduced them to dire straits, they resorted to all manner of expedients to check the advance of Alfonso V. Accordingly, they renewed their claim to Guinea, not because they believed in it, but with a view to distracting the invading monarch. Now it is true that their position was indeed serious in the early months of 1475,[3] and their need obliged them, therefore, to use every available resource. But arguments may be adduced to show that the Guinea policy of the Castilian rulers was the result of careful

[1] *Ibid.*, iii. 465–8.
[2] Palencia, *op. cit.*, iv. 128–9 ; Ortiz de Zúñiga, *Annales de Sevilla*, bk. XII, pp. 373–4.
[3] R. B. Merriman, *The Rise of the Spanish Empire*, ii. 51.

THE CHALLENGE OF CASTILE 47

and deliberate thought. Men knew that the treasury of Portugal drew a considerable revenue from the profits of the traffic of Guinea, and especially from the gold. If, then, the annual Portuguese fleet which sailed home from Guinea could be intercepted and its gold, pepper and ivory confiscated, the Castilian government might succeed in undermining, partially at any rate, the financial staying-power of the enemy. We shall see that Ferdinand did, in fact, plan to cut off the return of the annual fleet in the winter of 1475–6. Furthermore, even after the checkmating of King Alfonso V at the battle of Toro (March 1476), Castilian aims in Guinea were not abandoned. These facts tend surely to reveal that the deliberate object of Ferdinand and Isabella was, after due consideration, to expel the Portuguese from Guinea and to take it for themselves.

In point of fact, they were not treading upon very sure ground, when they proclaimed their rightful possession of the conquest of Guinea. Ever since the capture of Ceuta in 1415, the Portuguese had led the way in the opening up of the African coast. They were, then, rulers of the parts of Guinea by virtue of prior discovery. Papal sanction was also theirs, not only by the doubtful early concession of Pope Martin V, but also by the celebrated bulls of 1455 and 1456, bulls which had set their claim upon a pretty firm foundation. Should the catholic sovereigns question the validity of these grants, they would incur the charge of heresy. True they might reply that, in the bull *Dudum cum* (31 July 1436), Pope Eugenius IV had admitted the " conquest of Africa " to pertain to King John of Castile.[1] Yet, this bull having seen the light even before the discovery of Senegambia, it could not be supposed that the territory designated therein by the word 'Africa' included also Guinea. For these reasons, therefore, Ferdinand and Isabella found it difficult to justify their claim.

Nevertheless, their challenge was prosecuted vigorously. Apparently they made a profit from the collection of the ' fifth '.[2] During the four years of the war, besides enjoying success in the Iberian peninsular, they increased their control over Castilian trade with West Africa. Having occasion to emphasize the freedom of Castilians to make the Guinea voyage, provided first

---
[1] *Alguns Documentos*, p. 4.
[2] Pulgar, *Chronica de los Reyes Católicos*, pt. II, ch. lxii.

the royal permit should be obtained, Queen Isabella bade all merchants enter recognizances of good behaviour. Further, she decreed that licensed traders should refrain from business with enemy states, particularly Portugal and France, and insisted, above all, that they must not carry either Portuguese or French goods or men in their ships. To check evasion, she ordered that every prospective licensee must make a full declaration of his cargo to her receivers in Seville (4 March 1478).[1] A year later, a new order was published in which the Queen commanded that gold and other wares, acquired in Mina and on the coasts of Guinea, should be carried direct to Castile and not to other parts (17 February 1479).[2]

These measures exemplify a spirit and a policy of great caution. They show the crown taking elaborate care to regulate and subordinate the new trade. We may presume that many of the Andalusian sailors were little better than pirates. Some of the merchants behind them, in financing their earlier voyages, had encouraged an illegal and dangerous traffic. Was it surprising, then, that both merchants and seamen should seek now to avoid the payment of duties to the Castilian monarchy? One obvious channel of evasion was to transport their cargoes to non-Castilian ports; another was to falsify returns and so hoodwink the customs officers; and a third was to carry goods belonging to foreign merchants. All these dodges the wily traders seem to have tried. However the queen, by her laws of March 1478, and February 1479, sought to foil such malpractices, but with what success we cannot tell. Moreover, one clause of the first of these two edicts, which forbade licensed Castilian ships to take on board the subjects of enemy states, may have been directed against a more treacherous kind of evil work. It suggests that Portuguese were sailing in caravels, which belonged to a faction among the grandees of Castile, who favoured Alfonso V's claim to the throne.

The Marquis of Cadiz was prominent among those of high birth, who were not averse to a liaison with the Portuguese invader. Alonso de Palencia records that he did, in fact, support Alfonso V.[3] It would appear that he hoped to make

[1] Navarrete, *Colección de Viages*, ii. 386–9.
[2] *Ibid.*, i. xxxix.
[3] Palencia, *op. cit.*, iv. 214–5.

THE CHALLENGE OF CASTILE

political capital out of the rivalry between the two royal opponents. He was evidently acquainted with the plans of that group of Portuguese merchants, who traded to Guinea, and may even have adventured his money in the traffic.

The facts which suggest his treachery are these. In 1474, as we saw before, Prince John of Portugal was entrusted with the administration of the contracts of Guinea.[1] Palencia declares that Prince John took over because Fernão Gomes, whose ships had suffered at the hands of the Andalusians, was unable to bear further losses; but evidence of this kind, emanating from a Castilian source, cannot be accepted without confirmation; and, in any case, the contract of Gomes terminated in October 1475. However, doubtless in view of his knowledge and experience of the navigation of West Africa, the Lisbon merchant was commissioned by the prince to equip the annual trading fleet for the season of 1475–6. The Portuguese caravels set out for Mina in the autumn of 1475. Meantime, in Seville harbour the preparations were going forward of the armada which King Ferdinand had ordered to intercept this fleet on its return. Now, as luck would have it, the Marquis of Cadiz chanced to hear of these preparations. Grasping Ferdinand's intention, he sent two fast caravels from Cadiz to warn Fernão Gomes of the impending attack.[2] It so happened that the departure of the armada from Andalusia was delayed until the following year, and so the Mina fleet was able to return to Portugal without molestation. But how may one explain the action of the marquis ? Clearly he knew about the annual fleet which left Lisbon for Mina each autumn; further, there were pilots in his service who were familiar with the navigation of Guinea; and, lastly, for an unknown reason, he was uneasy for the safety of the annual Guinea fleet. Unfortunately, it is impossible to determine whether his anxiety for the fleet resulted from sympathy with the Portuguese cause, or his sympathy with that cause was partly a consequence of his direct interest in the fleet. Still, had sympathy with Alfonso V's dynastic claim been his primary motive, surely he would have contented himself with informing the Portuguese government of the armaments in Seville. Instead, he equipped caravels and sent

[1] *Vide supra*, p. 34.
[2] Palencia, *op. cit.*, iv. 214–5.

them direct to Guinea. These considerations and the marquis's apparent knowledge of and interest in colonial affairs, lead us to venture to suggest that a commercial link, whose nature we cannot discover, must have existed between him and the Portuguese merchants who traded to Guinea.

The attitude of Henry de Guzman, second Duke of Medina Sidonia, is even more difficult to understand. A tradition of rivalry estranged his family from that of the Marquis of Cadiz. Accordingly, in the War of Succession, the marquis having favoured Joanna *la Beltraneja*, the reigning duke supported Isabella. Yet his relations with Guinea cannot be reconciled easily with his alleged loyalty to his feudal superior. There are three scraps of evidence which shed light upon his interest in Guinea : he desired to seize one of the Cape Verde Islands ;[1] he hindered the equipment of the Seville armada until his request for the island should be granted ;[2] and, six years afterwards, he encouraged two Englishmen, William Fabian and John Tintam, to make a voyage to West Africa.[3]

Palencia's account of the duke's island project is very vague. He records that Medina Sidonia petitioned King Ferdinand to grant him the island of Santiago, should it be captured by the armada, which was to sail from Seville. Pending the granting of his petition the duke hindered the departure of the expedition. The king, blissfully ignorant of what were to be the consequences of his bounty, soon yielded to the request of his vassal, and so Carlos de Valera then weighed anchor. Already, however, the delay had allowed Alfonso V's Mina fleet to get back safely to Lisbon. It was now May 1476. Furthermore, even when they did get away, contrary winds drove the Andalusians back to harbour. Nevertheless, they ventured forth once more, and shaped a course for the Cape Verde Islands. After plundering Santiago, they captured the two caravels sent by the Marquis of Cadiz, and found on board 500 Azenegue slaves. But disputes now broke out among them and so, presumably towards the end of 1476, they returned to Andalusia. Henry de Guzman was partly responsible for the comparative failure of this enterprise. His greed had delayed the departure

---
[1] *Ibid.*, iv. 216–7.
[2] *Ibid.*
[3] Resende, *Chronica do D. João II*, ch. xxxiii.

THE CHALLENGE OF CASTILE 51

of the ships and caused them to be diverted from Mina, their original objective, to the Cape Verde Islands. Yet it is doubtful whether he regarded his attitude as disloyal. As a mighty grandee, he could exercise of right a considerable degree of independence. Though the duke had spoiled Ferdinand's plan for intercepting the Mina fleet, his motive was to injure the Portuguese. Probably he observed the same rule of conduct now, as later when he encouraged the Englishmen. We may credit him, then, at least with the virtue of consistency.

The failure of the expedition of 1476 did not deter the Castilians. The equipment of a new armada was often considered in council by Ferdinand and Isabella and the royal ministers.[1] At the same time, trading caravels sailed frequently from the ports of the south coast. Some were pirates who ignored the decrees of 1475. The catholic sovereigns, therefore, appointed one, Luis Gonçalves, to be " Chief Clerk of all barks and especially of those which go to the trades of Guinea as far as Sierra Leone." This officer was to see that in every ship sailed a clerk, whose business would be to check cargoes and to prevent unloading at the ports before the payment of the ' fifth '. This order had to be made public in the ports of Seville, Jerez, Cadiz, San Lucar, Palos and Huelva, from all of which, presumably, caravels set out for Guinea (6 December 1476).[2]

The names of the pirates, against whom this order was directed, have not been preserved, but we may speculate that one of them was a certain Juan Diaz. This man was a Portuguese pilot and a renegade. Many years later he was guilty of helping a French crew to capture a caravel of the King of Portugal's Mina fleet.[3] For a reason unknown, he had fled from his native country and settled in Andalusia. In the spring of 1476, he was at sea with Sebastian Rodriguez, preying probably on Portuguese shipping off the coast of Upper Guinea. He was also guilty of robbing an Andalusian balinger, which Anton Martin Nieto, of Palos, had equipped " to make war against the Portuguese and Moors ", that is, we may presume, to seize Azenegues on the Barbary coast or negroes in Senegambia.[4]

[1] Navarrete, Colección de Viages, i. 423.
[2] Ibid., iii. 468–71.
[3] Ibid., iii. 505.
[4] Ibid., iii. 475–77.

Moreover, if Diaz was an interloper, Nieto was possibly a licensed trader.

More exact evidence remains of the conflict between the two states for the winter of 1478-9. Towards the end of 1478, a fleet of thirty-five caravels was assembled in Seville to go to the Mine and to expel the Portuguese. Pedro de Covides was given the supreme command. The ships departed with supplies of cheap goods like shells and old clothes, trafficked successfully on the coast, loaded a quantity of gold, and returned. But Prince John had been advised of the expedition. Accordingly, a Portuguese armed squadron, under captains Jorge Correa and Meni Palha, set sail to intercept them. The Andalusians ran straight into the trap, their ships, crews and cargoes were arrested, and all were taken to Lisbon.[1]

It turned out that this was the last Guinea expedition officially organised by the catholic sovereigns. Negotiations to end the war began soon after the ships of Pedro de Covides were brought captive into Lisbon harbour. Alfonso V's invading army had been checked at the battle of Toro (1476), his effort to secure French support proved barren, and a second invasion of Castile in the beginning of 1479 failed. Accordingly, in March, Queen Isabella and Princess Beatrice, sister-in-law of Alfonso V, discussed terms of peace at Alcantara.[2] A settlement was achieved at Alcaçovas in September. It was ratified by King Alfonso and Prince John at Evora on 8 September, and by Ferdinand and Isabella at Toledo (6 March 1480).

The Treaty of Alcaçovas ended the war. Alfonso V renounced his claim to the throne of his rival, Isabella of Castile, and the peace of 1431 between the two states was again confirmed. Articles VIII and IX dealt with the colonial disputes. In the first, the catholic sovereigns promised that neither they nor their successors would disturb, publicly or secretly, the Portuguese crown in its possession of " the trade, lands and barter of Guinea with its gold mines ", the islands already discovered of the Azores, Madeira and Cape Verde, or such other islands as might be found " from the Canary Islands towards Guinea " ;

---

[1] Pulgar, *op. cit.*, pt. II, chs. lxxvi, lxxxviii ; Ortiz de Zúñiga, *Annales*, bk. xii, p. 386 ; Pina, *op. cit.*, ch. ccviii ; Goes, *op. cit.*, ch. cciii.
[2] R. B. Merriman, *The Rise of the Spanish Empire*, ii. 52-4.

THE CHALLENGE OF CASTILE 53

neither would they interfere with the subjects of Portugal, who went to those parts, nor encourage others, nor go themselves. In return for these concessions, King Alfonso V withdrew his claim to the Canary Islands in article IX.[1]

The colonial question, which had long antagonised the two adjacent nations, was thus amicably settled. In effect, the papal bulls, which granted to Portugal the 'discovery and conquest' of all lands beyond Cape Bojador as far as the Indies, were now recognised by the rulers of Castile. The state which had first challenged, now accepted, and was later to champion, the claim of Portugal. Henceforward, the river of colonial development forked: one arm, controlled by Castile, streamed westwards from the Canaries, and the other, monopolised by Portugal, ran southwards from Cape Bojador.

Yet the Castilians had been loth to surrender the Mine. This is evident from the prominence given in the records to the discussion of the question. It would appear that, before the peace negotiations began, Ferdinand had sought papal sanction for the right to issue licences to his subjects to go to Mina.[2] His ships had sustained their challenge in spite of great danger; for the methods of the Portuguese had been calculated to still their ardour. "They were in the habit of torturing and killing some of the Castilians, whom they caught beyond the Canaries," wrote Alonso de Palencia, "and, in order to instil constant horror in the rest, they used to cut off the legs and arms of others."[3] Moreover, chroniclers, both Castilian and Portuguese, referred to the gold as if it were an important point of dispute. Hernando del Pulgar, for example, when describing the conclusion of peace, does not mention the word ' Guinea ': the treaty required, he says, " that the mine of gold should belong to the King of Portugal and to the prince his son."[4] Andrés Bernáldez followed the same line of approach: " there was great division between the Castilians and the Portuguese ", runs his chronicle, " touching the mine of gold ".[5] Even in the Treaty of Alcaçovas, the reference to Guinea was coloured by the addition " with its gold mines ", which would seem to

[1] Davenport, i. 36–48.
[2] Davenport, i. 33, note 2.
[3] Palencia, *op. cit.*, iv. 128.
[4] Pulgar, *op. cit.*, pt. II, ch. xci.
[5] Andrés Bernáldez, *Historia de los Reyes Católicos*, ch. xlii.

signify that the diplomats were concerned especially with the fate of Mina. These illustrations leave little room for doubt that the gold trade was the chief point in the colonial dispute, and suggest that Castile was very unwilling to yield her claim.

Still, the main question was settled, as we saw, when the treaty was ratified finally by Ferdinand and Isabella at Toledo in March 1480. But, as is often the case, certain subsidiary problems arose out of the agreement. The demarcation of the exact boundaries between Castilian and Portuguese dominion beyond the Canaries was to provide ample cause of discussion. Moreover, certain Andalusian caravels were trading in Guinea even while the peace talks were proceeding. Eustache de la Fosse, a Fleming who has left a valuable record of a voyage to Guinea in 1479–80, mentions how he met one of these caravels.[1] The government of Castile knew that some Andalusian ships were in Guinea, for a royal order of February 1480 referred to " three caravels and . . . other caravels whatsoever, which went to the said Mina."[2] A few of them had already returned before the order was made, but others were still trafficking along the coast. Presumably, they had left Castilian ports in the fall of 1479, intent upon loading a last cargo of gold ere the peace treaty should be finally ratified.

Now the Portuguese government, as soon as peace had been concluded, issued new orders to all its captains, who habitually navigated along the Guinea Coast. They were instructed, " for the defence, protection and preservation of the contracts of Guinea," to cast into the sea the crews of all " caravels or ships of any of the people of Spain or of any other country," encountered in Guinea, and to arrest the ships and illicit cargoes (April 1480).[3] Prince John, having secured full recognition of his monopoly from Ferdinand and Isabella, was obviously determined to enforce it. But there were Andalusian caravels still trading " beyond the Canaries towards Guinea ". Perhaps the prince had been warned of their presence. At any rate, the unfortunate men, who happened to trade in the prohibited area during the early months of 1480, were thus faced with certain death, if they should be caught.

[1] Eustache de la Fosse, "Voyage", (*Revue hispanique*, 1897, pp. 174–201).
[2] Navarrete, *Colección de Viages*, ii. 395–6.
[3] *Alguns Documentos*, p. 45.

Accordingly, transitional arrangements were made for these voyagers. King Ferdinand, in a letter to Alfonso V and to Prince John, asked that security should be granted to the Andalusians, provided that the proper duties were paid to the Portuguese government. He argued that Diego Diaz and Alonso de Avila, two of the merchants concerned, had " sent the said two caravels to the said Mina del Oro and the trade of the Isles of Guinea " before peace was proclaimed and, therefore, were entitled to leniency. It appears that his request was granted, and that letters of safe-conduct were sent to the interested merchants. Ferdinand's argument is not, in fact, entirely satisfactory, because caravels, which were still trading in Guinea in February 1480, must have left Andalusia during the peace negotiations and, perhaps, even later. Moreover, one of the merchants whom he helped, Alonso de Avila, appears to have been a high government official. One of the queen's secretaries bore the same name,[1] and seems to have resided at Valladolid, while the Alonso de Avila, who sent his caravel to the Mine, was a merchant of Valladolid. One suspects that a measure of government influence may be discerned in Ferdinand's letter to the Portuguese rulers. Two other caravels, *la Bolandra* and *la Toca*, whose owners were given similar letters of safe-conduct by Prince John, arrived in Andalusia from Mina after the peace treaty was signed. A possible reason for Ferdinand's favour was that, besides paying a ' fifth ' to the Prince of Portugal, the owners also paid a fifth of the value of their cargoes to the King of Castile.[2] After this, however, no further evidence of regular Castilian voyages to Guinea has been found. We may conclude, therefore, that the granting of safe-conducts to these merchants completed the transitional measures.

So ended the first serious attempt on the part of a foreign power to compete with the Portuguese in West Africa. Castilian traders, following close upon the heels of the Portuguese, had tried to prevent the creation of a monopoly by their rivals. In so doing, they differed from those other challengers, French, English and Netherlander, who came after them, for these found a monopoly and tried to destroy it. But Castilians and Portu-

---

[1] Navarrete, *op. cit.*, ii. 389, iii. 468.
[2] *Ibid.*, ii. 395-6.

guese fought for half a century in what was almost an open colonial field, the latter always leading and the former always pursuing. Even as they competed in North Africa and the Canaries, so they did in West Africa. Each claimed sole possession in Guinea, and each tried to exclude the other.

This feature of the struggle was illustrated well in the War of Castilian Succession. A consideration of the administrative measures of the two states brings out the similarity of their methods. Both claimed Guinea; both tried to regulate the trade; both used a system of licences for this purpose; both demanded recognizances of good behaviour from all licensees; both appointed receivers and clerks to supervise and assess cargoes; both required a full declaration of all merchandise carried by sea; both imposed customs duties on imports from Guinea; and both sent out armed fleets to enforce their decisions and to expel the ships of the rival state from West African waters. Yet, if Castile pursued a policy similar in many ways to that of Portugal, she was, after all, only copying the methods of the sister state. She would appear, in fact, to have followed the lead of Portugal, and to have modelled her own regulations upon those of her greater rival.

The truth was that the Portuguese had an insuperable advantage in the struggle, based upon their priority in the discovery, their greater zeal for empire and their numerical superiority in those parts. In the race to Guinea, the Castilians brought up the rear only as a feeble second. Their efforts shone with the reflected light of Portugal. Moreover, the strength of the Church Universal, in the form of papal bulls, was asserted justly on the side of Portugal, bequeathing to the House of Aviz all lands beyond Cape Bojador. These grants were, in effect, recognised by Ferdinand and Isabella in 1480, though the Canaries remained in Castilian hands by way of just consolation. The challenge of Castile was thus effectively assuaged. It only remained to see for how long the Portuguese might preserve intact the monopoly, which they proceeded to consolidate.

CHAPTER IV

THE CONSOLIDATION OF THE PORTUGUESE MONOPOLY,
1480-1530

THE Portuguese, having disposed of the Castilian claim to Guinea, now devoted more time and energy to discovery and colonisation. They also secured, from the papacy and from King Ferdinand of Spain, confirmation of their territorial monopoly, and they devised new regulations, which supplemented Alfonso V's laws, for the organisation of the trade of West Africa. These measures, of course, strengthened only the legal basis of their rights over Guinea, but the Portuguese fully realised the need of executive force. Accordingly, they built fortresses at various places on the coast, and equipped armadas to convoy their trading fleets and to patrol the shores of Guinea. Dame Fortune was kind, for she granted them half a century of peace there so that they could complete this work. Not one of the other maritime powers of Europe laid claim to Guinea from 1480 to 1530, although interloping ships, it is true, sometimes appeared in the prohibited seas. Consequently, when the French challenged the Portuguese empire early in the reign of John III, the trade, organisation and defence of Guinea had all been greatly changed. We must describe, therefore, the legal consolidation of the monopoly, the expansion of trade, and the building of fortresses and fleets, in order to prepare the way for the story of the political and commercial struggle in the sixteenth century. This chapter will be confined to an account of the legal consolidation of the monopoly.

The events of the war with Castile had shown that, if the Guinea monopoly was to be upheld, steps must be taken to protect it. Moreover, there were signs of unwelcome activity in the ports of Flanders and England, and indications that Florentine, Genoese, English and Flemish merchants wanted to share in the gold trade. These reasons, combined with vague fears of what the future might have in store, drove the Portuguese, immediately after the return of Columbus from his first voyage of discovery to the west, to seek a confirmation of their monopoly. Their efforts were rewarded in 1493-4 by papal bulls and the Treaty of Tordesillas.

Let us first consider those unlicensed English and Flemish voyages to West Africa, which aroused the fears of the Portuguese and thus led them to strengthen their monopoly. The narrative of a Fleming, named Eustache de la Fosse, proves that Flemish merchants evinced an interest in Guinea gold, and also that voyages were actually undertaken from Flanders to Mina.[1] Eustache de la Fosse seems to have been an educated citizen of Tournai. Early in the year 1479 he left Bruges to sail to Mina. His master, whose name we do not know, had sent to Seville the merchandise, which was to be taken to the mine of gold. Accordingly, Eustache interrupted his journey and paid a necessary visit to Spain. A factor of his master, who lived in Seville, had freighted and equipped a caravel for the voyage. Eustache embarked and, eventually, in the middle of October, his crew got under way. On the Barbary coast they encountered two Portuguese caravels, but they passed them by, for the Portuguese were their enemies. Sailing south-westwards, they touched at the Canaries, and then made their way to the Rio do Ouro. Here, Eustache relates, the Spaniards were accustomed to fish every year. It would seem, then, that Castilian fishermen were ignoring the Portuguese claim to a monopoly of the trade, fisheries and conquest of all land, discovered or to be discovered, beyond Cape Bojador. The Fleming proceeds to describe how Cape Barbas, just north of Cape Verde, was negotiated, and he says that here perished one, Henry, the factor of Thomas Perrot, a merchant of Bruges. Off Cape Verde, Eustache fell in with two other caravels, one of which had been fitted out at Cadiz and was also going to Mina. Apparently, they sailed on together, turned south-east at Sierra Leone, and so reached the Malagueta coast. Eustache's caravel hurried on to the Gold Coast, but one of the other two caravels delayed to purchase malagueta pepper and also slaves, which they intended afterwards to barter for gold when they should reach Mina. Meantime, while the second caravel traded at

[1] Eustache de la Fosse, "Voyage", (*Revue hispanique*, 1897, pp. 174–201).

CONSOLIDATION OF PORTUGUESE MONOPOLY 59

Samma, the Flemish ship loaded 12 or 14 pounds of gold near the Village of Two Parts. But then, unfortunately, a Portuguese armed squadron, commanded by Fernand de les Vaux[1] and Diogo Cão, set upon them. The interlopers were arrested and, ultimately, the ringleaders were taken to Portugal. After trial, all were condemned to death for having traded to the Mine without the licence of the King of Portugal. But Eustache seems to have bribed his gaoler, and, one Saturday night, he escaped from his prison and fled across the frontier into Castile. Many years later, certainly not before 1516, as a reference in his narrative to a work published in that year by Amerigo Vespucci proves, Eustache sat down to write the story of his adventures.

The importance of Eustache's tale is considerable. Besides the expedition from Flanders to Mina in 1475, recounted by Duarte Pacheco Pereira,[2] we have proof here of a second voyage in 1479-80, and evidence of a third, not long before 1479, during which Henry, employed by another merchant of Bruges, had been shipwrecked just north of Cape Verde. Moreover, the Flemish traders of 1475 and 1479 sought help in Castile. Pacheco states that the Flemings, who were shipwrecked on the Malagueta coast, obtained a Castilian pilot. Eustache de la Fosse records the presence of a Flemish factor in Seville, who equipped the caravel for use in the Guinea enterprise, and perhaps he, too, employed a Castilian pilot. It would seem that merchants of Flanders and Andalusia pooled their knowledge and experience, when preparing these interloping voyages. We find, again, that Eustache knew that winter was the best time for sailing to Guinea: he set out in the middle of October and reached Mina in the middle of December. His narrative further reveals an exact acquaintance with the chief trading resorts around the coast, Cape Verde, Sierra Leone, Malagueta, Cape Threepoints, Mina whose two chief commercial centres, Samma and the Village of Two Parts, he also mentions, and the Rio dos Escravos. All these facts cannot be mere coincidences;

[1] Can this possibly be a variant spelling for Fernão do Po ? There is some ground for thinking so, because elsewhere Eustache says that Fernand de les Vaux had to sail 200 leagues to the east, and Fernão do Po discovered the island in the Gulf of Benin, which bears his name and which also lies to the east. May we even antedate the discovery of Benin, and assume that its coast had been navigated by 1479 ?
[2] *Vide supra.* p. 37.

they suggest a greater trade between Flanders and Guinea from 1475 to 1480 than extant records nowadays reveal.

Moreover, at this same time, there were plans afoot in certain English ports for at least one voyage to Guinea. An English fleet lay ready, perhaps anchored in the Thames, to sail to West Africa in 1481. This is revealed by the wording of King John II's well-known protest to Edward IV. The King of Portugal, hearing, apparently, of these naval preparations, sent ambassadors to the English king to "confirm the ancient leagues". The envoys, after showing their master's title to the overlordship of Guinea, asked Edward IV to forbid voyages to Guinea, and requested especially the dismantling of a fleet which, under the commission of the Duke of Medina Sidonia, had been equipped by John Tintam and William Fabian for a trading voyage to West Africa. Edward IV conceded all their demands. Richard Hakluyt, who incorporated these facts in his *Principal Navigations*, copied them from Garcia de Resende's Chronicle, published in 1545. But the earliest record of the episode may be found in Ruy de Pina's *Chronicle of King John II*, which was written probably at the very beginning of the sixteenth century.[1]

New evidence, mainly circumstantial, which has recently come to light, suggests that one voyage to Guinea had been completed before the Portuguese protest. Attempts to trace William Fabian and John Tintam have not met with much success. No evidence of the Tintams has been found. However, a citizen and merchant of London, named Thomas Fabian, received a grant of land at Harringay in 1467,[2] and in 1481 a certain Thomas Fabian, alias Fabyane, who was a merchant of the Staple at Calais, received a general pardon from Edward IV.[3] Moreover, in 1470, a John Fabian, citizen and freeman of London, was exporting bales of striped and undyed cloth, embarking them on Venetian galleys, which called at Southampton.[4] Thus, while Thomas exported wool to Flanders, John exported cloth, apparently in the Venetian galleys, either to Flanders or

---

[1] Hakluyt, vi. 123-4 ; Pina, *Chronica del Rey D. João II*, ch. vii ; Resende, *Chronica do Rey D. João II*, ch. xxxiii.
[2] *Catalogue of Ancient Deeds*, i. 489.
[3] *Cal. Patent Rolls*, 1476-85, p. 284.
[4] Petty Customs Accounts, Southampton Municipal Records : Edward IV, Book B, 20 June ; Book D, 12 December.

directly to the Mediterranean. We cannot be sure that Thomas and John Fabian were related. Yet we may infer that William, also a Londoner, may have been connected with either Thomas or John, and perhaps with both. If William were related to John, then, he too was perhaps dealing in the Mediterranean trade, and it was not a very long shot to venture also in the Guinea trade. On the other hand, if he were related to Thomas, presumably he may have heard tales about the gold of Mina from Flemish merchants, who, as we have seen, had sent ships to Mina as early as 1475.

All this, though very speculative, shows at least how news of profits in gold might have reached the ears of John Tintam and William Fabian. There was a considerable reshuffling of ideas among Englishmen, who were acquainted with the seas, because of their expulsion from the Iceland fisheries just at this time, and the victory of the Hansa in the Baltic. John Lloyd set out from Bristol to find the "island of Brasylle" in 1480, and a similar expedition was undertaken in 1481. It is just possible, again, that English ships visited Barbary in 1465 and 1469.[1] Was William Fabian also one of the pioneers? Did he make a voyage to Guinea in 1480–81? It so happened that, contemporaneously, the Portuguese Cortes protested against Castilian, English and Flemish intruders into West Africa.[2] Moreover, on 27 February 1481, Edward IV informed Pope Sixtus IV that "he willingly permits his subjects to pass over to any parts of Africa for traffic, and the exchange of baser merchandise for nobler, provided this be sanctioned by the pope's authority", and he prayed "His Holiness that no suspicions might attach to this voyage, and to grant letters for the aforesaid purpose, to date from the 1st of November last."[3] Now it would be plausible to maintain that Edward IV's letter had no connection with any voyage of Tintam and Fabian. Yet three facts are curious: that the papal provision was to have dated from 1 November, that is, from a time when, owing to the phenomenon of the 'Guinea season', it was customary and necessary to leave Europe; that Edward IV

[1] D. B. Quinn, "Edward IV and Exploration", (*Mariner's Mirror*, 1935, pp. 275–84).
[2] Santarem, *Memorias para a historia das Cortes Geraes*, pt. II, pp. 200–1 E. Prestage, *The Portuguese Pioneers*, pt. 196.
[3] *Cal. S. P. Ven.*, 1202–1509, no. 474.

should have believed it incumbent upon him to secure letters from the pope for " this voyage . . . to any parts of Africa for traffic " ; and, thirdly, that the object of the voyage was to have been " to exchange baser merchandise for nobler ", perhaps beads for gold. We may also suspect that the Duke of Medina Sidonia had invited the English merchants to undertake the expedition, and had supplied them, perhaps, with details of the navigation and an experienced Andalusian pilot.

These speculations suggest that certain English merchants, possibly Tintam and Fabian, made a voyage to West Africa in the winter of 1480–1. Perhaps the expedition was a minor episode in the struggle between Portugal and Castile and, for this reason, the Duke of Medina Sidonia, who was certainly responsible for the preparations of 1481, was also behind the earlier adventure. The Portuguese learnt of the voyages, either from their sea-captains or from the negroes in Guinea, and so a public protest against the intrusion of English ships was made in the Cortes. Moreover, John II, knowing about the successful voyage of 1480–1, and hearing through one of his ubiquitous spies of the preparations of Tintam and Fabian for another illicit voyage, sent his ambassadors to Edward IV. Much of this is admittedly pure hypothesis. Yet, behind the bleak bare facts, there may well be hidden an extraordinary story.[1]

It was revealed in the Cortes of 1481 that Florentines and Genoese, who lived in the dominions of Portugal, were finding out secrets about Mina.[2] May we deduce from this that Genoese seamen, like Flemings and Englishmen, were making illegal voyages to Guinea ? Perhaps this is to stretch the evidence unduly. But we do know that many Genoese sailed to Guinea in the early days of the discovery. A Genoese was the first to purchase pepper on the Malagueta coast in 1471.[3] Another Genoese sailed on the same ship as Eustache de la Fosse in 1479, and disembarked at the Canary Islands.[4] These men, and others like them, may conceivably have initiated illegal voyages beyond Cape Bojador. If this be so, then the Portuguese had good cause for examining the problem of defending Guinea.

[1] An anonymous pamphleteer of the middle-seventeenth century states that Fabian and Tintam did go to West Africa. *Vide* " The Golden Coast, or a description of Guinney ", London, 1665, pp. 84–8.
[2] Santarem, *Memorias*, pt. II, pp. 200–1.
[3] Pacheco, II. iii. [4] Eustache de la Fosse, *op. cit.*

CONSOLIDATION OF PORTUGUESE MONOPOLY 63

A more serious danger, which the Portuguese feared, was that another maritime state might challenge their monopolistic position. Accordingly, they tried to conceal facts about their oversea dominions and to exclude interlopers. King John II was obliged to deal ruthlessly with certain of the powerful feudatories of his country in order to achieve these ends. The Count of Penamacor and the Duke of Braganza toyed with the idea of gaining outside help against the crown, by the concession of commercial privileges in Guinea. One of the salient features of John II's policy was the curbing of the power of the feudal nobility. Penamacor and Braganza opposed him vigorously. Braganza entertained the proposition of Castilian participation in the Guinea traffic in 1483. A contemporary alleged that the duke promised to co-operate with Queen Isabella of Castile in war against John II, should the latter refuse to allow Castilian merchants to trade in Guinea, even though they should offer to pay the customary duties.[1] However, with the help of the municipalities, the King of Portugal overcame the disloyal duke and, on 30 May 1483, he was executed at Evora. Queen Isabella would seem from the evidence to have been a little disappointed over the abandonment of her earlier Guinea claim. The Braganza episode emphasized that John II must strengthen his monopoly, and, if possible, secure a confirmation from Castile.

The moral was set in relief once again in 1488. Count Penamacor, having incurred the displeasure of John II by his resistance to the royal policy of centralisation, was obliged to flee the country. First, he took refuge in Flanders, but, later, after taking the name Pero Nunez, he landed in England. Then he began to assemble a fleet to go to Guinea, and to urge shipowners in both Flanders and England to adventure in the African traffic. John II soon discovered the count's alias and, therefore, sent a special envoy, Alvaro Rangel, a knight, to reveal the identity of Pero Nunez to Henry VII of England. Henry VII favoured his royal ally by imprisoning the count in the Tower of London, whence he was transferred, afterwards, to Portugal. No evidence has been discovered, so far, to throw light upon the maritime preparations which, presumably, were undertaken soon after the count landed in England.[2]

[1] Pina, *Chronica del Rey D. João II*, ch. x.
[2] Resende, *Chronica do D. João II*, ch. lxxiii; *Cal. S. P. Span.*, 1485-1509, p. 15.

John II could not hope to preserve secrecy about Guinea, while recalcitrant grandees, like Braganza and Penamacor, thus collaborated with foreign merchants. Indeed, strive as they might, the Portuguese were unable to prevent the leakage of facts. Many foreigners, resident in Portugal, collected scraps of information about Mina. Others enrolled in the crews of Portuguese caravels.[1] Moreover, a few Portuguese pilots and sailors were deserting their country's service already, in spite of government measures to prevent them selling abroad their navigational knowledge and maritime experience.[2] Thus, for example, Lorenzo Artero, a pilot of Lagos, left his own country and settled in the Canaries, where he would seem to have met a Castilian merchant, named Alonso de Morales. Artero agreed to pilot one of de Morales's ships on a slave-raiding expedition to Guinea in the winter of 1494–5.[3] Here, in embryo, is the type of project, which John Hawkins undertook for the English so successfully three-quarters of a century later. Hawkins generally employed Portuguese renegade pilots, even though, in his day, far more was known by non-Portuguese about West Africa. The escape of a few deserters, like Lorenzo Artero, in the early period of Portuguese enterprise in Guinea, must have provoked intense anger among those who remained loyal to the policy of national secrecy.

Yet, the Portuguese crown itself was not entirely blameless for the leakage. Occasionally, Alfonso V and John II took foreign correspondents into their confidence. Alfonso V made a gift of a manuscript of Azurara's *Chronica de Guiné* to the King of Naples in 1453 ;[4] and John II sent samples of the pepper of Benin to Flanders and to other parts in 1486.[5] Admittedly, the crown did not reveal vital information about winds, currents, rhumb-lines and harbours by gifts of this kind, but the effect was to arouse curiosity among the merchants of the other maritime states.

A gauge of the leakage is provided by a comparative study of contemporary maps, charts and globes.[6] The well-known

---

[1] Santarem, *Recherches sur la priorité de la découverte . . . au dela du Cap Bojador*, pp. 194–5. [2] Navarrete, *Colección de Viages*, iii. 127–9.
[3] *Ibid.*, iii. 502–5. [4] Santarem, *Recherches*, pp. 144–5.
[5] Pina, *Chronica del Rey D. João II*, ch. xxiv.
[6] *Vide.* G. H. T. Kimble, " The Mapping of West Africa in the 14th and 15th Centuries," ch. viii. (An unpublished thesis in the University of London).

CONSOLIDATION OF PORTUGUESE MONOPOLY 65

chart of Andrea Bianco, produced in London in 1448, is almost identical with that of Benincasa, which was drawn in 1467 : so that, during the interval, foreign map-makers were able to obtain, apparently, only a very few new facts about the configuration and navigation of Guinea. But a second chart, drawn by Benincasa in 1468, advanced the southern limit of nomenclature from the region of Cape Verde to the Cape of Santa Maria beyond Sierra Leone. Moreover, the 'Guinea Portugalexe', a chart of Venetian origin (1489), mapped the entire West African coast to a point beyond Cape Lopo Gonçalves. The additions in Benincasa's second map suggest that he had somehow gained access to charts, drawn by a fellow-voyager with Pero de Cintra, the Portuguese navigator, who reached the Cape of Santa Maria in 1462. It is plain also that, by 1489, exact reports about the discoveries, undertaken by the agents of Fernão Gomes, had reached Venice, and we may presume that the Venetians spared no efforts to penetrate the Portuguese secrets, because of their interest in the eastern spice traffic. Lastly, the Cantino map, which was sent from Lisbon to the Duke of Ferrara before 19 November 1502, names correctly practically all the capes and bays, native villages, places of traffic and Portuguese stations around the coast, and includes legends, which reveal the value of the gold trade of Mina. It would appear, from an examination of the Cantino map, that by 1502 foreign navigators must have known a great many facts, which the Portuguese had tried to keep secret.

One of the reasons for the gradual dissemination of knowledge was that private Castilian merchants continued to ignore article VIII of the Treaty of Alcaçovas. Andalusian fishermen still resorted to the valuable banks between Cape Bojador and Cape Verde. Eustache de la Fosse, writing after 1516, alleged that "the Spaniards have the custom every year of going to fish" in the Rio do Ouro.[1] Moreover, in 1501, the King of Castile forbade fishing between Cape Bojador and the Rio do Ouro, an order which seems to imply that certain of his subjects had broken the agreement with Portugal.[2] After the discovery of America, furthermore, some Andalusian merchants began to seize slaves on the coast of Guinea. Alonso de Morales, a native of Cadiz,

---

[1] Eustache de la Fosse, " Voyage ", (*Revue hispanique*, 1897, pp. 174-201).
[2] *Alguns Documentos*, p. 126.

equipped a caravel for this purpose, and, employing a Portuguese renegade pilot, sailed to Guinea, where he captured many negroes in the autumn of 1494.[1] The King of Portugal complained to Ferdinand and Isabella about the infringement of the agreement of 1479–80. King Ferdinand ordered the seizure of Alonso de Morales and his accomplices. But even Ferdinand's unconditional recognition of the Portuguese monopoly did not deter a few bold interlopers. It was, perhaps, at the request of King Manuel, the Fortunate, that Ferdinand again confirmed the Treaty of Alcaçovas in 1503, because some ships from Castile had sailed to Guinea, and " the island of Fernando Po, and to the trades of that coast ".[2] There is evidence also that Castilian pirates traded in Guinea in 1547, 1549 and 1558.[3] It is probable that many of the trained pilots of southern Castile, when unemployed, could not resist the temptation to hazard the profitable Guinea voyage in the first half of the sixteenth century.

Portugal could not suffer unmoved the exploits of interlopers. She found herself unable to check the gradual accumulation in foreign ports, of a store of vital facts which related to her empire. In 1495, a French ship, piloted by a Portuguese renegade, captured one of the royal caravels from Mina, which carried on board 20,000 dobras of gold and, possibly, one of the secret charts of the Guinea navigation.[4] There was danger in such accidents. Portugal needed a new guarantee of her monopoly.

Accordingly, John II began to seek for a new means of preserving the *status quo* in Guinea. The first voyage of Columbus, and the continued activity of Castilian fishermen beyond Cape Bojador, provided him with a suitable occasion for resurrecting the subject of his monopoly. There could be no doubt that the fishermen had violated the Treaty of Alcaçovas. But Columbus's voyage raised a new issue. Columbus had been driven into the Tagus upon his return, and John II, when he heard about the discovery, " showed that he felt disgusted and aggrieved, because he believed that it was made within the seas and

[1] Navarrete, *Colección de Viages*, iii. 502–5.
[2] *Alguns Documentos*, p. 132.
[3] Andrada, *Chronica do rey D. João III*, pt. IV, ch. xxxvii; *Quadro Elementar*, ii. 102–3.
[4] Navarrete, *Colección de Viages*, iii. 505.

bounds of his lordship of Guinea."[1] His claim, however, was repudiated by Ferdinand who, to ensure his possession of the new lands, immediately appealed to Pope Alexander VI.[2] Nevertheless, John II was well on the way to achieving at least one goal : even an admission of Ferdinand's claim would probably involve a demarcation of territory, and a confirmation of the Portuguese monopoly in Guinea.

The pope could not arbitrate easily between the claims of the two monarchs. What was the position in 1493 ? The papal bulls of 1455 and 1456, and a later bull of 1481 which confirmed the Treaty of Alcaçovas,[3] had not contemplated a longitudinal division of discovered lands. These bulls had established a latitudinal demarcation only : all lands south of Capes Bojador and Nam had been granted to Portugal. Yet the bull *Inter Caetera* of 15 March 1456 had ceded, specifically, to Alfonso V, and his successors, all lands " as far as to the Indies " beyond Cape Bojador. Contemporaries generally, if not Columbus himself, believed that the land, which he had discovered, bordered upon the Indies. Accordingly, by virtue of *Inter Caetera*, did not the new territory appertain to John II ? The case for Portugal was strong. John II was not advancing a purely upstart claim. He based his demands upon papal bull and public treaty.

Yet Alexander VI gave a decision in favour of Castile. Four papal bulls, bearing upon the dispute,[4] were promulgated in 1493. By the third, *Inter Caetera*, which was dated 4 May but was not expedited until June, Castile was granted the government of all islands and mainlands, towards the west and south of " a line from the Arctic pole . . . to the Antarctic pole . . . distant 100 leagues towards the west and south from any of the islands commonly known as the Azores and Cape Verde ". Thus, the discoveries of Columbus were assigned to Castile.

But, at the same time, the active interests of King John II

---

[1] Pina, *Chronica del Rey D. João II*, ch. lxvi.
[2] H. Vander Linden, " Alexander VI and the bulls of demarcation ", (*A.H.R.*, xxii. 13).
[3] Davenport, i. 49–55 ; *Alguns Documentos*, pp. 46–55.
[4] Davenport, i. 56–83 ; *vide* Vander Linden, *op. cit.*, who argues that the bulls were not an instance of papal arbitration, but " acts of papal sovereignty in favour of a single power ", and that it was Alexander VI's interest to favour Ferdinand and Isabella. He also discusses the order of despatch of the four bulls.

were safeguarded. All the papal bulls specifically excluded lands in the actual possession of a christian prince from the grant to Castile. Even the bull *Dudum siquidem* of 26 September 1493 contained a clause to this effect, although it revoked all former papal grants to Portugal which might seem to give her rights in the western seas. Moreover, the trade and territories of Guinea lay to the east of the line of demarcation, established by *Inter Caetera*, while, as if to give double assurance to John II, King Ferdinand was conceded rights over his new dominions, which were identical with those already exercised by the King of Portugal in " Africa, Guinea and the Gold Mine." By implication, therefore, Pope Alexander VI's bulls recognised the special monopoly of Portugal:

A new Castilo-Portuguese treaty also confirmed that monopoly. King Ferdinand feared lest John II should send an armed fleet to take possession of the Columbine territories; John II, on his side, desired a settlement of the disputed right of fishing beyond Cape Bojador. Ferdinand wanted treaty recognition of his title to oversea dominions; John II would admit the title only on condition that the line of demarcation should be moved further west. Accordingly, negotiations between their plenipotentiaries began at Barcelona in August 1493. They were completed at Tordesillas on 7 June 1494. The two monarchs, by the Treaty of Tordesillas, agreed to remove the line of demarcation 370 leagues west of the Cape Verde Islands.[1] Article I conferred upon the King of Portugal and his successors for ever " all lands, both islands and mainlands, found and discovered already, or to be found and discovered hereafter, by the King of Portugal and by his vessels, on this side of the line . . . toward the east, in either north or south latitude." Castile thus recognised the Aviz lands in West Africa. Meantime, a separate convention solved the problem of the Barbary fisheries in favour of Portugal.[2] Pope Julius II confirmed the Tordesillas treaty by the bull *Ea quae* of 24 January 1506.[3] In this way, the occidental land dispute between the two Iberian powers was amicably and finally settled.

It is difficult to determine whether the other maritime powers

[1] Davenport, i. 84–100.
[2] *Alguns Documentos*, pp. 80–90.
[3] *Ibid.*, pp. 142–3.

of Europe recognised the Portuguese monopoly. Since they had not been signatories to it, the Treaty of Tordesillas did not bind there. Admittedly, that treaty was important, because, afterwards, Spain directed almost all her colonial energies to the exploitation of the new world, and she began to realise that a common interest existed between herself and her former rival in the defence of their monopolies. The two powers ceased, after 1494, to compete in West Africa. Nevertheless, a bilateral treaty was insufficient to deter the governments of France and England from encouraging their mariners to venture in the Guinea tiaffic. It is also highly doubtful whether contemporaries held the papal bulls, which first created the Portuguese monopoly, to be universal in their effect. During the sixteenth century, the kings of Portugal, when protesting against the infringement of their monopoly, sometimes appealed to the papal division of the world beyond the seas. Not unnaturally, John III and Sebastian referred more frequently to the bulls in their negotiations with the catholic ruler of France than did Sebastian in his correspondence with the protestant Queen Elizabeth of England. But we may question whether contemporaries accepted the bulls of 1493 as binding.

The papal right to dispose of new lands was based on the temporal sovereignty of the papacy, and the mediatory power which that involved. Many jurists disputed this claim, but favourable jurists alleged that the Donation of Constantine provided legal justification for the land grants of the medieval popes.[1] The original Donation was not a very satisfactory foundation for the later grant of all the mainland of West Africa to Portugal, yet precedents undoubtedly existed for the bulls of 1455, 1456 and 1493. The popes claimed the right to dispose of Saracen provinces during the crusades. Less authentic papal grants were those of the island of Sardinia to the Pisans in 1016 and 1045, and that of Ireland to Henry II of England in 1155. Lastly, Pope Clement VI's grant of Lançerote island to Don Luis de la Cerda in 1344 represented an incontestable precedent for the bulls of the fifteenth century.

The pope could also claim sovereign arbitral power as the spiritual father of the world. He was the representative of

[1] E. Nys, "La ligne de démarcation d'Alexandre VI ", (*Revue de droit international*, xxvii. 474–91).

Christ on earth. Surely, then, it was incumbent upon him to decide the ownership of new-found lands! His mediatory decisions could be sanctioned by oath, which he would administer, by excommunication and by interdict, and the temporal influence of the whole ecclesiastical hierarchy could be brought to bear upon a transgressor. Moreover, it was his prerogative to regulate relations between christian and non-christian peoples. The Council of Lateran (1179) had forbidden trade between christians and Saracens in arms, iron, wood and all that could be used in warfare. In 1307, Pope Clement V had forbidden all trade with the Infidels, though later popes issued trading licences to particular persons and particular corporations.[1] The pope even exercised the treaty power by intervening between warring states to restore peace: the diplomats of Pope Eugenius IV were among the principal architects of the Congress of Arras (1435).[2] It would seem, therefore, that there was also a theological foundation for the papal claim to dispose of new lands.

Yet arguments may be adduced to show that, in practice, the *plenitudo potestatis* of the papacy had almost vanished by 1493. Even in the fourteenth century the government of Venice had ignored papal prohibitions upon trade with the Saracens, and the licence system was developed partly to paper over the cracks.[3] Popes began to take sides in political disputes in Italy in the last quarter of the fifteenth century, and thus undermined their former mediatory prerogative. Professor Vander Linden considers that the bulls of 1493 were purely arbitrary decisions in favour of one power, to whom Alexander VI could refuse nothing.[4] The removal of the line of demarcation 270 leagues further west beyond its original position, by article I of the Treaty of Tordesillas, independently negotiated between Ferdinand and John II in 1494, is a strong argument in favour of the decline of the binding power of papal decisions. Neither Ferdinand nor John II appear to have referred to Alexander VI for permission to alter the maritime frontier, and the new treaty was not invalidated by the failure of the papacy to ratify it until 1506. So when it was convenient, even those monarchs,

---

[1] E. Nys, *Les origines du droit international*, pp. 284–5.
[2] M. de Maulde-la-Clavière, *La diplomatie au temps de Machiavel*, i. 37–9.
[3] G. B. Depping, *Histoire du commerce*, pp. 174 *et seq.*
[4] Vander Linden, *op. cit.*

CONSOLIDATION OF PORTUGUESE MONOPOLY 71

in whose interest the papal demarcation was first established, ignored the so-called international sovereignty of the popes.

All this would suggest that in 1500 the monarchies of France and England cannot have attributed universal validity to the bulls of 1493. Perhaps this is why neither power appears to have protested against them. Unfortunately, there is no evidence of the French, and very little evidence of the English attitude. Edward IV of England seems to have acquiesced in the Portuguese claim, when he forbade English voyages to Guinea in 1481, yet he had previously assumed the right to permit his subjects to trade to any part of Africa.[1] Perhaps we may argue that Henry VII tacitly accepted the doctrine of monopoly, when he confined the Count of Penamacor to the Tower in 1488.[2] Moreover, though it has been suggested that the Cabot patent of 1496, which empowered John Cabot and his three sons " to navigate in any seas to the east, north and west ", was an intentional disregard of the papal division,[3] the Cabots could not go to Guinea, for that clearly would have entailed a voyage to the south. Another interesting patent is that of 19 March 1501, which forbade its recipients, Richard Ward, Thomas Ashurst and John Thomas, of Bristol, and three Portuguese squires from the Azores, to sail to lands already known to any christian power. This excluded them from Guinea. These grants of 1496 and 1501 suggest that Henry VII admitted the Portuguese claim, but there is a more important patent of 9 December 1502, which utterly vitiates the theory of English recognition. Thomas Ashurst, and another Bristol merchant named Hugh Elliott, with two Portuguese, were authorised to make discoveries, provided they should not enter lands already in the possession of a friendly power.[4] The wording of this grant differs markedly from that of the others, and suggests that Henry VII had now determined not to recognise prior discovery as a just title to possession, except it should be supported by effective occupation. Now, at that time, King Manuel

---

[1] Pina, *Chronica del Rey D. João II*, ch. vii; *Cal. S. P. Ven.*, 1202–1509, no. 474.
[2] Resende, *Chronica do D. João II*, ch. lxxiii; *Cal. S. P. Span.*, 1485–1509 p. 15.
[3] A. P. Higgins, " International Law and the Outer World," (*Cambridge History of the British Empire*, i. 184).
[4] Rymer, *Foedera*, xiii. 37; J. A. Williamson, *The voyages of the Cabots*, *passim*.

of Portugal had occupied effectively only a very few isolated places along the Guinea Coast. Accordingly, we must presume that, if the question had been raised in 1502, Henry VII would have denied his ally's possession of the rest of the West African coast. In fact, there was no controversy, because the English King was busy restoring order after the wars of the Roses, and the English people as a whole were not interested in the outside world. Nevertheless, so far as a conclusion is possible, we may affirm that Henry VII did not recognise formally the Portuguese monopoly.

The kings of Portugal, while striving to secure international recognition of their exclusive possession of Guinea, also built up an elaborate system of regulations to put an end to the activities of interlopers. This policy had been undertaken earlier, but the illicit voyages, described above,[1] showed that the steps already taken were partially ineffective. Article VIII of the Treaty of Alcaçovas had forbidden voyages to 'the trade of Guinea' and to the islands, by " foreign people ", who might live in Castile, or who might provision and equip ships in the ports of Castile,[2] but this had not checked the interlopers. Accordingly, new laws were formulated to enforce the monopoly.

The trade of Guinea became a personal monopoly of the Portuguese crown in 1481. King Alfonso V, considering that the administration of Guinea would provide his son with a good training in the art of government, granted Prince John " the said trades of Guinea and the fisheries of the seas thereof, not only those of Mina and Arguin, but also of all other rivers and other places whatsoever, where there is now a trade or can be a trade by water or by land ". This was evidently a confirmation of the earlier grant of 1474. Existing individual privileges were to revert to the prince upon the fulfilment of their terms. The administrative powers, originally exercised by Prince Henry under the patent of 1443, were transferred to Prince John. Furthermore, the privilege of sending ships to trade or to fish was to be vested solely in him. John's rights were to be as exclusive over the fisheries as over the land traffic, and those who should traffic or fish in the Guinea trades, without his licence or commission, were to be severely punished.[3] It so

---

[1] *Vide supra*, pp. 58-62, 65-6.   [2] Davenport, i. 44.
[3] *Annaes Maritimos e Coloniaes*, série V, no. 2, p. 37.

SECTION OF THE LUIS TEIXEIRA MAP, c. 1602

II

happened that Alfonso V died, soon after conceding these powers to his son. The prince became King John II, and since he did not delegate their administration, the supervision of the Arguin and Guinea trades was included among the departments of royal government.

Nevertheless, the Portuguese crown often retained little more than a mere, indirect supervision over certain sections of the Guinea trade. The trades of Upper Guinea, Mina and São Thomé island were periodically leased to contractors. An anonymous Portuguese pilot, who sailed frequently to São Thomé, has left a brief, but valuable, description of the route, written probably in 1554, in which he refers to these contracts. He records that the Guinea Coast " up to the Kingdom of Manicongo " was divided into two parts, each of which was leased, every four or five years, to the highest bidder, and that no others were allowed to trade there.[1] There is some confirmatory evidence, though we cannot be sure of the territorial limits of these contracts. The Santiagians, who enjoyed special commercial privileges in Upper Guinea by the grant of 1466, did not lose them, when King John II personally administered the entire coast after 1481. Moreover, two Antwerp merchants, Diego and Christobal de Haro, with several other merchants, contracted before 1515 with King Manuel " to have the right of carrying on the trade for a few years in certain rivers of Guinea ", though in that year, as they complained, a Portuguese captain plundered some of their ships.[2] The de Haros were, probably, members of a company of contractors. It is also plain, from the fact that these brothers lived in Antwerp, that foreigners were not excluded entirely from the privileges of trading in Guinea.

Most contractors, however, were Portuguese. A very prominent Portuguese merchant, who frequently adventured in the contracts of Guinea, was Affonso de Torres of Lisbon. He would seem to have been one of the merchants, who farmed the contract of Mina in 1541,[3] and, ten years afterwards, privileges, which he had enjoyed as a contractor of the trade of the island of São Thomé, came to an end.[4]

[1] G. B. Ramusio, *Navigationi et Viaggi*, i. 126.
[2] *Alguns Documentos*, pp. 397-8.
[3] H. P. Biggar, *A Collection of documents relating to Jaques Cartier and the Sieur de Roberval*, pp. 172-3.   [4] J. D. M. Ford, *The letters of John III*, p. 382.

All this indicates that the contract system, known to have been applied in the organisation of the Portuguese East Indies, obtained also in West Africa. It was continued throughout the sixteenth century. King Sebastian leased the Mina traffic to a group of his subjects in 1567.[1] Among the contractors, who farmed the rivers and the "maritime shores" between Cape Verde and Sierra Leone in 1562, were Antonio Gonçalves de Guzman and Duarte Leo, and they seem to have been the farmers as late as 1568.[2] Lastly, evidence of the existence of the contract system in 1592 is furnished by Richard Rainolds and Thomas Dassell, who made a voyage from the west of England to Guinea: they referred to the "Renters of the Castel de Mina and other places, where golde is upon the coast of Guinea".[3]

The policy of the crown, in creating these territorial monopolies, seems to have been to obtain as high an income as possible. Contractors were allowed to farm the trade of certain regions in West Africa, at a yearly rent, payable in cash and sometimes in slaves. We are uncertain of the number and the allocation of these contracts. Ramusio's pilot says that the Guinea Coast was divided into "two parts". But there were at least three contracts. The de Haro brothers enjoyed the privilege of trading to "certain rivers of Guinea". This is vague, but we may deduce that they were not contractors in the Mina gold trade, for, in that event, a reference to Mina would almost certainly have been included. Affonso de Torres, however, was a Mina contractor, and, at a different date, farmed the contract of São Thomé. Mina and São Thomé were distinct contracts. The Mina contract probably involved the exclusive right to purchase gold on the richest part of the coast, while the São Thomé contract allowed those who farmed it to buy slaves from the negro merchants on the coasts of Benin and Gabun.[4] The other contract, as farmed between 1562 and 1568, included Cape Verde, and "the rivers and maritime shores of Guinea, S. Domingo and Sierra Leone".[5] This seems to signify the entire coast of Upper Guinea, south of Cape Verde. But

---

[1] L'Abbé Douais, *Dépêches de M. de Fourquevaux*, pp. 288, 301.
[2] P. R. O., S.P.70, 99, ff. 1-49.
[3] Hakluyt, vii. 98-9.
[4] J. D. M. Ford, *op. cit.*, pp. 266-7.
[5] P. R. O., S.P. 70, 99, f. 2.

CONSOLIDATION OF PORTUGUESE MONOPOLY 75

the farm of 1562-8 did not supersede the special privileges of the Santiagians, for one of the merchants, whose ships were robbed by the English in 1562-3, was an inhabitant of Santiago.[1] We may conclude, therefore, that there were at least three contracts, those of Upper Guinea, Mina and São Thomé, and that special circumstances governed that of Upper Guinea, where the islanders of Santiago could also trade.

To be a contractor in one of the Guinea trades, however, did not imply a position of entire freedom within the territorial limits of the farm. A collection of regulations bound all those, who engaged in the Guinea traffic. These regulations were fully codified in the early sixteenth century, and published as part of the Ordinances of King Manuel.[2] They show that three classes of persons were associated with the Guinea trade, royal officials, contractors and licensees. The first class included the officers and clerks of the Lisbon House of Guinea (*Casa de Guiné*) whose duties consisted in the administration of Guinea for the crown, a judge whose special function was the settlement of disputes arising out of infringements of the regulations, those captains who commanded royal ships in West Africa, together with their crews, and officers, who were resident in Guinea generally for periods of three years, like the governor, the factor, the magistrate and the minor officials of the castle of São Jorge da Mina. The second class included individuals or groups, like Affonso de Torres and Christobal de Haro with his colleagues, who farmed the contracts in Guinea. The licensees, constituting the third group, included all those private merchants who purchased special licences from the crown to make particular voyages to Guinea. Except for these privileged persons, no others were permitted to trade on the West African coast.

Armed forces were used to execute the regulations early in the evolution of the monopoly organisation. De Prado had suffered punishment of death in 1460, and Diogo Cão had patrolled the Mina coast with an armada in 1480. An important statement on Portuguese policy was included in Alfonso V's instructions to sea-captains of 6 April 1480. He commanded his captains to seize all foreign caravels, which they might encounter in Guinea, and to cast their crews into the sea. These

[1] *Ibid.*, ff. 2-3.
[2] *As Ordenações del Rey D. Manoel*, bk. V, ff. 83, 91-7.

methods, it was explained, were to be adopted for the defence and protection of Guinea, its trade and gold mines, all of which belonged by right solely to Portugal.[1] Similar methods were employed throughout the sixteenth century, with reference to all interlopers. The royal instructions of 1480 were not the result of a sudden decision : they were part and parcel of a general policy of exclusion. All intruders, even though they could produce authentic letters of marque from a European potentate and claim to be privateers and not mere pirates, were reckoned pirates by the Portuguese and, as such, were punished without mercy.

Severe penalties for infractors had been included in the laws for the regulation of the Guinea trade, which had been published in 1474. Moreover, in 1480, King Alfonso V forbade the illegal and subterranean traffic in shells, between the Canary Islands and the Guinea Coast, on pain of confiscation of goods, public whipping and seven years' exile to Alcacer.[2] The negro merchants of Guinea were very eager to buy shells in exchange for their gold, slaves, ivory, pepper and gum. Consequently, this particular form of evasion of the monopoly would seem to have flourished, and, to check it, John II of Portugal even attempted to occupy the Canaries in 1481.[3] The Ordinances of King Manuel, to strengthen the sanction of force behind the regulations, threatened with death and the loss of all their possessions, whoever attempted to trade or to pillage in Guinea.[4]

But these Ordinances did not insist that all interloping ships and their crews should be sunk. Portuguese captains were instructed to bring infractors back to Lisbon. Those interlopers, who were caught when actually trading without a licence or robbing and raiding in Guinea, were to receive summary treatment : the crews were to be put to death, and the crown was to appropriate their goods. But the crews of all ships, encountered in the Guinea seas, which were not actually trading or plundering, were to be properly examined before the Judge of Guinea in Lisbon. Furthermore, it was realised that the royal officials in Guinea might co-operate with interlopers, that licensees and contractors might exceed the limits of their con-

[1] *Alguns Documentos*, p. 45.
[2] Barcellos, p. 38.
[3] Pina, *Chronica del Rey D. João II*, ch. viii.
[4] *As Ordenações del Rey D. Manoel*, bk. V, ff. 91-7.

CONSOLIDATION OF PORTUGUESE MONOPOLY 77

cessions, that captains might traffic to forbidden places or in forbidden articles, and that attempts might be made to avoid the payment of the royal dues on goods, which were brought back to Portugal, either by the production of false cargo returns or by the smuggling of cargoes on land in places remote from Lisbon. Laws were directed against all these avenues of evasion, and special precautions were taken to prevent the violation of the regulations for the Mina traffic. All the new provisions were included in the Ordinances. An all round and determined effort was thus made, in King Manuel's reign, to tighten the monopoly.

A further aspect of this strengthening of the royal control was the official policy of secrecy. Although there were exceptions, the whole country generally collaborated in an attempt to conceal information. A national policy was adopted and pursued for the suppression of the truth about the Portuguese empire. Facts about the discoveries were deliberately misrepresented; sailors were warned to be silent; contemporary chronicles were carefully garbled; maps and charts of navigation were extracted from contemporary books, like the *Esmeraldo de Situ Orbis*; and the making of globes, maps and charts became the privilege of a single family, whose loyalty to the Portuguese crown was unquestioned.[1] That the nation co-operated with the crown upon these matters is suggested by a protest of the Cortes in 1481 against the residence of foreigners in the Portuguese dominions on the ground that they discovered news about Mina.[2] It would seem that the Portuguese feared lest the spread of knowledge about their empire, and the appearance of rivals in the forbidden seas, should prove inevitable consecutives. The appearance of rivals could not be avoided except by the maintenance of secrecy.

Lastly, an efficient espionage organisation was created. Evidence exists, which shows that the kings of Portugal deliberately employed spies in foreign countries to find out the intentions of their enemies. Alfonso V employed a Castilian, who acted as " reader of the chronicles and books of Castile ".[3] It was probably a Portuguese spy in England, who reported the naval

---

[1] J. Cortesão, *The national secret of the Portuguese discoveries in the fifteenth century*, (translated from the Portuguese by W. A. Bentley).
[2] Santarem, *Memorias para a historia das Cortes Geraes*, pt. II, pp. 200-1.
[3] E. Prestage, *The Portuguese Pioneers*, p. 168.

preparations of John Tintam and William Fabian in 1481. John III developed the spy system considerably, and his successor, King Sebastian, was able to use Spanish agents besides Portuguese in England and France. The chief Portuguese factor in Antwerp sometimes fulfilled the function of co-ordinating head of these multifarious, if secret, activities. Spies were employed in foreign courts, and in the ports of the interloping countries, to keep a close watch upon maritime preparations, and their reports would be transmitted via Antwerp to Lisbon. Machinery could then be set in motion to frustrate or to counter the intending infractors. The Portuguese monopoly did not dissolve for lack of precautionary measures.

Extremely complex, then, was the monopoly, which French interlopers began to violate after 1530. Its character was twofold; it was national and royal. The discoveries of Prince Henry the Navigator and the papal bulls of 1455 and 1456 determined, in the beginning, its national bias. We have seen that all land beyond Cape Bojador was granted to the Portuguese, and, though later papal bulls and the Treaties of Alcaçovas and Tordesillas amended the territorial limits, the original principle was upheld that the subjects of other christian princes were to be excluded. The royal bias in the monopoly derived from the dual system of contracts and licences. Theoretically, this system might be regarded as an outcome of the prevailing feudal doctrine that all land was held of the crown. This would explain the territorial grant to Prince Henry in 1443. In practice, however, the contracts and the licences resulted from the profiteering policy of the Portuguese crown. High profits would accrue to the royal treasury only by the maintenance of a close regulation of the traffic. Accordingly, royal was added to national exclusiveness, though the distinction was not altogether clear to contemporary minds, nor were foreign merchants always denied the right to farm contracts. The crown exercised, continually, a general supervision over the traffic of West Africa, and discriminated, in most cases, against foreigners and to the advantage of its own subjects. The monopoly was thus consolidated.

CHAPTER V

TRADE AND FORTIFICATION IN WEST AFRICA, 1480–1578

AFTER the settlement of the dispute with Castile, Portuguese merchants, encouraged by the crown, proceeded to build up a flourishing trade in West Africa. Most of their ships brought gold, ivory, slaves, pepper and some minor commodities direct from Guinea to Portugal, but a good deal of local trading was undertaken. In the islands of Guinea certain small industries were organised, particularly that of sugar, while in the neighbouring seas fishing proved valuable. Between 1500 and 1530 the trade of Guinea was exceedingly profitable. After 1530, however, a slight decline set in, and by 1578 a definite fall in the total value of the Portuguese traffic is discernible.

It is not possible to estimate accurately the volume of the trade, and we cannot launch upon an elaborate description of its diversity. This is because the records are not very full, though useful material, so far untouched, probably exists in the Lisbon archives.[1] But some light may be thrown on these problems by Duarte Pacheco Pereira's *Esmeraldo de Situ Orbis*. His information can be supplemented by brief references to trade in contemporary Portuguese chronicles and histories, especially the *Da Asia* of João de Barros, in the correspondence of King John III, and in one or two other contemporary documents. Bearing in mind that the printed sources of evidence at our command are very limited, let us examine the nature and extent of Portuguese trade in West Africa during the century after 1480. First, we shall try to describe direct trade between Portugal and West Africa, and then we shall proceed to local traffic in West Africa.

A direct trade from Guinea to Portugal was carried on in gold, pepper, ivory, slaves, sugar, wax, fish, and one or two

[1] *Vide* F. Figueredo, " The Geographical Discoveries and Conquests of the Portuguese ", (*Hispanic American Historical Review*, vi. 47–70).

minor commodities like palm oil. Of these, the gold was long considered to be the most important, though, in point of fact, the pepper and slave traffics were probably more lucrative. Small quantities of gold were first brought to Portugal in 1441, but it was not until Fernão Gomes financed the discovery of the Mina coast that the gold trade came to be really important. After 1471, however, the value of the annual shipments of gold rapidly increased. The first profitable trade in gold was opened up at a village, called Samma, near Cape Threepoints, and, a few years later, the Portuguese began to trade at the Village of Two Parts, farther east, where the fortress of São Jorge da Mina was built. These were the two chief trading places, but gold could be bought along the shore for about 160 miles, from Axem, to the west of the Cape, as far as the Cabo das Redes to the east.[1] The Portuguese called this part of the Guinea Coast ' the Mine ', or Mina.

Small quantities of gold could be purchased at many other places around the West African coast. A little was obtainable in Senegal, and rather more in the basin of the river Gambia. Sometimes, Portuguese ships would sail far up the Gambia, eighty leagues as the crow flies, to the native fair at Setuku, and Pacheco records that they were wont by this means to secure at least 5,000 dobras of gold per year.[2] But the navigation of the river was difficult, and an unsuccessful attempt was made to clear its channel in the reign of King John II.[3] Further south, lured by the red cloth, the linen and the stone beads, which the whites offered them, the negro merchants of the tribes, who lived on the banks of the Rio Grande, would bring small sums of gold down to the shore.[4] Some of the purest gold was bought from the Teymenes in the region of the Rio de Case;[5] while in Sierra Leone the Bouloees provided the merchants with a little 23 carat gold.[6] More gold could be purchased at Cape St. Anna and near the Rio dos Sestos.[7] At many places round the coast, then, it was generally possible to pursue a little traffic in gold.

Both Castilian and Portuguese annalists refer to the gold

[1] Pacheco, II. iv.
[2] Ibid., I. xxvi, xxix.
[3] Barros, I. iii. 8.
[4] Pacheco, I. xxxi.
[5] Ibid., I. xxxii.
[6] Ibid., I. xxxiii.
[7] Ibid., II. i, ii.

TRADE AND FORTIFICATION

traffic, as if it were centred at a huge mine. The former speak of " *la mina del oro* ", the latter of " *a mina* ".[1] Even King John III, in a letter of 5 February 1551, mentioned certain " new mines ", which had been found fifty leagues from Mina.[2] But, in reality, no mine ever existed. The gold was purchased from the natives, so that the phrase "the purchase of the gold ",[3] used by the Portuguese historian, João de Barros, was more truly descriptive : Mina was the region where gold could be purchased. Gold seems to have been obtained in two ways. First many of the natives habitually wore gold bangles and bracelets, for which the white traders would barter. Thus, one of the Portuguese captains, Fernando de Montaroio, was able to return to his country in 1502 with a cargo of gold bracelets, bangles and other ornaments, worth 250 marks.[4] Secondly quantities of gold dust were gathered regularly in the river basins. Running streams washed the gold down from the mountains of the interior, and, on the lower slopes of the hills and also on the shore, the natives patiently sifted the soil to extract the gold dust. Nuggets were very rare ; practically all the gold was in dust form. The native merchants carried it down to the shore, where they would bargain with the Portuguese, and then exchange it for articles which they considered more valuable.

It is not unlikely that the Castilians were genuinely ignorant of the real character of the so-called ' Mine '. The Portuguese chroniclers, however, may have used the word out of habit rather than for lack of accurate information. John III's reference to the " new mines " must be understood to mean that a place had been found on the coast, where the natives were ready to sell a considerable quantity, not only of gold dust, but also of gold ornaments of various kinds, which they had accumulated. Lopo de Sousa, captain of the castle of São Jorge, was commanded forthwith to keep the discovery secret, lest interlopers should hear of it.[5] In due course, the royal ships from

---

[1] Pulgar, *Chronica de los Reyes Católicos*, pt. II, ch. lxii ; Andrés Bernáldez, *Historia de los Reyes Católicos*, ch. vi ; Pina, *Chronica del Rey D. João II*, ch. ii.
[2] Ford, *The Letters of John III*, p. 376.
[3] " *O resgate do ouro*," Barros, I. ii. 2.
[4] Barros, I. vi. 2.
[5] Ford, *The Letters of John III*, pp. 376, 394.

Lisbon would embark the gold, and take it back to Portugal without loss to the crown.

Indeed, the entire gold trade was closely supervised by the kings of Portugal. Admittedly, gold was excluded from the list of commodities, in which traffic was unconditionally forbidden by the law of 1470, yet, by the Ordinances of King Manuel, no one could go to Guinea without a royal licence or, when the Mina traffic was in farm, without the permission of the contractor, and those who violated the Ordinances were heavily punished. In 1551 Simão Vaz was exiled to India for having purchased gold at Mina, on board the ship *Pantafa*, without a licence.[1] Moreover, royal ships were probably used to bring home the gold. As soon as a ship from Mina arrived in Lisbon, the king would be informed, and his representatives, clerks and customs officers, would go on board to receive a declaration of the cargo. Eustache de la Fosse tells us that this was the usual procedure even in 1480,[2] while the Ordinances of King Manuel show that, by 1521, more stringent regulations had been devised to prevent the smuggling of gold into Portugal.[3] The crown appropriated regularly one-twentieth of all gold, imported from Guinea. Moreover, certain ships were accustomed to make the Guinea voyage every year; the letters of King John III show that the same ships repeatedly sailed to Mina. As early as 1497 Bartholomew Diaz was captain of one of the ships, which " usually went to São Jorge da Mina."[4] Five years later Vasco da Gama remarked to a group of Indian ambassadors that " twelve or fifteen ships usually came over every year from Guinea ".[5] A legend on the Cantino map, which was drawn before 19 November 1502, refers to the castle of Mina " from which twelve caravels carry gold each year to the most excellent Prince Manuel of Portugal ". Obviously, an annual fleet to transport gold from Mina to Portugal had been organised by the beginning of the sixteenth century. It is also plain that an inclusive system was instituted to regulate ships, men and cargoes.

We have not managed to calculate how much gold was

---

[1] Viterbo, i. 42.
[2] Eustache de la Fosse, " Voyage ", (*Revue hispanique*, 1897, pp. 174–201).
[3] *As Ordenacções del Rey D. Manoel*, bk. V, ff. 91–7.
[4] Barros, I. iv. 1.
[5] *Ibid.*, I. vi. 2.

TRADE AND FORTIFICATION

brought into Portugal. Probably the total varied from year to year. Pacheco records that 170,000 dobras of pure gold were carried annually to Portugal after 1481, and a modern historian accepts this estimate.[1] Another piece of evidence has come to light, which suggests that Pacheco's estimate was not exaggerated. One of the royal caravels from Mina was captured by a French pirate in 1495, and 20,000 dobras of gold were found on board.[2] This may have been an unusually large cargo for one caravel, but it would follow that the annual fleet must have imported at least 200,000 dobras in that year. A decline in the total amount of gold, brought from Mina, may have occurred after 1530. King John III, in a letter of 3 February 1533, agreed that no ship need carry more than 10,000 dobras of gold, but expressed a hope that in future improving circumstances would allow the fleet to load as much gold as in earlier years.[3] Actually the decline was not serious until the end of the sixteenth century.[4]

This lucrative traffic, in its heyday, occupied a prominent place in the royal accounts. There are indications, in the correspondence of King John III, that the crown came to depend upon a regular annual supply of gold from Mina, and loans would be raised to tide over temporary financial difficulties on the credit of the anticipated receipts from the gold.[5] From this we may conclude that the supervision and regulation of this branch of the royal revenue formed a not insignificant part of government administration at Lisbon.

Equally important, apparently, from 1470 to 1506 was the pepper traffic. King Alfonso V's law of 19 October 1470, which converted the trade of malagueta pepper into a government monopoly, shows that its value already must have been considerable.[6] It is possible that Alfonso was alarmed by the growing size of the pepper cargoes, which privileged merchants were bringing from Sierra Leone. After the discovery of the Malagueta coast in 1469-71, the volume of the trade must have jumped up to a hitherto unparalleled figure. Most of the malagueta pepper was taken on board at a place, situated thir-

[1] Pacheco, II. v ; Almeida, *Historia de Portugal*, iii. 554.
[2] Navarrete, *Colección de Viages*, iii. 505.
[3] Ford, *The Letters of John III*, pp. 84-5.
[4] Azevedo, *Epocas Economico*, p. 81.
[5] Ford, *op. cit.*, pp. 308, 315.
[6] *Alguns Documentos*, p. 33.

teen leagues east of the Rio de São Vicente, but it was procurable, generally, along the entire coast from Sierra Leone to Cape Palmas.[1] Before Indian pepper was brought via the direct sea-route to Europe, this product of Guinea found a ready market in Flanders.[2] It is not surprising, therefore, to find that Alfonso V should have created a royal monopoly of its trade.

Malagueta was not a true pepper. Yet there was real pepper to be had in Benin. João Affonso de Aveiro navigated, and apparently charted, the Benin coast in 1486, and he also opened up a trade in Benin pepper.[3] The Portuguese called this genuine pepper *pimenta del rabo* to distinguish it from malagueta. It was a particularly pungent species, and, proving extremely valuable, its trade rapidly expanded. A factory was established at Gató, which was the port of the city of Benin, and a few Portuguese, some of whom intermarried with the natives, remained there to help in the promotion of the trade.[4] But Benin was a very unhealthy region, and was situated even farther from Portugal than Mina. Sailors, who brought back the pepper, underwent grave risks. Probably, a high rate of mortality obtained, and provided a strong deterrent against venturing to Benin. Moreover, after 1498, Vasco da Gama showed that a sea-route was possible to the East Indies, and a less hazardous, and more lucrative pepper trade was opened up. Indian pepper fetched a higher price at Antwerp,[5] and the Benin pepper trade did not prove so profitable as had been expected. King Manuel controlled the transport of pepper from both India and Benin. Not wishing to see the European market for Indian pepper ruined by competition with that of Benin, he prohibited the extraction of the latter in 1506.[6] It was only between 1486 and 1506, then, that the Benin pepper traffic flourished.

The trade of malagueta, however, had a much longer life than that of Benin pepper, and was pursued throughout the sixteenth century. A Portuguese historian has assembled valuable figures to indicate the quantity of the traffic. Between 1498 and 1505,

[1] Pacheco, II. iii.
[2] Azevedo, *Epocas Economico*, p. 173.
[3] Barros, I. iii. 3 ; Pina, *Chronica del Rey D. João II*, ch. xxiv.
[4] Barros, I. iii. 3 ; Pina, *Chronica del Rey D. João II*, ch. xxiv ; Resende, *Chronica do D. João II*, ch. lxiv.
[5] Azevedo, *Epocas Economico*, p. 81.
[6] G. B. Ramusio, *Navigationi et Viaggi*, i. 126.

2,000 quintals of malagueta were consigned to the chief Portuguese factor at Antwerp, an average of 250 quintals per year. Only 75 quintals of Benin pepper were annually consigned to the factor over the same period. The quantity of malagueta was probably greater than that of Benin pepper throughout the twenty years before 1506. Moreover, 454 quintals of malagueta was the average figure for the years 1509-14.[1] In 1537 King John III sold 400 quintals at the rate of 12 cruzados per quintal, and this would suggest that there had been no appreciable fall in the annual amount of malagueta, imported since the beginning of the century.[2] If this be a correct surmise, it is also a remarkable one, for French traders in Guinea often carried away most of the available malagueta after 1530, and their intrusion must surely have had a detrimental effect upon the value of the Portuguese trade.

After an early boom, profits from the malagueta trade seem to have fallen. It would appear that the negro merchants soon grasped the value of their wares and raised their prices. Pacheco illustrates this price revolution in a passage about the trade of the Rio dos Sestos: formerly, one alquier of malagueta could have been bought for one pewter manilla, but, when he wrote[3] (c. 1505), the negro merchants demanded 5 or 6 manillas for the same measure of Guinea pepper. The black merchants would carry their pepper in baskets out from the mainland in their canoes, which they called *almadias*, and would haggle with the Portuguese traders until they should have made a satisfactory bargain. Probably, interlopers were partly responsible for the acumen of the natives. However, the fall in profits on the Guinea Coast was paralleled by a similar fall on the Antwerp bourse. One pound of malagueta fetched 12 dinheiros in 1511, but only half that sum in 1517. A recovery occurred later in the century, so that in 1578 one pound was priced at 28 dinheiros.[4] These price fluctuations were incidental to the main importance of the trade, its value to the crown. Malagueta remained a royal monopoly throughout the sixteenth century.

The slave trade between West Africa and Portugal began in 1441, when Antam Gonçalves brought the first cargo to Lisbon.

[1] Azevedo, *Epocas Economico*, pp. 80, 81, 118.
[2] Almeida, *Historia de Portugal*, iii. 554.
[3] Pacheco, II. ii.
[4] Azevedo, *Epocas Economico*, pp. 80-1.

This was the beginning of a steady flow of slaves to Portugal for two generations. The Arguin factory was the original centre for the trade on the West African coast, but, as more land was found, the commercial centre of gravity tended to move southwards. Senegambia became a valuable field for slave-raiding; so, later, did the Rio de Casamansa, the Rio de Case, Cape St. Anna, the Rio dos Sestos and, ultimately, all the coast of Benin.[1] It is probable that the slave trade of Upper Guinea was flourishing by 1470, but that of Benin was not opened up until 1486, when the factory of Gató was built. During the sixteenth century, thousands of slaves were obtained on the coast of the Kingdom of Angola, and Loanda, which was founded in 1578, grew to be the largest sea-port of that province, and became the centre , a very flourishing commerce.[2] The fortunes of Angola were thereafter largely dependent upon the Portuguese colony of Brazil, because of the slave trade between them. It was, however, the island of São Thomé, which first came to be the centre of the slave traffic in the Gulf of Guinea. Negroes were taken to São Thomé from Benin and from many places on the coast between Benin and Cape St. Catherine, while slaves from Angola, called Angolares, were also carried to the island. Most of these unfortunate captives were shipped either to Portugal or to Pernambuco in Brazil. The trade expanded considerably during the century, so that, by 1602, a number of slave marts had been established by the Portuguese all round the coast of the Gulf. It would seem, indeed, that permanent factories were actually maintained in one or two places, like the earlier one at Gató.[3]

The negro merchants raised the price of slaves, as of malagueta, after only a few years of trading. It was possible to buy eighteen Moors for one horse at Arguin in 1455, but half a century later, a horse would only purchase twelve negroes near the Senegal.[4] A similar change occurred at the Rio dos Sestos, where the price of one slave rose from two shaving basins to four or five.[5] The native merchants of Porto d'Ali demanded a horse for six slaves in 1505 and, by that year, the former slave

---

[1] Pacheco, bk. II, *passim*.
[2] C. P. Lucas, *A Historical Geography of the British Colonies*, iii. 48.
[3] P. D. Marees, *Beschryvinge van het Gout-custe*, pp. 229–50.
[4] Ramusio, *op. cit.*, i. 104 *et seq.*; Pacheco, I. xxvi.
[5] Pacheco, II. iii.

trade six miles south of Cape Verde had even been abandoned.[1]

This evidence suggests that, towards the end of the fifteenth century, the slave trade declined. An examination of the figures for slaves, imported into Portugal, at first sight tends to confirm the decline. Cadamosto recorded that in his day 700 or 800 slaves were annually carried to Lisbon. The researches of Lucio de Azevedo show that 448 slaves, belonging to the crown alone, were imported annually between 1486 and 1493, and an average of 500 during the years 1511-13.[2] Now all these figures seem to indicate that fewer slaves were imported after the generation of Cadamosto. Moreover, this conclusion is specially attractive, because it confirms the theory of a decreasing volume of traffic just before the opening up of the market in the new world for West African negroes.[3] But, how unreliable such casual estimates can be is revealed by collating Cadamosto's evidence with Pacheco's reckoning that, " when the trade of Upper Guinea was well-ordered, in each year more than 3,500 slaves were drawn from it ".[4] His statement appears to be irreconcilable with the rest of the evidence, except it be considered a gross exaggeration. Nor can we ignore the probable effect of the discovery of Benin in 1486, for the Benin slave trade must surely have augmented the total volume of the traffic. Probably, the number of imported slaves varied from year to year, and a tendency to decline was checked, firstly by the opening up of Benin and, secondly, by the demand for native labour in the new world.

The first batch of negroes was purchased in Lisbon for the West Indies in 1510, and the licence system was inaugurated three years later.[5] Thereafter, the revenue from the slave traffic was an important royal asset, but it was soon found necessary to restrict the purchase of negroes. An edict of 15 March 1518 regulated the price of slaves, and forbade merchants to penetrate into the interior of Guinea to get them.[6] Some of the Santiagians, who enjoyed special privileges in Senegambia, seem to have penetrated up country to trade, while there were renegades and degraded whites, who mixed with the inland

[1] *Ibid.*, I. xxviii.
[2] Azevedo, *Epocas Economico*, p. 73.
[3] A. Helps, *The Spanish Conquest in America*, i. 52-3.
[4] Pacheco, I. xxxiii.
[5] E. Donnan, *Documents illustrative of the history of the slave trade to America*, 15.
[6] Azevedo, *Epocas Economico*, p. 74.

native tribes, and negotiated trade between interlopers and negro merchants to the crown's disadvantage. Later writers refer often, and generally with scorn, to these men,[1] against whom the law of 1518 was directed. A royal pardon was offered to those, who would return at once, provided they should surrender up one-half of the wares which they had already bought. Behind the law would seem to be the fact that the demand in the West Indies for blackamoors was growing, and on every licensed shipload of slaves, which came to Portugal, the king imposed a freight charge. It is patent how an increase of interloping traffic, or a consequent fall in prices, was liable to deprive the crown of revenue.

The number of slaves exported from West Africa rose rapidly after the opening up of the transatlantic market. In the four years 1513-16, more than 700 slaves were carried annually to Portugal and Spain from Santiago alone.[2] The island of São Thomé flourished, since it was the centre of the African slave trade until 1578. By 1540 the export of slaves, in some years, may have reached 10,000.[3] In the middle of the century, slaves were transported directly to the West Indies from São Thomé. Some have wondered whether it was not the general rule for slaves to be taken first to Portugal, and then reshipped for Brazil and the West Indies. This may have been so, but some slaves were carried straight across the Atlantic, for King John III, in one of his letters, refers to " the slaves which go from the island of São Thomé to the Antilles ".[4] The end of the century saw an amazing expansion: in 1595, when the *asiento* was leased to Gomez Regnal, it was stipulated that 4,500 slaves should be imported to the new world annually for nine years.[5] Although many of these slaves were secured in Congo and Angola, the number is sufficiently high to indicate how far the Guinea slave trade had expanded.

The slave trade was in many ways the most important branch of the traffic of Guinea. It was the earliest to prosper; it proved to be more reliable than others, like gold and mala-

---

[1] Almada, *Tratado breve dos Rios de Guiné*, pp. 14-15 ; Guerreiro, *Relaçaões Annuis*, ii. 130.
[2] Azevedo, *Epocas Economico*, p. 75.
[3] Donnan, *op. cit.*, i. 17.
[4] Ford, *The Letters of John III*, p. 382.
[5] Donnan, *op. cit.*, i. 17.

gueta, which tended to decline after 1530; and it provided a greater source of income for the crown, which continued to draw revenue from it for over two centuries.

Of the ivory trade there is strangely little evidence. Martim Boviage held the right to purchase all the ivory brought from Guinea in 1469, so that Fernão Gomes was unable to exploit it.[1] When Pacheco wrote his *Esmeraldo*, elephants' teeth could be bought at many places along the coast of Upper Guinea, ivory collars from the Teymenes at the Rio de Case, and a good deal of ivory in the Kingdom of Benin.[2] The absence of any references to trade along the modern Ivory Coast suggests that this region was unfrequented by the Portuguese. Pacheco asserts that the negroes were untrustworthy: " Seven villages are to be met with from the Rio de Laguoa forward for seven leagues ", he writes, " and here there is no trade and the negroes are treacherous ".[3]

Yet the evidence of Pacheco can only be taken as accurate for the early sixteenth century. Long before 1600 the Portuguese had begun to trade off this part of the coast, and at the end of the century the Hollanders began to displace them.[4] Moreover, English interlopers purchased ivory there as early as 1555, securing a considerable quantity of ' teeth ' at a village, which was situated thirteen leagues east of Cape Palmas.[5] Accordingly, it may be assumed that the Portuguese opened up a valuable ivory trade on the Ivory Coast before the middle of the century. This did not lead to the abandonment of the older, if smaller, trades, for Portuguese merchants were still working the traffic at the Rio de Nuno and in northern Sierra Leone in 1594.[6] Unfortunately, no exact evidence has been found of the value of the ivory trade. It was not converted into a government monopoly, and this would suggest that the crown attached less importance to it than to malagueta.

Gold, pepper, slaves and ivory were the chief products of Guinea. Fishing also prospered. The most valuable fishing grounds were the Barbary banks, between Cape Bojador and the

[1] Barros, I. ii. 2.
[2] Pacheco, I. xxxii, xxxiii ; II. x.
[3] *Ibid.*, II. iv.
[4] Barbot, *Description of Guinea*, bk. II, ch. ix.
[5] Hakluyt, vi. 190.
[6] Almada, *Tratado breve dos Rios de Guiné*, pp. 69 *et seq.*

Rio do Ouro. It was the right to fish in this region, which had been disputed for many years in the late fifteenth century between Castile and Portugal. The dispute was finally settled in favour of the latter power. Coastal fishing was also important off various parts of the shore of Guinea. The natives had probably fished near their villages, in their little canoes, for many centuries; the Portuguese, for their part, encouraged fishing, not only because those whites, who settled on the mainland and in the islands, included fish in their diet, but also because the royal officials imposed tolls on native fishing. Among the best fisheries were those of the Cape Verde archipelago, Sierra Leone and near the mouth of the Rio dos Camarões.[1]

Fishing near the Cape Verde Islands would seem to have been very profitable. Europeans as well as natives took part, though, unfortunately for the Portuguese, many of their caravels were seized by interlopers after 1530 and, towards the end of this century, Frenchmen and Hollanders, successively, engrossed these fishing grounds. Negro fishermen were to be found all round the Guinea Coast. They would go out in the morning from their villages, and return at sundown with their catches. Tradition, as set down by Nicolas Villaut and Jean Barbot, recorded that the Portuguese, like their Dutch dispossessors in the seventeenth century, collected dues from the natives for the right to fish in the vicinity of their stations.[2] It would appear that this tradition was not unfounded, for at Arguin, in 1506, the Azenegue fishermen were compelled to pay the Portuguese a due of one-fifth for the same privilege.[3] Wherever they could, the Portuguese probably exacted these tolls.

A number of minor products were imported from Guinea. Great quantities of salt were gathered in the island of Sal, one of the Cape Verde group, and taken direct to Lisbon.[4] Civet was highly valued and its trade became a government monopoly in 1470.[5] The Ordinances of King Manuel specifically forbade all and sundry to trade in civet. Moreover, some of the by-products

---

[1] G. B. Ramusio, *Navigationi et Viaggi*, i. 125 ; Pacheco, I. xxxiii ; II. x.
[2] Villaut, *Relation des Costes d'Afrique*, p. 431 ; Barbot, *Description of Guinea*, bk. III, ch. vi.
[3] "Narrative of Valentim Fernandez Alema", December 1506 (ed. Dr. J. Schmeller), p. 45.
[4] G. B. Ramusio, *Navigationi et Viaggi*, i. 124-5.
[5] *Alguns Documentos*, p. 33.

of the palm were also imported, such as palm mats and palm oil,[1] and a kind of soap, which was manufactured at Cape Verde.[2] A little silver and indigo, and quantities of amber, wax and hides figured among the imports from Guinea, hides being more important, apparently, towards the end of the sixteenth century.[3] Lastly, fine cotton silk, produced in certain parts of Guinea, was also valued.[4] The total value of these minor products was probably not very great, but their number emphasizes that the traffic was by no means confined solely to the four stock commodities of gold, slaves, pepper and ivory.

In addition to the direct trade with Portugal, there was a little local trade in West Africa. The Santiagians early opened up a trade with the mainland of Guinea. This commerce was encouraged by the special privileges granted to the islanders in 1466.[5] It appears to have prospered at the end of the fifteenth century, and Santiago became the entrepôt of a valuable traffic. During the year 1514, at least nine caravels left the island carrying hides, skins, rice, ivory, wax, wooden-bowls and millet, products which had been purchased in Upper Guinea.[6] But abuses soon crept into the trade with the mainland: dues were not paid to the crown; some of the Santiagians penetrated far inland; and prices began to fall because of evasions of the law. Consequently, the privileges of the islanders were curtailed by royal decrees in 1517-18.[7]

These restrictive regulations throw much light upon trade in this part of Guinea. They show that commodities, like wax, iron, ivory, and slaves, were bought or sold in spite of prohibitions; they suggest that half-breeds, and perhaps negroes, engaged in the traffic; and they indicate that the provisions of the 1466 grant were often ignored. Accordingly, when the decrees of 1517-18 were issued, trade with Sierra Leone was forbidden, and various minor restrictions were enforced.

These changes did not end the connection between Santiago and the mainland. On the contrary, a considerable trade grew up between Santiago and Cacheo, which was the largest Portu-

---

[1] Pacheco, I. xxxii; II. viii.
[2] Ramusio, *op. cit.*, i. 124-5.
[3] Almada, *Tratado breve dos Rios de Guiné*, pp. 69-73; Barros, I. iii. 12.
[4] Pacheco, I. xxxiii.
[5] *Vide supra*, p. 31.
[6] Barcellos, p. 72.
[7] *Ibid.*, pp. 84-9.

guese settlement on the mainland, and was situated on the banks of the Rio de S. Domingo.[1] This trade was almost uninterrupted until 1560, when French interlopers began to traffic regularly at Cape Verde. Captain André Alvares d'Almada, whose book was written in 1594, seems to have remembered the time when the Santiago-Senegambia trade flourished. "When King Noghor reigned in Boudoumel", he records, " it was with his subjects that the inhabitants of the isle of Santiago made their chief traffic. . . . This prince was a great friend of the Portuguese. Every year a great number of vessels, loaded with horses and other merchandise, left Santiago to trade on the coast ". But the French ousted the Portuguese, who therefore abandoned the traffic.[2] Hakluyt's *Principal Navigations* confirm the evidence of the captain. When Robert Rainolds went to Guinea in 1591, he found that the French of Dieppe and Newhaven had traded to the Gambia and the Senegal " above thirty yeares ", and "commonly with foure or five ships a yeare ".[3] A contemporary cause in the English Admiralty Court disclosed, incidentally, the same fact.[4] So it was apparently that the ancient trade between the island of Santiago and Guinea of Cape Verde suffered a decline towards the end of the sixteenth century.

South of Senegambia, the Portuguese developed a local trade, which flourished even at the end of the century. Captain Almada records how his countrymen sold slaves to the natives at the Cabo de Verga, and purchased surplus rice farther south at the Rio da Furna. This rice was carried " to parts where it is more needed ".[5] No proof has been found that this trade had been instituted earlier, though it was probably at least as extensive in the middle of the century. The Ordinances of King Manuel provided that those ships, which were sent to embark slaves at São Thomé, O Principe and Annobon might by special permission purchase maize and meat on the outward journey at Beziguiche and its hinterland,[6] and this suggests that some local trade was organised before 1521 in Upper Guinea. Perhaps,

---

[1] *Ensaios*, I. i. xv.
[2] Almada, *Tratado breve dos Rios de Guiné*, p. 14.
[3] Hakluyt, vii. 91.
[4] P.R.O., H.C.A. 24, file 59, ff. 17-20.
[5] Almada, *Tratado breve dos Rios de Guiné*, pp. 71-2.
[6] *As Ordenações del Rey D. Manoel*, bk. V, f. 94.

TRADE AND FORTIFICATION

then, local trade between the Senegal and Sierra Leone was fairly regular in the sixteenth century. If so, its volume can have been only small.

A similar local trade was pursued between Benin and the Mina coast, for slaves, bought by the Portuguese in Benin, were sold to native merchants at Mina. This trade probably began as soon as the coast of Benin had been fully explored, and in 1486 it would seem also that the factory of Gató was used by the promoters. Pacheco, who tells us that he was four times in the city of Benin, describes how native wars facilitated the trade, for prisoners of war were sold to the Portuguese at reduced prices, one slave costing from twelve to fifteen bracelets of brass or copper.[1] Cotton cloths, panther skins and palm oil were also purchased. These products were then carried by ship to the castle of São Jorge, where the factor sold them to negro traders for gold.[2] The slaves were specially coveted by the black merchants of Mina, since they brought no asses to the castle, when they came down from the interior, and therefore needed slaves for carriers on their return to the uplands.[3] In consequence, slaves fetched a price at Mina double that obtainable in Portugal. The Benin-Mina trade naturally prospered.

The island of São Thomé shared in this trade, for the complete transaction seems to have been of a triangular character. Many of the slaves, taken from the Benin coast, were first carried to the island and from there transported to Mina. São Thomé was, in fact, an entrepôt for trade in the Gulf of Guinea, as Santiago served Upper Guinea. But the factory of Gató was abandoned in the reign of King John III, mainly because of the fever-ridden climate, and this led to the end of the Benin-Mina slave trade.[4] We do not know whether the local trade in cotton cloths, panther skins and palm oil was also abandoned.

Close as was the commercial dependence of Santiago and São Thomé upon their neighbouring mainlands, these islands, like a few of the smaller ones, preserved their separate identities. Let us examine first the Cape Verde group. Santiago, with its chief town and harbour in the south at Ribeira Grande, and the smaller town of Alcatrazes on the other side of the island,

[1] Pacheco, II. vii.
[2] *Ibid.*, II. viii.
[3] Barros, I. iii. 3.
[4] Pina, *Chronica del Rey D. João II*, ch. xxiv.

seems to have been the home of a small but prosperous community. The improvement of its trade in the early sixteenth century attracted settlers from Portugal and slaves from Guinea.[1] Many ships, carrying Guinea cargoes, annually returned from its ports to Portugal and Castile.[2] By 1497 it had already become sufficiently important to have an hospital of its own, though this is significant of a less pleasant feature of Portuguese enterprise in Guinea.[3] A little over a generation later, Ramusio's pilot gave a glowing account of the fertility of Santiago. To be sure, his estimate that 500 Castilian and Portuguese families of distinction resided in the town of Ribeira Grande alone may be an exaggeration of the truth, but it is at least indicative of the quondam prosperity of an island, which to-day is regarded as comparatively barren. Altogether, Santiago seems to have been the home of a vigorous and energetic community.[4]

The other Cape Verde Islands counted for little. Fogo seems to have been the least insignificant ; it was settled soon after its first discovery (1461) ;[5] by 1517 its inhabitants shared in the trade of Senegambia ;[6] and in the reign of John III this trade was still being pursued.[7] Boavista was settled from Santiago (1490).[8] Maio was used by the Santiagians for grazing cattle and raising cotton crops in the sixteenth century, and was certainly peopled by 1576.[9] São Nicolão was settled during the century, and a grant of Antão in 1538 suggests that it, too, was also peopled.[10] Moreover, the fact that the islands of Sal, Brava and Santa Luzia were leased by the crown in 1545 suggests that they were settled by that time, and yielding a small profit ; certainly the supplies of salt in the island of Sal must have given some financial advantage to the lessee.[11] But Santiago overshadowed all the smaller islands of the archipelago. In these others, a few inhabitants probably lived a solitary and semi-civilised existence. Only in Santiago was there an organised community.

[1] *Ensaios*, I. ii. 8 ; Barcellos, p. 72.
[2] *Ibid.*
[3] *Ibid.*, p. 54.
[4] G. B. Ramusio, *Navigationi et Viaggi*, i. 125.
[5] *Ensaios*, I. ii. 23.
[6] Barcellos, pp. 84–5.
[7] Ford, *The Letters of John III*, p. 132.
[8] Barcellos, p. 51.
[9] *Ensaios*, I. ii. 31–3 ; Hakluyt, x. 83.
[10] *Ensaios*, I. i. xii ; I. ii. 72.
[11] Barcellos, pp. 120–2.

TRADE AND FORTIFICATION

São Thomé dominated the group of four islands in the Gulf of Guinea, as Santiago overshadowed the other Cape Verde Islands. Its colonisation and trade were encouraged by a number of grants from the crown between 1485 and 1500, allowing its inhabitants special commercial privileges on the mainland.[1] A patent of 26 March 1500 summarised most of these concessions : Fernão de Mello was confirmed in his office of captain of São Thomé, and the inhabitants of the island were privileged for ever to trade on the mainland " from the Rio Real and the island of Fernando Po up to the land of Manicongo ", but they were not to trade where gold was available, except by special permission of the crown. They were permitted, all the same, to sell provisions, fruits and vegetables, produced in their island, to the city of São Jorge da Mina, and to receive gold in exchange. Transactions at Mina castle were to be supervised by the royal officials, and subjected to the same conditions as bound the royal caravels and ships, which customarily sailed from Portugal to São Jorge.[2] Should the crown, at some future time, decide to lease the trades of the mainland beyond the Rio Real, the rights of the islanders were not to be violated.

These grants laid the foundations of prosperity in the island, for a profitable slave trade was opened up with the mainland, to which the islanders were thus allowed to traffic. Some of the slaves, who were brought from Angola and Benin, were employed on the sugar plantations and in the sugar mills, which Fernão de Mello built early in the sixteenth century.[3] A flourishing sugar industry resulted. Sugar and slaves constituted the two chief sources of wealth in the island which, despite a wasting fire in 1512, became one of the leading oversea possessions of Portugal. The graph of its prosperity would seem to have attained its peak sometime between 1530 and 1560. Unrepentant Jews and convicted men were sent to swell the population, and mulattoes, who could withstand more easily the asperities of the climate, were given equal privileges with the white settlers.[4]

---

[1] *Ensaios*, II. ii. 3–6 ; *Alguns Documentos*, p. 57.
[2] Arch. Nac. da Torre do Tombo, Livro das Ilhas, f. 81.
[3] Pacheco, II. ii.
[4] Pina, *Chronica del Rey D. João II*, ch. lxviii ; Resende, *Chronica do D. João II*, ch. clxxix ; *Ensaios*, II. ii. 6–7.

The Portuguese pilot, whose record has been preserved by Ramusio, drew a picture of a prosperous São Thomé in 1554.[1] In the port of Povoasan, on the north side of the island, the ships of many nations, including Portugal, Castile, France and Genoa, would congregate. They brought food and provisions such as wines, oil, cheese, leather and flour to the islanders; they carried away the sugar, about 150,000 arrobes per year, mainly to Antwerp; and the slaves, obtained in Guinea and Angola, they transported mostly to the West Indies. Admittedly, the happiness and prosperity of the island were sometimes threatened by the discontent of the slaves, but in 1554 there seem to have been a large number of sugar plantations, on some of which over 300 slaves were employed. Royal officials administered the island, because in 1522, São Thomé had reverted from the possession of a private donee to the crown.[2] Afterwards, contractors regularly farmed its trade. The island continued in this condition until the death of John III.

The importance of the other three islands does not warrant more than a brief reference. O Principe was settled in the reign of King John II, and in the middle of the next century was the scene of a small sugar industry. The dues of this island were granted to the King of Portugal's eldest son.[3] The island of Fernando Po only acquired a small population and that mainly of coloured slaves, who were employed on sugar plantations.[4] There may have been some commercial connection between it and the coast of Benin, for it was the northernmost of the four islands in the Gulf of Guinea. By virtue of its strategic position, Fernando Po was important both as a base for attacks upon the mainland and as a factory for the traffic of the Gulf. For these reasons, it played a small part in the international struggle after the middle sixteenth century. Annobon, which lies to the southwest of São Thomé, was the least valuable of the four islands. It remained practically desolate, save for a short-lived attempt to settle it in 1506,[5] a few exiled Portuguese, and a few fishermen from São Thomé, who used it as a landing ground.[6]

[1] G. B. Ramusio, *Navigationi et Viaggi*, i. 126–7.
[2] *Ensaios*, II. ii. 7–8.
[3] Pacheco, II. ii; G. B. Ramusio, *Navigationi et Viaggi*, i. 126.
[4] Pacheco, II. x.
[5] "Narrative of Valentim Fernandez Alema", December 1506 (ed. Dr. J. Schmeller), p. 43.
[6] Ramusio, *op. cit.*, i. 127; *As Ordenações del Rey D. Manoel*, bk. V, f. 92.

The total value of Portuguese trade in West Africa in the sixteenth century does not bear easy comparison with that of the East Indies. A report relevant to this matter is included in the Cotton MSS. in the British Museum. It reveals that in the last quarter of the century, while the East Indies yielded an annual revenue of two million cruzados, the value to the crown of the entire trade of West Africa was only 280,000 cruzados. Of this sum, 120,000 cruzados was drawn from Mina, 60,000 from Cape Verde and its mainland trade, and the rest from São Thomé and Angola. The total, according to the report, was even less than the revenue accruing from Brazil by 20,000 cruzados. It only amounted to 14 per cent of the East Indies revenue.[1] These figures reveal the relative insignificance of the Guinea trade, even though we allow a certain element of inaccuracy in them. But, it should be remembered that the heyday of the Guinea traffic for the Portuguese ended soon after 1530. For many years before the East Indies trade was opened up, Portuguese merchants were reaping profits from the region between Arguin and Cape St. Catherine. The relative importance of the Guinea trade was considerable between 1450 and 1530.

Most of the Portuguese discoverers and traders, inspired by the Henrician tradition of peace and evangelisation, seem to have tried to avoid wars with the natives. But so variegated a traffic, as they created, brought in its wake its toll of frequent skirmishes with the negro tribes. There was unfortunate bloodshed early in the days of discovery, and scattered snippets of evidence show that lives were sometimes lost after the organisation of the regular trades. Thus Simão da Cunha, the commander of one of the royal fleets in Guinea, died there, fighting " in the service of his king and of his country " before April 1492.[2] Pacheco records that ships in distress could not always take refuge in the rivers of Senegambia " owing to the disorders of the natives ".[3] Certain negro tribes would seem to have contemplated an attack upon the castle of São Jorge in 1503. The Kingdom of Jalofo was the scene of a native succession struggle in 1487-8, and there were many negro wars in Benin.[4]

---

[1] B.M., Cotton MS. Nero B. 1, ff. 240-5
[2] Viterbo, ii. 184-5.
[3] Pacheco, I. xxvi.
[4] *Alguns Documentos*, p. 133 ; Barros, I. iii. 6 ; Pacheco, II. vii ; Resende, *Chronica do D. João II*, ch. lxxvii.

Stability was lacking among the native tribes. The invasion of a new and warlike people from the heart of Africa was always liable to overthrow the more settled negro kingdoms on the coast. We shall see that great dislocation resulted from one of these periodic invasions in the middle of the sixteenth century. For the Portuguese, instability involved commercial uncertainties, and the danger that their settlements, and the warehouses which they built, might be attacked by warring tribes. Portuguese relations with the negroes, then, led to the building of a number of forts on the coast, quite apart from the need of defence against interlopers,

São Jorge castle, the giant among the Portuguese establishments in Guinea, was founded in 1482. Vivid descriptions of the circumstances of its origin are given in contemporary Portuguese chronicles. Interlopers, lured by the magnetism of gold, seem to have threatened destruction to the Portuguese monopoly soon after João de Santarem and Pero de Escolar discovered Mina. Perhaps negro wars embarrassed the white traders on the Mina coast. Whatever the cause, there would seem to have been great commotion among the nation and in the royal court. Apparently, John II, first as prince and then as king, determined upon a mighty effort to strengthen his monopoly. To emphasize his rights, he sent ambassadors to England and Castile, and possibly to the pope.[1] He tried to snatch the Canary Islands from Castile "for the greater security of Guinea".[2] Then, after considering the problem in council, he ordered the building of the castle of São Jorge da Mina. Simultaneously, the celebrated instructions to sea-captains were issued on 5 April 1480 ; Diogo Cão, commanding a Portuguese fleet in Guinea, apprehended Eustache de la Fosse in the winter of 1479–80 ; and the Cortes protested against foreign activity in the Portuguese dominions.[3]

It was while the national enthusiasm for empire was thus raised to a high pitch that King John II took the momentous step of commissioning Diogo d'Azambuja to go to Mina to build a fort on a convenient site. Pope Sixtus IV, probably in response to a specific request, conceded a full indulgence for

[1] Pina, *Chronica del Rey D. João II*, chs. vii, viii ; *Quadro Elementar*, x. 95.
[2] Pina, *op. cit.*, ch. viii.
[3] *Vide supra*, p. 77.

their sins to all christians, who might die in the castle of the Mine (18 September 1481).[1] Thus fortified, Diogo d'Azambuja set out with 600 men, on board a fleet of ten ships and two barks. The voyage to Mina was uneventful. When they arrived, the Portuguese went on land and negotiated with the local king, Caramansa, for permission to erect a fort and, after this was obtained, the stone-workers, masons and carpenters began the building. Within a few weeks of landing, they had erected a chapel, an encircling wall, a huge central tower and a spacious warehouse, which seem to have been the chief features of the new castle. Then, the main part of the expedition returned to Portugal. But sixty men and three women remained in the castle under the captaincy of Diogo d'Azambuja.

The first captain returned home two years and seven months later to be honoured by the king for his great services.[2] Shortly afterwards, the privileges of a city were conferred upon the castle (1486),[3] and John II assumed the title 'lord of Guinea'.[4] It is to be regretted that the historian, João de Barros, should have been so laconic in his reference to the elevation of São Jorge to the status of a city. We cannot be sure what privileges were conceded to the defenders. In fact, the change probably involved the granting of a certain degree of self-government to the negroes of the neighbouring town as well as to the citizens of the castle. The site of the castle belonged, apparently, to the tribes of the Fetu and the Comani, and the Portuguese, in accordance with an agreement made between Diogo d'Azambuja and King Caramansa, seem to have rented it from them. The agreement, contained in what was later known as the Elmina 'Note', caused a lot of trouble between the Europeans and the local tribes in the eighteenth century.[5] Even in the sixteenth century, the Portuguese had to make gifts to the princes of the Fetu and the Comani, each of whom owned one half of the site of Mina town. This may have been the origin of its first name, for it was called the Village of Two Parts before the castle was built. A century after 1482 the town had be-

[1] *Quadro Elementar*, x. 95.
[2] *Alguns Documentos*, p. 56.
[3] Barros, I. iii. 2.
[4] Pina, *Chronica del Rey D. João II*, ch. xix.
[5] H. A. Wyndham, *The Atlantic and Slavery*, p. 13; Dapper, *Description de l'Afrique*, p. 283.

come the 'Commonwealth of Mina', from whose detribalised negro inhabitants the Portuguese garrison of the castle was largely recruited for defence against neighbouring tribes like the Fetu.

More contemporary information remains to us about this castle than about any of the smaller ones, sufficient indeed to produce something like a connected account of its history throughout the sixteenth century. São Jorge was the oldest of the Guinea forts; it dominated the Gold Coast; and it was the mightiest of all the permanent fortifications. Moreover, it was the strategic heart of rivalry around the Mine and so became the centre of the hostile attentions of the interloping powers. The size of the garrison, maintained by the Portuguese, fluctuated, but it would seem to have averaged about sixty, apart from the negro auxiliaries. There is evidence to show that São Jorge provided a base for occasional efforts to evangelise the local tribes.[1] Gifts of trinkets and the sale of spirits were used to passify the warlike tribes and, sometimes, the Portuguese tried to play off one tribe against another. Daily troubles weakened the garrison: fresh water was difficult to obtain; except for fish and cargoes of fruit from São Thomé, the residents depended upon annual supplies of fresh food from Lisbon; fever was always prevalent; many of the whites were convicts or political exiles, and some of them expressed their dissatisfaction with their fate by engaging in private trade to the detriment of the royal dues; while their corporate morale was always being undermined by alarms about negro attacks upon their fort, and their endurance tested continually after 1530 by the unending vigil in the tower, where they watched for interlopers. All things considered, it was a wonderful achievement, on the part of the Portuguese, to have kept up this establishment so long. São Jorge, after a century and a half of Portuguese rule, was captured by the Dutch in 1637.

The power of the Portuguese did not extend beyond the walls of São Jorge, and they soon discovered that only one fortress was of very little avail for protecting 2,000 miles of coast. Andrés Bernáldez, the Castilian chronicler, astutely pointed out this weakness as early as 1513, when he declared that the Portuguese were not lords of the land where the gold was

[1] *Alguns Documentos*, pp. 133-4.

TRADE AND FORTIFICATION 101

collected, " save only for their trade in a fortress, which they have recently erected ".[1] A similar criticism was levelled against the Portuguese defences more than half a century later by Martin Frobisher, the famous English privateer.[2] By that time, however, several more smaller forts had been built to remedy the defect.

The first of the minor forts was Axem, built originally in 1503 on a site to the west of Cape Threepoints. Both Pacheco and de Barros were familiar with it, and a document in the Portuguese Torre do Tombo contains a description of its foundation.[3] It was attacked by negroes in 1515 and, therefore, was moved to a more strategic position. The Portuguese made some alterations in its structure in the middle of the century.[4] In 1602 a Dutch writer described Axem as "a little fortress... very ill-defended ".[5]

Two additional 'strong houses' were built on the Gold Coast: Samma and Accra. Unfortunately, we cannot be sure when these two lodges were first fortified.

Samma village lies just east of Cape Threepoints. Perhaps, the Portuguese factory was built soon after 1471, when the Mine was discovered. Pacheco records briefly that Samma was the village where the first gold trade was made. De Barros confirms this, but in words that suggest he may have drawn his information from the same source as Pacheco or from the *Esmeraldo* itself.[6] The apparent familiarity of both writers with the place-name, Samma, might be regarded as an indication that the native town included a Portuguese establishment. However, the earliest definite evidence of a fort at Samma may be found in Hakluyt's *Principal Navigations*: when John Lok sailed to Guinea, the inhabitants of Samma " shot off their ordnance "; they had " two or three pieces of ordnance and no more " (12 January 1555).[7] These facts seem to prove that Samma was not fortified until the reign of King John III, when it was found necessary to strengthen the defences against French

---

[1] Andrés Bernáldez, *Historia de los Reyes Católicos*, ch. vi.
[2] B.M., Lansdowne MS. 171, ff. 148-9.
[3] Pacheco, II. iv ; Barros, I. ii. 2 ; *Alguns Documentos*, pp. 133-4.
[4] Welman, *The native states of the Gold Coast. II. Ahanta*, p. 14 ; Barbot, *Description of Guinea*, bk. III, ch. ii.
[5] P. D. Marees, *Beschryvinge van het Gout-custe*, pp. 15, 81-2.
[6] Pacheco, II. 11 ; Barros, I. ii. 2.
[7] Hakluyt, vi. 160.

interlopers. There were only a few Portuguese stationed in the fort even at the end of the century. Pieter Marees describes Samma as a place " where the Portuguese have another strong house, and because the region is very fertile, three or four Portuguese dwell there to collect the toll of the fish, and to buy several other food products on the coast, which they send daily to the castles of Axem and Mina ".[1] Samma had evidently become an auxiliary to the other forts.

The last of the fortified stations on the Gold Coast was Accra. It has been found as difficult to date accurately the origin of Accra as of Samma. Jean Barbot, whose evidence on this point cannot be regarded as entirely reliable, states vaguely that " some years after 1484 the King of Portugal formed a Guinea Company, with the sole privilege of trading there, ... which at first made a considerable profit, and caused fort St. Anthony to be built at Axim, another small one at Accra, and a lodge at Sama ".[2] His indiscriminate association of Samma and Accra suggests a contemporaneity of origin, which is not borne out by the facts. Neither Pacheco nor de Barros refers to Accra, though both mention Samma. This suggests a later origin for the former. Even Martin Frobisher, who was asked to declare what he knew of the Portuguese stations in Guinea in 1562, did not refer to Accra, though his demonstrable inaccuracy in other respects makes his statement untrustworthy.[3] In fact, we have no unquestionable evidence of the existence of Accra until 1576, when the Portuguese were attempting, apparently, to extend its defences. Negroes attacked it and razed it to the ground in the same year.[4]

It is probable that, in Portuguese eyes, their defences on the Gold Coast ranked first in importance. Nevertheless, some fortifications were erected in Senegambia, the Cape Verde Islands, Sierra Leone and the island of São Thomé. A native succession dispute was mainly responsible for a project to build a fort at the mouth of the Senegal. Twenty caravels sailed from Portugal for the Senegal, under the command of Pero Vaz da Cunha, to restore Prince Bemoij, who was the unsuccessful claimant, to build a fortress, and to open up the way to Tim-

[1] Marees, *op. cit.*, p. 82.
[2] Barbot, *Description of Guinea*, bk. III, ch. vi.
[3] B.M., Lansdowne MS. 171, ff. 148–9.
[4] Marees, *op. cit.*, pp. 88–9.

TRADE AND FORTIFICATION

buktu. João de Barros dated the enterprise in 1485-6, Ruy de Pina two years later; the former records that the fort was to be built on the banks of the Senegal, the latter that building was begun at its mouth.[1] In the end, however, the whole scheme was abandoned, for Bemoij perished or was murdered, and Pero Vaz returned to Portugal. A start appears to have been made in the building operations, for Jean Barbot asserts that in his day at Byhurt, at the mouth of the Senegal, were " still to be seen the ruins of a fort ", which, he continues, was almost finished by the Portuguese in the reign of King John II.[2] The projected fort at Byhurt is the only known instance of an attempt by the Portuguese to fortify Senegambia.

The Cape Verde archipelago was of greater strategic importance. Portuguese caravels, bound for Brazil, regularly called at Santiago Island. Portuguese fleets, which returned from São Thomé and the East Indies, also made for the islands. They stood, then, at the confluence of several of the chief highways of the sea. Moreover, interlopers, when they grasped the strategic significance of the archipelago, would hide in neighbouring creeks and inlets, ready to pounce upon fishing caravels and isolated trading caravels and carracks, should any be separated from the annual fleets. It is no wonder that fortifications were built in Santiago. Fort St. Martha was erected on one side of the town of Ribeira Grande in the sixteenth century.[3] Little is known about the details of this fort, but it would seem that few improvements were made until the third quarter of the century.

A fort was built in Sierra Leone in the reign of King John II, but this must have proved too expensive. After a few years the king ordered its abandonment.[4] The Malagueta coast was never fortified, although at least two expeditions were sent from Portugal to establish forts in 1532 and 1540.[5] We have seen that the slave and pepper trades of Benin were stabilised by the building of a factory in Gató village, which was kept up for fifty years after 1486. But there is no ground for supposing that Gató was ever fortified. More important was the island of São

---

[1] Barros, I. iii. 7-8 ; Pina, *Chronica del Rey D. João II*, ch. xxxii.
[2] Barbot, *op. cit.*, bk. I, ch. i.
[3] Barcellos, p. 159.
[4] Pacheco, I. xxxii.
[5] *Vide infra*, pp. 126-7.

Thomé, especially after the expansion of the slave trade with the new world, and, accordingly, more careful thought seems to have been devoted to the problem of its defence. Plans for a fortress were considered in 1493, when Alvaro de Caminha, the captain of the island, was appointed governor of " the fortress which was to be built ".[1] Materials for building were sent out and, by 1506, a small fort appears to have been built in the capital, Povoasan.[2] Afterwards, however, the defence of the island was neglected, until a fearful raid by French interlopers in 1567 roused the inhabitants and the crown to a sense cf their responsibilities. A handsome castle, named after the king, was then erected.[3]

No other forts were built between 1454 and 1578 though, occasionally, various schemes seem to have been considered. Thus, for example, one for defending Malagueta was submitted by a contemporary in 1542.[4] The chief obstacle to fortification was probably expense. This would explain why the only permanent forts on the mainland on Guinea were situated along the Mina coast, which was, relatively, the richest part of West Africa. On the other hand, the attempts to establish forts on the Senegal, in Sierra Leone and on the Malagueta coast, would suggest that the Portuguese attributed considerable importance to the rest of Guinea.

Only a few historical narratives have so far been written, which have attempted to describe in detail, the early trade and the forts of the Portuguese in West Africa. Historians have generally shown more interest either in the slave trade between Angola and Brazil, or in the Portuguese empire beyond the Cape of Good Hope. The history of Guinea in the sixteenth century has been regarded rather as auxiliary to one of these two themes than as an independent story. Consequently, there has been a tendency to ignore the importance of Portuguese enterprise in Guinea. Their achievements in West Africa have been overshadowed, either by placing an exaggerated emphasis upon the slave trade to the new world, or by the greater glory of their empire, which circumnavigated the Indian Ocean. It is time a sense of proportion was introduced.

---

[1] *Ensaios*, II. ii. 4.
[2] " Narrative of Valentim Fernandez Alema", December 1506 (ed. Dr. J. Schmeller), p. 42 ; Peres, *Historia de Portugal*, V. 445.
[3] *Vide infra*, p. 183.   [4] M. de Sousa Coutinho, *Annaes de João III*, p. 405.

Admittedly, it would be an equal distortion of the truth to deny the pre-eminence of the slave traffic in the economic life of West Africa in the eighteenth century. Nor could it be claimed that the volume of Portuguese commerce in Guinea approximated to one tithe of that with the East Indies. Yet it may be suggested that the monopolistic organisation of the Guinea trade provided both Spain and Portugal with precedent, example and experience, when they began to build up their empires in the East and West Indies. Moreover, a good deal of material has been marshalled here to show that, in the period 1480–1578, Guinea enjoyed a vigorous and separate life, and was by no means entirely dependent upon the transatlantic market. Its gold, ivory and pepper, together with its minor products, like hides and ambergris, were valuable both before and long after the new world was discovered. Nor did the expansion of the American slave market adversely affect the pursuit of the other kinds of traffic. On the contrary, evidence is available to show that the Portuguese, in the later sixteenth century, followed a positive policy of expansion in Guinea, constructing forts south of the Gambia, continuing their local trades, and even attempting settlements in Sierra Leone.

Trade preceded fortification in West Africa, but it is doubtful whether the building of forts increased the profits from the trade. A vicious circle stultified the efforts of the Portuguese merchants. We shall see how trade attracted French and English interlopers after 1530. Forts were built, therefore, mainly to exclude them, but a few forts were quite useless to protect 2,000 miles of coast. Furthermore, fortification involved expenditure, and so the profits, which were made in the trade, were consumed in the defence of the trade. True, this may not apply to the first half century from 1480 to 1530, when few interlopers troubled the prosperous pursuits of the contractors and the licensees. But the gradual decline of the net value of Portuguese trade in West Africa after 1530 may be attributed partly to this paradox. If we regard the Portuguese empire in Guinea as a vast commercial business, we may say that overhead charges steadily increased until they equalled and even exceeded production. That is why, towards the end of the sixteenth century, some sections of the Portuguese trade were run at a loss, and some were altogether abandoned.

CHAPTER VI

FRENCH INTERVENTION IN WEST AFRICA, 1530–1553

FIFTY years of quiet consolidation in Guinea came to an abrupt end in 1530. We have tried to show that after 1480 the governments of France and England, if they did not recognise, at least refrained from interference in the monopoly beyond Cape Bojador. Moreover, the wealth of the new world diverted the Castilians from Guinea. Portuguese merchants, thus left alone, seized their opportunity to build up a profitable trade, and Portuguese missionaries undertook the evangelisation of many of the negro tribes. Their achievements revealed great qualities, energy, initiative, enterprise, courage, and diplomatic subtlety in their relations with the natives. But one *sine qua non* of successful empire-building would seem to have been neglected : the Portuguese had not created an effective system of defence. The result was that, when French interlopers began to traffic in increasing numbers to Guinea, the Portuguese were unable to exclude them.

Until 1553 the part played by Englishmen in West Africa was negligible. The major threat to Portuguese supremacy came from the French. These twenty-three years may be regarded, then, as a period when the Portuguese monopoly was subjected to a French challenge. Unlike the earlier challenge from Castile, the second did not end in a Portuguese victory. On the contrary, the volume of French interloping trade began to multiply after 1553, while English traders henceforth made regular voyages to Guinea. Again, the new challenge was not a territorial struggle between relative equals, in which each submitted similar claims. The Castilo-Portuguese conflict had resolved itself, in a sense, into a race for possessions and trade, starting from scratch. But there was no race about the rivalry after 1530. The later struggles were the outcome of acts of pure aggression, perpetrated by groups of enterprising merchants and sailors in England and in France, against imperial Portugal. Dynamic interlopers assailed a static empire.

It is generally agreed that Jean Ango, who lived in Dieppe, inspired the remarkable outburst of French maritime enterprise in the early sixteenth century. Jean Ango was an influential ship-owner and a man of powerful mental vision. He was particularly interested in the oversea wealth of Portugal and Spain, and his inventive mind devised various projects for penetrating into the Indies. In the ports of Brittany and Normandy numerous ships were equipped, under his supervision and with the aid of his money, to attack the returning Indian fleets.[1] Many of these expeditions were directed to the islands near the West African coast, which provided shelter for the pirates, lying in wait for the unsuspecting flotillas. Other French ships sailed farther south down the African coast.

In these circumstances, regular French incursions into Guinea began in the 'thirties. As early as 1492 French pirates had seized a Portuguese caravel, returning from Mina with a cargo of gold.[2] Similar captures were made in 1495 and 1522, and King John III seems to have taken special exception to the robbery in 1522, for he ordered João da Silveira, his ambassador in France, to try to secure reparations.[3] The loss of a single Mina caravel threatened the Portuguese monopoly. Navigation charts might be captured with a caravel, and so the national policy of secrecy might be undermined.

Franco-Portuguese relations were far from amicable in the ten years before 1530, because of mutual seizures. Jean Fleury, one of the leading French privateers, had ravaged Portuguese shipping on a large scale off the African coast.[4] Indeed, more than 300 Portuguese ships were captured by French pirates and privateers between 1500 and 1531.[5] Moreover, the preparations in Rouen for the voyage of Giovanni da Verrazano in 1523 may have been the occasion of great speculation among the Portuguese. Did he propose to traffic to Guinea?[6] Six years later, the brothers Parmentier, apparently already familiar with the

[1] P. Gaffarel, "Jean Ango", (*Le Bulletin de la Société normande de Géographie*, 1889).
[2] Resende, *Chronica do D. João II*, ch. cxlv.
[3] Navarrete, *Colección de Viages*, iii. 505; *Alguns Documentos*, p. 459.
[4] Roncière, iii. 251 et seq.
[5] Ford, *The Letters of John III*, p. 8.
[6] Roncière, iii. 270.

Guinea Coast, rounded the Cape of Good Hope and penetrated into the East Indies.[1] It is not surprising, therefore, that John III sanctioned reprisals. One of Jean Ango's ships, the *Marie*, of Dieppe, whose captain was Jean Faim, was seized near the Portuguese coast and its crew imprisoned. This arrest caused a great outcry among the Norman ship-owners, and was condemned generally as an iniquitous violation of neutrality.[2] Jean Ango, whose shipping was especially endangered by the counter-measures of the Portuguese, evidently complained to the King of France. King Francis I listened with sympathy to the accusations of his mariners and merchants, and so, on 27 July 1530, the Dieppe shipping magnate was given a letter of marque, authorising him to recoup himself at the expense of Portuguese maritime trade to the value of 220,000 ducats.

The government of John III of Portugal was fully alive to the dangerous situation, created by this unforeseen development. It was clear that a French intervention in Guinea must be considered and, if possible, prevented. Portuguese policy was directed, therefore, towards securing the revocation of Jean Ango's letter of marque and, further, obtaining from King Francis I a promise to prohibit all voyages from Normandy and Brittany to Brazil, Guinea and the other oversea dominions of Portugal.

Accordingly, in April 1531, John III commissioned Count Antonio d'Ataide and Dr. Gaspar Vaz to go to France as ambassadors, and to try to secure the abrogation of the letter of marque. Concurrently, knowing of the presence of French corsairs, he sent despatches to the authorities in all his seaports, commanding them to warn ship-owners, masters and mariners, who were there, to arm their vessels before sailing (23 April 1531).[3] The King realised that effective force must be combined with diplomatic pressure in order to protect his empire.

His actions suggest that French interlopers were already trading and pillaging in Guinea, as well as on the Brazilian coast. Of this a little evidence exists. A Breton corsair carried out a raid on Portuguese shipping near the Cape Verde Islands early in 1529, according to a reference in the extant narrative of the

---
[1] *Ibid.*
[2] Roncière, iii. 252.
[3] M. de Sousa Coutinho, *Annaes de João III*, p. 376.

Voyage of the Parmentiers, and, soon after, the brothers Parmentier themselves navigated part of the Upper Guinea Coast during their celebrated voyage to the East Indies.[1] These are the earliest visits to Guinea by Frenchmen, of which we have irrefutable evidence. Some voyages may have been made before 1529, because French pirates attacked the Brazilian coast between 1527 and 1528, while the Cape Verde Islands provided a half-way house en route for Brazil. Moreover, French captains, who later engaged in the Brazil trade, nearly always trafficked first on the Guinea Coast. There is no reason to suppose that the earlier adventurers in the Brazil trade ignored the commerce of Guinea.

Trading expeditions to Guinea became more regular after 1530. It is known that, at the beginning of September 1531, a ship reached Rouen from Guinea with a cargo of malagueta, cotton, ivory and hides, obtained by violence as the Portuguese alleged.[2] The cargo does not provide a key to the region from which this ship returned, but the Cape Verde archipelago was probably where the piracies were committed. Moreover, winter was the only safe time for Guinea traffic so that, chronologically, the out-voyage may have preceded the Portuguese mission to France in April. It is further recorded that, in this same month, four ships, equipped by M. de Navarre and M. de Chateaubriand and commanded by De la Motte, who was a member of the queen's household, were prepared ready in Brittany either to go to Malagueta or, by virtue of Jean Ango's letter of marque, to plunder Portuguese shipping in the African seas.[3]

Another point is worthy of consideration with regard to the interloping traffic in Guinea in the winter and spring of 1530-1. Dr. J. A. Williamson has described how the elder William Hawkins, who was interested in the Brazil trade, sent out the *Paul*, a goodly tall ship of 250 tons, to Brazil in 1530, and how her crew purchased malagueta pepper at the Rio dos Sestos. He has also shown that French and English navigators collaborated in the planning of the double Guinea-Brazil voyage, and that the main initiative in their schemes seems to have come

---

[1] L. Estancelin, *Recherches sur les Voyages des Navigateurs normands*.
[2] *Quadro Elementar*, iii. 241.
[3] E. Guénin, *Ango et ses pilotes*, p. 91.

from the French.¹ One is led, therefore, to suspect that in the autumn of 1530 French ships, destined for Brazil, may also have called at Sierra Leone. If this be so, it would follow that the five ships, referred to above, were not the only French vessels, which traded in West Africa in the nine months before mid-summer 1531.

This French intrusion was, doubtless, one of the immediate reasons why the Portuguese envoys attended upon the King of France. John III's despatch of 23 April 1531 appears to throw further light upon the French activities in Guinea. Moreover, the cargo, which was brought back to Rouen in September, seems to have been obtained by piracy rather than by peaceful traffic on the coast. Perhaps a Portuguese ship had been seized and sunk, and its merchandise confiscated. Accordingly, all Portuguese vessels were to go armed, in future, when they should sail to Guinea.

Meanwhile, in the summer of 1531, Count Antonio d'Ataide and Dr. Gaspar Vaz, John III's envoys, pursued their negotiations. At Fonte Nables they met their French rivals and, despite the grant of fresh letters of marque to the great Dieppe privateer on 12 March, they managed to secure a revocation of all the previous concessions to Jean Ango (11 July 1531).²

Nevertheless, preparations went on in the French ports for expeditions to both Guinea and Brazil. Many voyages were undertaken in the autumn of 1531. In a letter to the King of Portugal of 18 August, Count Antonio d'Ataide reported that Jean Ango was believed to be equipping four ships to go to Guinea and to return via the coast of Malagueta, that many more ships were being equipped in the ports of Brittany, and that, as he heard, a great fleet was being made ready in England. He would investigate the reason for the English fleet and, if anything of interest to Portugal should be divulged, he would at once report.³ His letter is instructive, for it reveals that the Portuguese feared an English intervention. We may speculate whether news had come through of the first voyage of William Hawkins. His information about the French preparations for Guinea was not quite accurate. These were not limited to four vessels. At least ten ships, four at Harfleur and six at Rouen,

---

¹ J. A. Williamson, *John Hawkins*, pp. 9–11 ; Hakluyt, xi. 23.
² M. de Sousa Coutinho, *Annaes de João III*, p. 374 ; Roncière, iii. 278–87.
³ *Quadro Elementar*, iii. 239–40.

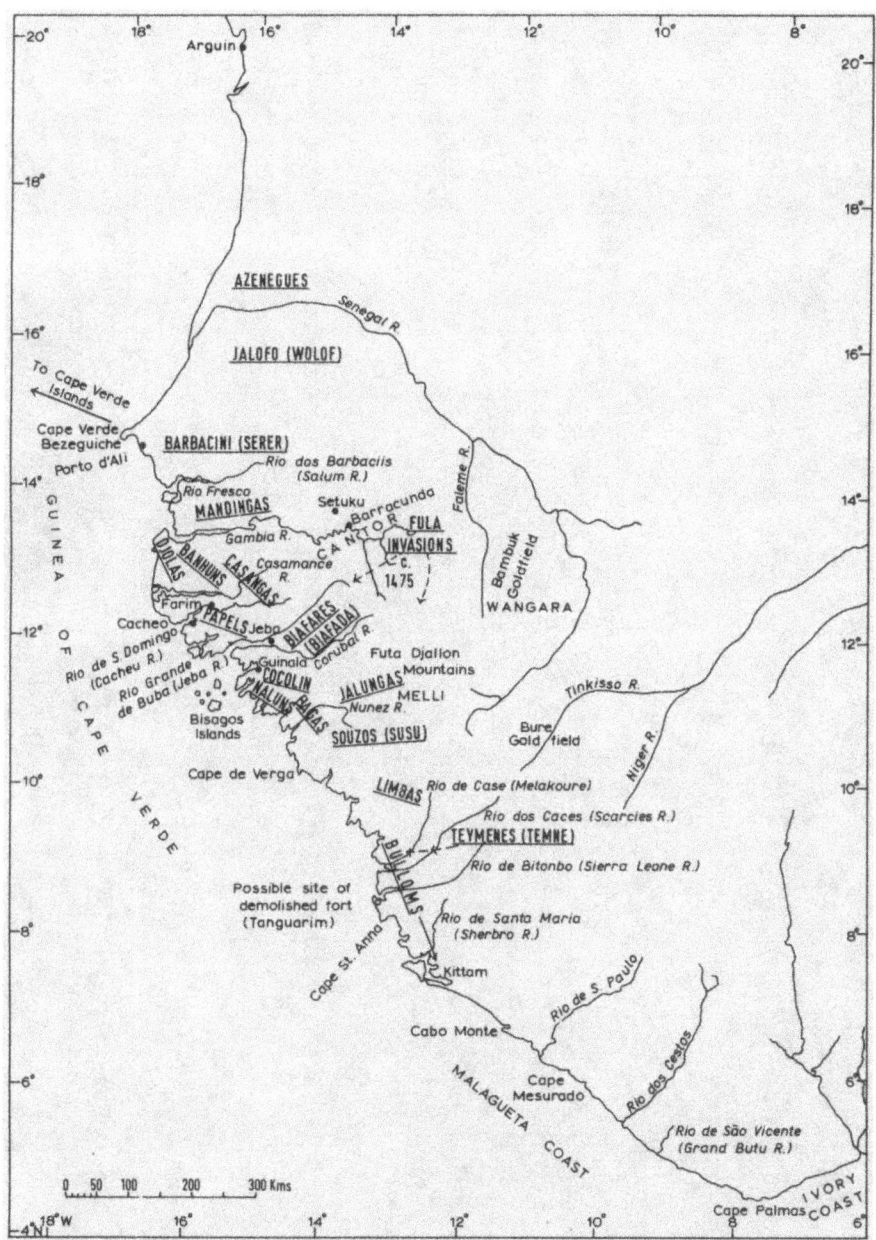

GUINEA OF CAPE VERDE AND THE MALAGUETA COAST
States shown in capital letters
Peoples shown in capitals underlined

III

were being equipped to go to Guinea and Brazil.[1] Plans were being laid, apparently, for an extensive descent upon the West African coast in the coming autumn.

This evidence makes it abundantly clear that the mission of Count Antonio d'Ataide and Dr. Gaspar Vaz had not achieved its fundamental purpose, though Jean Ango's letter of marque had been revoked. French ships still sailed to Guinea, and new expeditions were still being planned. The envoys, then, must try to persuade Francis I to forbid all voyages by his subjects to Guinea. If he would do this, perhaps the growing interference of a dangerous rival to the Portuguese in West Africa might be checked. There were obvious difficulties, such as the opposition of those who were interested in the financial side of these French maritime adventures. The first and greatest obstacle was the attitude of the King of France. Could he be won over to the Portuguese point of view, so that the veto, if and when it should be issued, would be effective?

The attitude of King Francis seems to have been governed mainly by his position in Europe. His wars with the Emperor Charles V caused him to cherish the alliance of Portugal; he repeatedly spoke of his wish to preserve " good friendship " with King John III.[2] Yet Charles V and John III were drawn together by their common interest in upholding the two imperial monopolies, created by the papal bulls and the Treaty of Tordesillas (1493–4). The King of Portugal, for his part, justified the monopoly by drawing a distinction between free and closed waters. In a letter to Ruy Fernandes, on 2 May 1534, he wrote that " the seas which all ought and can navigate, are those, which always were known by all and common to all; but those others, which never were known, and did not seem to be navigable, and were discovered with such great labour by me, are [closed] ".[3] Presumably then, the free seas were only those of Europe, since they had always been known to all. On the other hand, the seas of Guinea, Brazil and the Indies were the exclusive preserve of the Portuguese. John III's argument was a convenient version of the doctrine of a ' *mare clausum* '.

But Francis I championed the opposed doctrine of a '*mare*

---

[1] Roncière, iii. 285, note (1).
[2] *Quadro Elementar*, iii. 241.
[3] Gomes de Carvalho, *D. Joao III e os Francezes*, p. 64.

apertum '; he affirmed that all could " navigate the common sea ".[1] Like John III, he supported the theory which suited him best, but it involved a sharp conflict with a state, whose alliance he desired. Consequently, he did not pursue the point too far. French trade in Guinea was not, in his eyes, sufficiently important to warrant or risk a rupture with the King of Portugal. Therefore, his policy fluctuated. He did not always support and befriend his Norman and Breton subjects; sometimes, when the attitude of the Portuguese government was unusually menacing, he would make a show of rebuffing them.

This, indeed, seems to have been what happened in August 1531. For some time after the revocation of Ango's letter of marque, the Portuguese envoys appear to have pressed in vain for a veto on all voyages to Guinea and Brazil. At length, a bribe of 10,000 cruzados won over the influential Chabot, the Admiral of France, and it was he, apparently, who persuaded King Francis I to yield.[2] Accordingly, a royal proclamation, issued from Fonte Nables, forbade all French ships to go to traffic in the lands of the conquest of the King of Portugal, under pain of confiscation of goods and the arrest of the disobedient crews (3 August 1531).[3]

A Portuguese effort to secure a change in the phrasing of the prohibition does not appear to have been successful, but in due course it was published in Picardy and in some parts of Normandy.[4]

In the ports of Normandy and Brittany the veto met with an extremely hostile reception. Indeed, it was actually ignored. The Norman ship-owners, at the same time as they sent envoys to Paris to press for the raising of the embargo, also seem quietly to have continued their preparations for the Guinea voyages. Four ships, piloted by João Affonso, a renegade Portuguese, slipped out of Harfleur harbour on the way to Malagueta in October.[5] A month later, ten more ships were equipped and ready to sail. In consequence of the arguments of the Norman envoys in Paris, these ships were apparently allowed to leave France, provided they should not go to the

---

[1] Roncière, iii. 291.
[2] Gomes de Carvalho, *op. cit.*, pp. 45–7.
[3] M. de Sousa Coutinho, *Annaes de João III*, p. 374.
[4] Ford, *The Letters of John III*, pp. 42, 57 ; *Quadro Elementar*, iii. 239.
[5] Roncière, iii. 285 ; Gomes de Carvalho, *op. cit.*, pp. 50–1.

lands of Portugal or pass beyond the Cape Verde Islands.[1]

Meanwhile, a dramatic commercial struggle appears to have broken out between the French and the Portuguese on the Malagueta coast. When the four ships left Harfleur in October, Dr. Gaspar Vaz pointed out that, " if these ships return and are not sent to the bottom, Your Highness will find it result that the trade of Malagueta will be lost and the pepper undergo a great decline ".[2] This was a very real danger. We have shown how interloping activity was partly responsible for the decay of profits in Senegambia towards the end of the fifteenth century.[3] Now, a similar situation was developing on the Malagueta coast. The new rivals to Portugal seem to have concentrated upon the traffic of Malagueta more than upon that of other districts. The chief object of the French interlopers was to obtain supplies of the celebrated ' grain of paradise '. Consequently, prices on this part of the Guinea Coast were suddenly threatened.

It is probable that, under the supervision of the crown, a policy of controlled prices regulated Portuguese trading in Guinea. All contractors and licensees offered the native merchants equal prices, so that the latter could not bargain. Profits were thus maintained. Probably however, French interlopers were now disturbing the equilibrium of the trade on the Malagueta coast, prices were beginning to fluctuate with a tendency to fall, and profits were falling with them. We may suspect also that the French traders were exploiting the ' gift system ' to the detriment of the trade of the Portuguese. One of the preliminaries to trade in certain parts of Guinea was the making of a gift to the local native prince or king.[4] The French captains, by offering superior gifts to the native potentates, could easily ingratiate themselves into the favour of the negroes, and thus displace their white rivals from the traffic. It is conceivable that they were now doing this on the Malagueta coast.

Direct evidence of the details of the struggle is lacking. Contemporary records leave no doubt that the French interlopers favoured especially the Malagueta coast, but we cannot go further than say that, probably, they tried to undercut the

[1] Roncière, iii. 285.
[2] Gomes de Carvalho, *op. cit.*, pp. 50–1.
[3] *Vide supra*, pp. 85, 88, 91.
[4] G. B. Ramusio, *Navigationi et Viaggi*, iii. 429.

prices of their Portuguese competitors. Price undercutting was a well-marked feature of commercial rivalry on the Guinea Coast after 1553, and the Hollanders employed the 'gift system' after 1595 in their struggle with the Portuguese. That these methods may have been used earlier in the century is suggested only by a vague and unreliable reference in Ramusio's *Viaggi*. A Dieppe captain, who had visited Guinea, there records that the Portuguese were unpopular, but that the French were eagerly welcomed by the chiefs of the land of Guinea.[1] Doubtless, his statement is biassed in favour of his own countrymen. Even so, it suggests that the French offered the natives cheaper goods and better gifts, and thus were more popular with them. Speculative though this may be, at least it is certain that the French were menacing the Portuguese traffic in malagueta pepper. Dr. Gaspar Vaz's comment, already quoted, provides sufficient proof of this and shows, further, that the Portuguese were well aware of the danger. More stringent measures would have to be taken against the rival traders.

Besides the French voyages to Guinea, the Englishman, William Hawkins, seems to have sent three expeditions between 1530 and 1532.[2] There must have been a large number of interloping ships in West Africa in the winter of 1531-2. In practice, the breach in the Portuguese monopoly was slowly widening. Malagueta pepper and the Malagueta coast were not the only objectives. Hawkins purchased ivory at the Rio dos Sestos on his second voyage, and, if the strategy of his voyage were copied from the French, it would appear that French traders also bought ivory in Sierra Leone. Moreover, although, by the amendment to the royal veto of August 1531, the French adventurers had been forbidden to sail beyond the Cape Verde Islands, did it not follow that they could still plunder in that archipelago? Perhaps the foundations of the later French pre-eminence in the region of the islands were already being laid. Furthermore, the Guinea voyage now represented a complete venture for them. Apparently, they forestalled the English in this, as in so many other ways, for to Hawkins Sierra Leone was only a convenient half-way house on the way to Brazil.

---

[1] *Ibid.*
[2] Hakluyt, xi. 23-4 ; J. A. Williamson, *John Hawkins*, pp. 9-11.

The stream of French activity in West Africa did not dry up in consequence of the embassy of Count Antonio d'Ataide. Although several prospective voyages were forbidden in November 1531, yet the following season produced a new crop of adventures to Guinea (1532-3).[1] The preamble to a letter of marque of 3 February 1543 reveals that Jean Ango sent at least three ships to Guinea in the autumn of 1532. One, *La Michelle*, loaded pepper, musk and ivory in West Africa, and then went on to Brazil after the manner of the Hawkins expeditions; the other two, *L'Alouette* and *La Musette*, were attacked in Guinea on 27 October 1532 by " the caravels and ships [of Portugal] fitted out for war ", and the first was fortunate to escape.[2] It was becoming more and more obvious that artless diplomatic protests were of little avail against the French interlopers.

Accordingly, the Portuguese experimented with several other suggestions for the maintenance of their imperilled monopoly. The agents of King John III put forward two proposals: one was that the vessels of Jean Ango should be bought by the Portuguese government; the other envisaged the sharing of the Antwerp trade between Rouen and Flanders.[3] The latter move " would content the French ", wrote Dr. Gaspar Vaz to John III on 19 October 1531. There was, in fact, much to be said for it. Most of the French voyages to West Africa, at this time, seem to have been directed to the Malagueta coast. The pepper of that region seems to have been the chief attraction. Now the greater part of all the malagueta pepper was carried to Antwerp, which was the general distributing centre. It would appear feasible, therefore, to believe that, had the townspeople of Rouen been given a share in the distribution of this commodity along with other less valuable articles, the merchants of Brittany and Normandy might have ceased their interloping traffic to Guinea. Unfortunately, the council of John III feared to alienate the Emperor Charles V by a measure, which would undoubtedly have conduced to French profit, and the creditors of the Flanders factory also seem to have opposed the project.[4] The scheme was thus abandoned. Of the other suggestion, nothing more appears to have been said. So the two

[1] E. Guénin, *Jean Ango et ses pilotes*, p. 198.
[2] *Ibid.*, pp. 149-54.
[3] Roncière, iii. 286; *Quadro Elementar*, iii. 24.
[4] Gomes de Carvalho, *op. cit.*, p. 52.

projects, which were to have operated in France to alleviate the tension in West Africa, were both shelved. Instead, more direct methods were adopted.

The way of negotiation having virtually failed, John III fell back upon that of force. Although he continued the negotiations at the French court, he now concentrated more attention upon two further aspects of the Guinea problem : the expulsion of the French from West African waters, and the protection, by means of a convoy system, of outgoing and returning Guinea fleets.

He employed various expedients to expel the French. First of all, his espionage organisation was improved. From many French ports men, in the pay of the Portuguese government, sent reports to the Portuguese agent in Paris about maritime preparations, and the information, thus collected, was transmitted to Lisbon. There was, indeed, an urgent need for this kind of work. Although Bernadim de Tavora was sent to France in 1533 to try, by diplomatic pressure and by bribing admiral Chabot, to stop the illicit voyages,[1] the Norman and Breton merchants and privateers continued to adventure in the Guinea traffic. The trial of admiral Chabot revealed that two merchants of Rouen, called d'Agincourt and Huet, bribed him on 19 May 1533 to allow them to send four ships to " *les terres de l' Affrique* ".[2] It was not difficult to place a wide interpretation upon the phrasing of this concession, and to send ships to Guinea. Moreover, a letter of King John III indicates that two French ships had left for the Malagueta coast, piloted by the renegade Portuguese João Affonso, in January 1533.[3] French voyages to Guinea were still unchecked.

The voyage of João Affonso in 1533 will serve to illustrate the working of the Portuguese espionage system. It seems to have been towards the end of January 1533 that João Affonso set out with two French ships. On 21 January the King of Portugal informed Count Antonio d'Ataide that one of his agents in France, Antonio Vaz de Lacerda, had reported that certain French ships were about to depart for India, and would reassemble probably off the Malagueta coast. The count was commanded to ascertain the precise rendezvous from Antonio

[1] *Ibid.*, pp. 52–3, 68–70.
[2] Guénin, *op. cit.*, p. 157.
[3] Ford, *Letters of John III*, pp. 79–80.

Vaz, and the time when the interlopers would be likely to arrive there. Duarte Coelho, one of the King's captains, would then be able to await the arrival of the French off that coast and so attack them. Secrecy was to be maintained and only trustworthy men employed.[1] A second letter of the same date gave more detailed instructions to the Portuguese minister.[2] But four days later, John III wrote again, this time to command Duarte Coelho to go to the Azores " with the fleet which is now ranging on the coast of Malagueta " to await the ships from India.[3] There was insufficient time, between the middle of January and the date of the return of the Indies fleet, for Duarte Coelho to deal with the French fleet separately, while cruising off the Malagueta coast, before returning to the Azores. Therefore, it was decided to recall him immediately to the Azores, so that he might meet the Indies fleet there and protect it from piratical French attacks. Accordingly, the original plan of awaiting Affonso's interloping fleet off Malagueta was abandoned. This seems to have been the reason for the change in the instructions which were sent to Duarte Coelho.

Having arranged for the interception of the interlopers, John III did not cease his vigilance. A letter of 27 January reveals that the Portuguese knew definitely, through Dr. Gaspar Vaz, of the departure of the French ships.[4] A few days later, the chief magistrate of the Algarve reported that the French had touched at the Canary Islands. Consequently, John III gave orders that the Mina fleet was to be warned of the dangerous presence of French privateers. This same letter indicates that he had not given up hope that Duarte Coelho might be able to stay in Malagueta waters to intercept the French, and then sail to the Azores in time to meet the returning ships from the East Indies.[5] In the end, however, Duarte Coelho does not appear to have stayed much longer in Guinea. He had been scheduled to remain there until the middle of April 1533 and, after that, was to make his way to the Azores. He received the order to leave Malagueta in May, and, presumably, he then met the Indies fleet, which he may have convoyed back to Lisbon. No evidence has been found to show that

[1] *Ibid.*, pp. 69–70.
[2] *Ibid.*, pp. 71–2.
[3] *Ibid.*, p. 73.
[4] *Ibid.*, pp. 79–80.
[5] *Ibid.*, pp. 81–2.

he ever encountered the two French ships. Nevertheless, the episode serves to illustrate the remarkable diligence with which the Portuguese watched the activities of French interlopers in Guinea.

A second method of forcibly excluding the French was the old one of casting ships' crews into the sea. Proof that this merciless punishment was still employed is provided by the remark, already quoted, of Dr. Gaspar Vaz regarding the four ships of Harfleur that, " if they are not sent to the bottom " the pepper trade would be ruined.[2] Several years later, Marino Cavalli, the Venetian ambassador in France, had occasion to refer to the perpetual struggle between the Portuguese and the French (1546). " If they encounter one another at sea and the French happen to be weak, the Portuguese attack them and send their ships to the bottom ", he wrote, alluding probably to the treatment dealt out by the Portuguese to Frenchmen, whom they chanced to catch in Guinea, Brazil and the Indies.[3] Furthermore, in 1552, the King of Portugal sent instructions to his captains to pursue and to sink all suspected French vessels in Guinea and Brazil.[4] This feature of Portuguese policy did not change throughout this period, 1530–53. That the captains of John III, who sailed the seas of Guinea, were sometimes neglectful of their duties is suggested by the order of 1552; but the official policy of the government remained constant. No mercy was ever shown to interlopers.

In the next place, squadrons of armed ships were maintained by Portugal in Guinea to attack and to destroy the interlopers. The evidence, submitted below, suggests that these armadas were neither regular nor permanent, but is insufficient to allow the drawing of definitive conclusions.

Duarte Coelho was cruising off the Malagueta coast with an armed fleet of seven ships in the winter and early spring of 1532–3. He had sailed from Portugal in October 1532, and throughout the ensuing winter he would seem to have remained off the Malagueta coast.[5] At the beginning of May 1533, as we have seen, he was recalled to meet the Indies fleet for the pur-

[1] *Vide supra*, p. 113.
[2] M. N. Tommaseo, *Relations des Ambassadeurs de Venise*, i. 292–5.
[3] Rebello da Silva, *Historia de Portugal*, iii. 133.
[4] M. de Sousa Coutinho, *Annaes de João III*, p. 377.

FRENCH INTERVENTION IN WEST AFRICA 119

pose of protecting it and, apparently, of convoying it back to Lisbon. One of King John III's letters, written on 6 July 1533, shows that Coelho did return to the island of Terceira and there met the fleet from the East Indies.[1] We hear no more of his operations in Guinea until 1543.

An inhospitable climate and the shortage of fresh water and fresh food complicated the problem of the defence of Guinea. It was exceedingly difficult to maintain permanent fleets. Accordingly, the Portuguese government was reduced to the expedient of stationing armadas off the Guinea Coast for short periods. Those periods were made to coincide, as far as possible, with the times when interloping ships were accustomed to frequent West African waters, that is, the eight months from September to April. This would explain why Duarte Coelho left Portugal in October and was recalled in May. Behind the scanty evidence, so far discovered, there would seem to be this story. Duarte Coelho was sent out with an armed fleet to range off the Malagueta coast and so preserve the pepper traffic, at that season of the year when the activity of French interlopers was likely to be most intensive. This manœuvre was carried out in 1532-3. In the spring, towards the end of the trading season, and when heavy rains and the terrific heat rendered further traffic far too dangerous, Duarte returned to the Azores to convoy the Indies fleet to Portugal. Whether this was a yearly feature of the Portuguese defence of Malagueta is not known. But an interesting repetition of the manœuvre has been found for the winter of 1540-1.[2]

More definite evidence exists for the Mina coast. A letter of the King of Portugal reveals that a permanent fleet of armed caravels was not maintained at the castle of São Jorge in 1534. "Because of the need arising from the long period which elapses, when there are no ships at Mina", wrote John III, "I strongly recommend that you order [the Mina fleet] to be made ready with the greatest possible speed". The existing practice was, apparently, for the Mina caravels to leave Portugal for the castle of São Jorge in October, the chief captain being provided with a full and explicit *regimentó*, or list of instructions, and, as soon as the gold, accumulated in the warehouse of the fort, had

[1] *Ibid.*, p. 378.
[2] *Vide infra*, p. 127.

been embarked, for the fleet to return to Lisbon. But John III realised the advantage of a permanent squadron at Mina. The same letter contains a request to Count Antonio d'Ataide that he should consider " whether some caravels ought to remain at Mina for some time ".[1] The minister, so addressed, replied, apparently, in the affirmative on 20 January, and so three days later the king ordered four ships to " remain on the coast, to serve in that which may be necessary ".[2] It is not unreasonable to suppose that this fleet was to be employed mainly to prevent French interlopers from buying gold from the negro merchants.

But this squadron cannot have been permanently stationed at Mina and provisioned from the castle. One of the four delegated ships was a galleon, called the *Trinidade*, but in 1537 this same ship was being armed " secure from the corsairs ", and equipped with provisions and merchandise in Portugal, to go to Mina, and to bring back all the gold which was stored in the warehouse.[3] Evidently, the squadron did not hold together for long in West Africa. It is probable that the incursions of the French were as yet not sufficiently serious to justify the attempt to maintain a permanent armada.

No additional evidence has been found of protective squadrons in West Africa until 1541–3. The persistence of French activity makes it almost certain that there must have been armed Portuguese fleets in Guinea despite the absence of records in the intervening years. Thus, a French fleet was known by the Portuguese to be at the Cape Verde Islands on its way to Malagueta in 1536.[4] William Hawkins may have sent a ship to the Rio dos Sestos in the same year.[5] Two years later, three vessels left Nantes for Malagueta,[6] and in 1540 Hawkins organised a further expedition to Brazil via Guinea.[7]

After 1540, so far as extant evidence indicates, the volume of French traffic rapidly grew. This was the year of the Chabot scandal, when the disgraceful bribing of the admiral was exposed. Accordingly, the embargo on Guinea voyages, which had been repeated in 1537–8–9, was lifted.[8] French merchants were

---

[1] Ford, *The Letters of John III*, pp. 153–6.
[2] *Ibid.*, pp. 157–8.
[3] *Ibid.*, pp. 305–6.
[4] *Ibid.*, p. 274.
[5] J. A. Williamson, *John Hawkins*, p. 12.
[6] M. de Sousa Coutinho, *op. cit.*, pp. 402–3.
[7] Williamson, *op. cit.*, p. 14.
[8] *Vide infra*, p. 134.

FRENCH INTERVENTION IN WEST AFRICA 121

thus enabled to plan new expeditions for West Africa with the favour, and no longer the opposition of their sovereign. Four French ships left Rouen for Guinea in 1541;[1] at Bordeaux and La Rochelle three ships were made ready in the same year to sail for the coast of Guinea; Jean Ango equipped fourteen or fifteen ships and galleons in the port of Dieppe, all of which left for Malagueta and Brazil;[2] and near the Cape Verde Islands a number of fights occurred during the ensuing winter between Frenchmen and Portuguese.[3]

Here, then, is evidence of a French descent upon West Africa almost as extensive as that of the English twenty years later. The evidence for the year 1542 is equally striking. One French ship visited Cape Threepoints probably to purchase gold dust; another caravel, whose master was Sebastian de Salme, pursued a very prosperous and varied traffic, its cargo including 157 cases of sugar, 50 quintals of wax, 20 cases of gum-arabic, 12 Guinea hens and 1,000 pounds of gold! Moreover, *la Grande-Martine* returned to Rouen with a cargo of Guinea pepper, while at the same time other French ships were purchasing pepper in Guinea.[4] The value of the French interloping traffic must have increased considerably after 1540. Perhaps, on the other hand, Portuguese profits fell.

It may have been for this reason that new measures were executed for the maintenance of armed fleets in West Africa. King John III often argued that the sea was so vast that defensive fleets were of no avail. It would not be possible in any case to catch the interlopers, because they could not be found. Yet in January 1542 he told Luis Sarmiento, the Spanish ambassador in Portugal, that, four or five months before, " he had despatched one of his captains with an armada to the island of São Thomé to remain upon those shores ".[5] His words suggest that the situation in Guinea was becoming so serious that a defence for São Thomé, in the heart of the Gulf, was considered necessary, in addition to the naval protection already provided for Malagueta and Mina. Consequently, in September

---

[1] E. Gosselin, *Documents pour servir a l'histoire de la marine normande*, pp. 143-4.
[2] Biggar, *Documents relating to Cartier and Roberval*, pp. 209-11, 263.
[3] Barcellos, pp. 116-18.
[4] Gosselin, *op. cit.*, pp. 144-5; E. Guénin, *Ango et ses pilotes*, p. 230.
[5] Biggar, *op. cit.*, p. 427.

or October 1541, an armed squadron was sent to defend the Gulf, using the island of São Thomé as its base of operations.

Moreover, we have evidence of armed fleets in Guinea in 1543. Duarte Coelho, who had commanded the expedition of 1532-3, was appointed chief captain of a fleet which seems then to have been at Mina. Two other fleets were also in Guinea, patrolling the Malagueta and Mina coasts respectively. The commander of the five caravels of the Mina fleet was captain Ruy Mendes de Mesquita. Fernão Rodrigues Barba, who had already served as commander of the armada of four ships sent to defend the Mina coast in 1534, was now captain of the Malagueta fleet; and it is interesting to notice that the galleon *São João*, which had been included in the armada of 1534, was now attached to the Malagueta fleet.[1] The apparent continuity in ships and personnel suggests a more regular system of naval defence than the printed records reveal.

One other point is worth noting in this connection. It is recorded in de Sousa's *Annals* that, from the time of the accession of King John III to 1544, " malagueta had not paid . . . one-fifth part of what it did formerly, and had cost for its defence 80,000 cruzados ".[2] The defence of empire trade was obviously proving expensive and part had already ceased to pay for itself. How had the 80,000 cruzados been spent? Later, it will be shown that considerable losses must have resulted from abortive efforts to fortify the Malagueta coast in 1532 and again in 1541.[3] Expense would also have been incurred in the arming of the convoys.[4] Nevertheless, a portion of this sum may have been consumed in the upkeep of occasional fleets. For this reason it seems probable that the Malagueta fleet of 1543 was delegated to remain off that coast for a specified period in order to protect the pepper trade from French interlopers. But, the absence of a factory, let alone a fortress, on the Malagueta coast made it impossible for the armada to cruise there permanently. The ships would be obliged to seek provisions either at the castle of São Jorge, or at Ribeira Grande in Santiago Island, or even at Lisbon in Portugal.

---

[1] Ford, *The Letters of John III*, pp. 157-8; M. de Sousa Coutinho, *op. cit.*, p. 411.
[2] *Ibid.*, p. 416.
[3] *Vide infra*, pp. 126-7.
[4] *Vide infra*, pp. 128-32.

FRENCH INTERVENTION IN WEST AFRICA 123

The Mina armada was, in this respect, more fortunate than that of Malagueta. Yet, such supplies as Ruy Mendes de Mesquita's fleet may have drawn from the castle of São Jorge could not have been very adequate. There are many indications in the letters of King John III that the castle itself was annually provisioned from Portugal. A system whereby a defensive squadron drew supplies from a fortress, which drew its supplies elsewhere, cannot have been very satisfactory. It is obvious, all the same, that the Portuguese government tried to arrange for a coast patrol, and that in 1543 two protective squadrons were organised to cruise respectively off the coasts of Malagueta and Mina.

We must turn next to 1547. In May of that year, captain Antonio Anes Pinteado was despatched with a fleet of warships from Lisbon to cruise along the Barbary coast, to seize interloping French ships, and then to sail on a trading voyage to Brazil.[1] Now it is possible that Pinteado had already commanded a defensive squadron in Lower Guinea. He was, like Duarte Coelho and Fernão Rodrigues Barba, one of the regular naval commanders in the service of Portugal, and by 1553 he had acquired a terrifying reputation for his successful patrol of the "coasts of Brazil and Guinea" against the French.[2] Admittedly, Pinteado did not go to Malagueta or Mina in 1547, but in 1553 he piloted an English fleet to Benin. Obviously then, he was familiar with the navigation of Lower Guinea. Accordingly, there is good reason for supposing that he had commanded either the Mina or the Malagueta armada before 1547.

The years 1550 and 1552 bring two pieces of evidence of doubtful value. The chronicler, Francisco de Andrada, records that in 1550 King John III sent two armed caravels, manned with nearly one hundred men, to Guinea, under the command of Captains Francisco Machado and Jeronimo Ferreyra ;[3] and in 1552 the naval commanders of Portugal, who were in Guinea and Brazil, were ordered to pursue and to sink suspected French vessels in those regions.[4] The extract from Andrada seems to provide an example of a small defensive squadron being sent to

---

[1] *Hans Staden. The True History of his Captivity*, (trans. and ed. by M. Letts), p. 34.
[2] Hakluyt, vi. 141–52 ; *Cal. S. P. Spain*, 1553, p. 14.
[3] Andrada, *Chronica del Rey D. João III*, pt. iv, ch. lxviii.
[4] Rebello da Silva, *Historia de Portugal*, iii. 133.

Guinea. John III's order to his captains shows that there must have been armed fleets in Guinea in 1552. In fact, seven additional warships were sent to Arguin, Cape Verde, Guinea and Brazil in that year.[1]

It must be admitted that all this evidence about the Portuguese armadas in Guinea between 1530 and 1553 is not very convincing. Scanty as it is, however, some conclusions may be drawn. John III obviously realised that defensive fleets were necessary, and he made occasional creative efforts. There were armed ships, patrolling parts of the coast in 1532-3, 1534, 1541, 1543, 1550 and 1552. A closer examination of the records shows that, to a degree, the same ships were employed and the same captains served for several years. This would suggest a more regular patrol system than we dare assert. Surely the odds are against a captain, like Duarte Coelho, who commanded a Guinea fleet in 1532-3 and again in 1543, having been transferred to the Brazilian or the East Indian service during the intervening years. More probably, though we do not hear of him, he continued in the Guinea naval service. Yet, we cannot be sure about the armadas. John III was unwilling further to increase royal expenditure. Doubting its value in the long run, he did not sympathise overmuch with the policy of huge armaments to defend the coast. Even if he sent annual fleets of armed ships, he does not seem to have maintained them in West African waters for more than a few months at a time.

A second method of protecting the coastal trade of Guinea was to repair existing fortresses and to build new ones. But neither King John III nor the contractors welcomed additional expenditure, and so work of this kind was not carried far. Nevertheless, Mina was regularly provisioned during these years, all the fortresses of Arguin, Cape Verde and Guinea seem to have been repaired in 1552, and two efforts were made in 1532 and 1540-1 respectively to build a fort on the Malagueta coast.

The upkeep of the castle of São Jorge da Mina was an important section of the Guinea administration. King John III, though he frequently sought the advice of his chief minister, Count Antonio d'Ataide, personally supervised its government and several royal letters show how interested he was in the well-

---

[1] Barcellos, p. 135.

being of the garrison of the castle. On 3 February 1533 he exhorted the count to see that " care be taken for the provision of Mina ".[1] Another letter, written five days later, reveals that the castle was in a condition of some disorder, for the captain was ill and the caravels, destined for Mina, were late. Accordingly, the king bade his minister see that order was restored.[2] A third letter of 1534 indicates the dependence of the garrison upon the provisions, which were annually brought from Portugal.[3] Again, the count, after consultation with John III, ordered the clerk of the Casa da Mina, Fernão d'Alvarez, to assign Tomas de Barros and Belchior Soarez to the provision ships for Mina in that year.[4] A secret hoard of more than 18,000 cruzados of gold in Mina city was reported to the king in 1536, and he at once issued orders for its collection and safe deposit in his treasury.[5] Fifteen years later a new gold mine was discovered 50 leagues from the castle ; Lopo de Sousa, the governor of São Jorge, sent news to John III, who commanded that the discovery should not be made public.[6] It is obvious that the king exercised a close personal supervision over the castle. Yet other evidence suggests that São Jorge was not always in good repair. Although it was the only substantial land defence for the Gold Coast, the personnel of its garrison had declined to thirty, if we may trust the report of a Dieppe captain who wrote in 1545.[7] This it may be which accounts for the instructions " sent by [John III] in 1552 to his captains to repair and garrison the fortresses, half abandoned, on the coast of . . . Guinea ".[8] Presumably, the depredations of the French had become so serious by 1552 that the king, in spite of his unwillingness to spend more money on his imperial defences, was obliged to carry out certain reparations.

Sierra Leone and Malagueta were even more vulnerable. A fortress in Sierra Leone was no longer used.[9] The Portuguese traded frequently at the Rio dos Sestos, but they possessed no

---

[1] Ford, *The Letters of John III*, pp. 84–5.
[2] *Ibid.*, pp. 91–2.
[3] *Ibid.*, pp. 153–6.
[4] *Ibid.*, p. 212.
[5] *Ibid.*, pp. 275–6.
[6] *Ibid.*, p. 376.
[7] G. B. Ramusio, *Navagationi et Viaggi*, iii. 429.
[8] Rebello da Silva, *Historia de Portugal*, iii. 133.
[9] Pacheco, I. xxxii.

fort to guard the land for themselves against the French.[1] Nor had they a fort on the Malagueta coast. But the fact that the French made a special point of trading to this region would seem to have galvanised King John III into action. A royal patent, issued on 21 October 1532, is printed in de Sousa's *Annals*. It empowers Duarte Coelho, who is sent with a fleet to the coast of Malagueta for the building of fortresses, to put on parole those persons who are to remain there.[2] At last, the king had resolved, apparently, to undertake the cost of building a fort on the Malagueta coast. It is interesting to notice that there were convicts or political prisoners among the men, who were to garrison the proposed fort. Duarte Coelho took them with him and was ordered to put them on parole. Perhaps then, the criticism, which was afterwards levelled against the garrison of São Jorge, was not unfounded; some of the defenders were criminals or political exiles. The Portuguese government was, in fact, obliged to recruit the garrisons of the forts in Guinea mainly from exiles and criminals. Other men were unwilling to serve in the inhospitable land of West Africa.

Unfortunately, no confirmation has been found of this early attempt to fortify Malagueta, but there is no reason to doubt de Sousa's evidence. Curiously, however, Duarte Coelho does not appear to have fulfilled his commission. No fortress was built. Count Antonio d'Ataide, writing just after the failure of a second attempt to build a fortress on that coast, lamented that no fort was ever established there. "The trade of Malagueta has been pursued for more than 28 years", he wrote, "the remedy was to have built a fortress in a convenient place on that coast . . . but nothing more was done" and so the traffic had declined.[3] What happened, then, to the equipment and to the men, taken apparently to Malagueta by Duarte Coelho in October 1532? No evidence has been found to shed any light upon the problem. We cannot even say whether the pilots of the expedition tried to find a suitable site on the coast for the intended fortress.

New preparations to fortify Malagueta were undertaken just at the time when the interloping trade and privateering exploits

---
[1] Ramusio, *op. cit.*, iii. 429.
[2] M. de Sousa Coutinho, *Annaes de João III*, p. 377.
[3] *Ibid.*, p. 405.

of the French were growing more serious than ever before. The second scheme was identical in many ways with that of 1532. King John III informed the Spanish ambassador at Lisbon on 30 September 1540 that " he had fitted out a fleet in Lisbon to proceed to the coast of Malagueta, there to build a fort at a certain spot, to prevent the French out there from putting in to procure a spice called ' malagueta ' ".[1] Two large and five or six small ships, with a total crew of 500 men, were to go. " Stone, lime and masons " were to be taken, " so that on their arrival the building could be commenced ". The captain of the expedition had been ordered to return afterwards with his ships to the Azores in March 1541 to meet the East Indies merchant fleet on its homeward journey.

Now we may suspect that the instructions, given to Duarte Coelho in 1532 must have been, word for word, practically the same. Coelho had gone out in October. He had ranged off the Malagueta coast until the beginning of May and then had returned to the Azores.[2] The new scheme followed a similar plan. There can be little doubt that, in 1540, the Portuguese monarch was drawing upon past experience. Yet this expedition achieved no more than did that of 1532. Indeed, its end was tragic. The fleet left Lisbon on or before 30 September, but ran into so violent a storm that one ship sank with all hands and the rest had to struggle back as best they could to Galicia.[3]

As far as we know, this was the last attempt made by the Portuguese to fortify the Malagueta coast in the sixteenth century. Its failure was significant of a wider movement. It was a sign-post on the road towards the ultimate break-down of the monopoly. The French could not be kept out by force, for distances were too great and land areas too extensive. Doubtless, some part of the 80,000 cruzados, mentioned by de Sousa, was consumed in this costly fiasco. The revenue derivable from Malagueta was insufficient to pay for its defence, and so the French were able gradually to spread their commercial net.

The activities, favoured by the French in West Africa, were of two kinds. On the one hand, they trafficked peacefully along

---
[1] Biggar, *Documents relating to Cartier and Roberval*, pp. 110–15.
[2] *Vide supra*, pp. 116-18.
[3] *Cal. S. P. Span.*, 1538-42, pp. 293-4 ; Biggar, *op. cit.*, pp. 171-3.

the coast or in the islands for malagueta pepper, gold, ivory, sugar and hides; the voyage of Sebastian de Salme is a good example of this (1542).[1] On the other hand, many captains went out with the deliberate intention, not of trading, but of preying upon the cargo-bearing caravels of Portugal. These captains paid particular attention to the Cape Verde Islands where, it was known, Portuguese caravels and carracks were in the habit of taking shelter. A marauding expedition of this type was undertaken in 1544. Antonio Correa de Souza, who was the captain of the city of Ribeira Grande, sent a letter to the King of Portugal on 30 October 1544, in which he reported that two French ships had entered among the Portuguese craft then at Santiago and Fogo Islands, and had captured, plundered and sunk many of them. Another French caravel, he wrote, had sailed into the harbour of Praia, after plundering three ships, and had anchored there, " since . . . here was the route of all the ships, which were destined for São Thomé and Brazil ". But while the pirate waited in Praia port, captain Antonio had attacked it, the Frenchmen had fled, and a prize had been recovered. The letter concludes with a significant appeal for artillery, " for the people of the land are scared at the coming of the Frenchmen ".[2]

Now the peaceful traffic of French interlopers could be checked, if not prevented, by the methods we have already described, elaborate espionage, armed fleets, the casting of crews into the sea, and the fortified posts on the land. But the Portuguese had to recognise that piracy could be effectively countered only by the arming and convoying of the fleets which went to Guinea. Accordingly, they devised and employed a regular system of armed convoys.

Yearly fleets had been sent to bring back gold from Mina as early as 1480.[3] A considerable expansion of this rudimentary system occurred under John III. Fleets were sent, probably annually, not only to Mina but also to Malagueta. The fleet, which sailed to Mina, carried out provisions for the garrison and commodities for sale to the negro merchants, and brought back the gold stored in the warehouse. There are numerous refer-

---

[1] *Vide supra*, p. 121.
[2] Barcellos, pp. 119–20.
[3] *Vide supra*, p. 37.

ences to " the fleet of Mina¹ ". " Regarding the fleet, which will sail to Mina, it seems good to me for the galleon *São João* to go therein ", wrote the king on 23 January 1534.² A few incidental phrases here and there indicate the importance attached to the gold, brought back by these fleets. The galleon *Trinidade*, which visited Mina in 1537, was to " carry all the gold which is at present at Mina ". Order was given to the captain that, when the ship should arrive at the castle, all the available gold was to be delivered to it.³ Another letter reveals that Count Antonio d'Ataide had borrowed 35,000 cruzados on the credit of " the gold of the caravels which are to come from Mina ".⁴ The Portuguese government seems to have looked to the return of the Mina fleet to replete its treasury each year, and to pay some of its debts.

There are fewer indications of a regular fleet being sent to Malagueta. Count Antonio d'Ataide asserted in 1542 that the trade of Malagueta had been opened up for only just over twenty-eight years,⁵ and, if by this he were referring to malagueta pepper, his statement was very inaccurate and possibly a deliberate misrepresentation of the facts. Traffic in malagueta had been made a government monopoly as long before as 1470, and in 1498 large quantities of malagueta had been imported.⁶ But, perhaps the count was thinking of the time, during which the traffic had been properly organised, At any rate, we have no evidence of a fleet, which sailed annually to Malagueta, until the reign of King John III. In January 1541, the king commended the count for withholding the order for the unloading of the " fleet of Malagueta, [which] had arrived ", until the royal command was given.⁷ It would appear that the Malagueta fleet had returned to Portugal earlier than usual. Three years later, John III is found issuing orders to the commander of " his fleet at Malagueta ".⁸ More certain proof of the existence of such a fleet is provided in 1536, when Manoel d' Albuquerque was commissioned to go with the ships for the coast of Malagueta,

¹ " *a armada da Mina.*" Vide Ford, *The Letters of John III*, p. 305.
² *Ibid.*, pp. 157-8.
³ *Ibid.*, pp. 305-6.
⁴ *Ibid.*, p. 315.
⁵ M. de Sousa Coutinho, *Annaes de João III*, p. 405.
⁶ *Vide supra*, pp. 84-5.
⁷ Ford, *op. cit.*, p. 357.
⁸ *Cal. S. P. Span.*, 1544, p. 375.

and provided with the usual list of instructions.[1] It may be assumed, therefore, that separate annual fleets now sailed to Malagueta and to Mina.

A rudimentary convoy system was organised even before 1540. Of this there is some evidence. When the Mina fleet was making for the Malagueta coast in the autumn of 1533, the king informed his ministers that the captains had received the "usual powers", by which he may have referred to certain convoy arrangements.[2] Further light is thrown on this type of precaution against French interlopers in a letter of the previous February. Two French ships were known to have been near the Canary Islands, when the Mina fleet set out for Guinea. Accordingly, the king gave orders that the fleet should be warned, should go "well-guarded", and should, if possible, make a junction with those ships, which were bound for the "Islands".[3] All might then proceed in company with greater security.

Another passage in John III's correspondence gives us an insight into the organisation of this Mina convoy. The fleet, which sailed to Mina in 1535, included the galleon *Trinidade*, certain caravels and the usual provision boats.[4] It is possible that the galleon went to guard the merchant fleet; the caravels may have carried out a few troops, convicts for the most part, to renew the Mina garrison, perhaps took back a few of the old garrison, who had completed their period of exile and had survived the dangers of a tropical climate, and also transported the gold of Mina to Portugal; while the provision boats took food, clothing and articles of merchandise, to be exchanged for the gold, to the isolated residents of the castle of São Jorge. Thus, we would venture to suggest, was the Mina armada organised.

A further aspect of the convoy system is suggested by a letter of 30 August 1536: the king ordered that those ships, which were bound for Mina and São Thomé, should sail "in company" with other ships, which happened to be voyaging down the Guinea Coast.[5] Trading caravels, engaged in the Brazil traffic, were probably intended to fall in with this convoy scheme, be-

---

[1] Ford, *op. cit.*, p. 286.
[2] *Ibid.*, p. 134.
[3] *Ibid.*, p. 82.
[4] *Ibid.*, pp. 211–12.
[5] *Ibid.*, p. 268.

FRENCH INTERVENTION IN WEST AFRICA 131

cause all could sail together at least as far as Cape Verde. If we recall also that in 1533, John III had commanded the Mina fleet to join with ships, bound for the " Islands ", we may see that three streams of maritime traffic were combined for common defence, those respectively of Guinea, Brazil and the African islands.

Admittedly, so far, the system was only embryonic. John III was experimenting, and the convoys may not have been fully organised before 1552. It is remarkable, nevertheless, that the early system, as devised empirically after 1530, would seem to have been similar, in fundamentals, to the completed one. King Sebastian, when issuing elaborate instructions in 1557 and 1571 relating to the maritime convoys, drew freely upon the experience of his great predecessor.[1] Accordingly, it would appear that, by 1540, the main foundations of the convoy organisation had been laid. The ships went in company as far as possible ; they went armed ; and the king kept them informed, by means of swift caravels, of the presence of interlopers.

More definite arrangements were made in 1552. By that time, the danger to shipping from privateers in the East and West Indies had grown considerably. So the Emperor Charles V and King John III now co-operated in defending their monopoly. As early as 1540, the King of Portugal had affirmed that his caravels would combine with those of the emperor against the French interlopers.[2] Charles V, even before this, had identified his imperial interests with those of Portugal.[3] Yet both rulers failed to reach a public agreement concerning a system of convoys until 1552, when a convention was concluded between them. This provided for combined Hispano-Portuguese naval forces to guard the Iberian coasts and the islands of the Azores against French attacks. Special clauses were included regarding the fleets of West Africa. Ships, bound for Arguin, Cape Verde, the trades of Guinea, Malagueta, Mina and São Thomé, were to come and go during the three monsoons of January, March and September. Armed ships, belonging to King John III, were to go with the fleets, and most of the merchant ships were to be armed.[4] The two Guinea caravels, which

---
[1] *Leys e Provisões del Rei D. Sebastião*, pp. 166–94.
[2] *Cal. S. P. Span.*, 1538–42, p. 292.
[3] Davenport, i. 210.
[4] *Ibid.*, i. 213–14.

Andrada mentioned in his *Chronicle*, may have been the armed convoys required to accompany the West African fleets by this agreement. The convoys would leave Portugal in September and return from Guinea in January or March. The fleet, which returned in March, was to join the East Indies fleet at the Azores. Thus, a more adequate protection for the annual trading fleets would be provided.

But, so far as the arrangements for Guinea were concerned, this agreement did not contain anything that was new in principle. It has been shown that the fleets were already in the habit of sailing " in company ". All ships had been obliged to arm by royal command as far back as 1531.[1] An armed convoy had sailed the seas of Guinea in company with the merchant ships of Mina in 1534 ;[2] while the months specified for the out-voyages and the return voyages were the accustomed ones, for they were determined by physical conditions. Closer naval cooperation with the fleets of the Emperor Charles V may be regarded as an innovation, but that in itself did not affect the convoys of Guinea to any great extent, for collaboration would only be effective between the Azores and the Iberian peninsula. Nevertheless, under the 1552 convention, all the details of the convoy system were assembled for coincident application, a stage in organisation not hitherto attained, if we may trust the available evidence. The convoy system was gradually developed until it was regularised in 1552.

Meanwhile, if we turn once again to Europe, we find that John III was continuing unabated his diplomatic pressure at the court of King Francis I. In spite of the bribing of admiral Chabot, fresh letters of marque were granted to Jean Ango in November 1533, and more French voyages were made to the forbidden seas.[3] João Vaz, a Portuguese agent in France, reported these events to John III, whereupon Bernadim de Tavora was sent to France in the following December to renew negotiations.[4] It was, furthermore, in accordance with this same line of action that John III had informed the most christian king, through the French ambassador in Portugal, of the demarcation of the

---

[1] *Vide supra*, p. 108.
[2] *Vide supra*, p. 120.
[3] E. Guénin, *Ango et ses pilotes*, p. 199.
[4] Gomes de Carvalho, *D. João III e os Francezes*, pp. 67-70.

seas, which had been made between the two Iberian states (January 1533).[1]

Neither measure had the desired effect. On the contrary, admiral Chabot was believed once again to be favouring the enterprises of the Norman and Breton privateers, on condition that he received one-tenth of the value of the cargoes brought home.[2] Moreover, unfortunately for Portugal, certain other interests affected her relations with France. The Venetian ambassador in France reported that the King of Portugal " very much feared the emperor " in 1535.[3] Also John III was very concerned for the safety of his spice fleets, which sailed every year to Flanders.[4] Consequently, he gave his support to France in the Hapsburg-Valois War of 1536 in the hope that, on the one hand, the Hapsburg power might be curtailed, and, on the other hand, the spice fleets should not be robbed by French privateers. Indeed, a Franco-Portuguese rapprochement was already apparent in 1535,[5] and in the following year the relations of the two countries were regulated by the Treaty of Lyons (14 July 1536).[6] But not one of the eleven articles in this treaty referred either to Guinea or to Brazil.

Shortly afterwards, however, the approximation between France and Portugal was cemented by an agreement concerning Guinea. Ruy Fernandes, the Portuguese ambassador in France, succeeded in bribing the admiral a second time,[7] with the result that Chabot persuaded his sovereign to agree to the Portuguese demands about Guinea. By letters patent of 26 August 1536 Francis I forbade all attacks upon Portuguese shipping in Guinea. Meanwhile, a conference was held at Bayonne to determine upon claims arising out of mutual seizures.[8] In the following year, on 30 May and also on 23 August, the French king prohibited all his subjects from sailing to Guinea and Brazil. But the publication of these letters patent, containing the veto on all such voyages, does not appear

[1] Ford, *op. cit.*, p. 79.
[2] Gomes de Carvalho, *op. cit.*, pp. 67-8.
[3] Relation of Marino Gustiano, 1535; printed in M. N. Tommaseo, *Relations des Ambassadeurs de Venise*, i. 86-9.
[4] *Cal. S. P. Span.*, 1536-8, p. 318.
[5] Tommaseo, *op. cit.*, i. 86.
[6] Davenport, i. 201-4.
[7] Roncière, iii. 292.
[8] *Quadro Elementar*, iii. 258-60, 262-80.

to have been effective, and consequently, once again on 20 May 1538, Francis I issued a new embargo.

The letter patent of 1538 is included in the Cotton collection of manuscripts in the British Museum. The preamble recites the protest of the King of Portugal and refers to the previous patents of 1537. It adds that, in spite of those prohibitions, certain Frenchmen have voyaged to the prohibited seas and, therefore, in order to preserve the ancient friendship of Portugal and France, it has been found necessary to repeat the embargo. French ships are then ordered not to go to Brazil, to Malagueta, or to any other lands, discovered by the Kings of Portugal, on pain of confiscation of their ships, money, merchandise and possessions and bodily chastisement.[1] The dating of the manuscript is curious, for, while the copyist dates it 20 May, the patent itself was issued from St. Germain on 22 December. More than one patent was evidently published in 1538, and another in January 1539, as a manuscript, which M. Charles B. de la Roncière has read, indicates.[2]

These royal decrees produced a struggle for the favour of the king at the court of France. The Portuguese ambassador competed with the representatives of the privateers of Normandy and Brittany.[3] For a time, the Portuguese were successful (1538–40). But the exposure of the corrupt practices of admiral Chabot produced a *volte-face*. On 13 November 1540 the embargo upon voyages to Malagueta and Brazil was raised and, in consequence, many ships left for Guinea.[4] Indeed, the changes of 1540 broke up the temporary rapprochement between France and Portugal. Henceforth, John III became more friendly towards the Emperor Charles V. A system of collaboration between the two imperial rulers, against French attacks upon the oversea monopolies, was gradually organised, reaching its culmination in the convention of 1552.

Peace was restored between the emperor and the King of France in 1544 by the Treaty of Crespy. A separate clause was included in the treaty which admitted the right of Frenchmen to trade in the Indies, East and West.[5] This clause, however,

[1] B.M., Cotton MS. Nero B. 1, f. 88.
[2] Roncière, iii. 292.
[3] *Ibid.*, iii. 296.
[4] Gosselin, *op. cit.*, pp. 144–5.
[5] Davenport, i. 209.

was not ratified. The emperor had inserted it in the treaty in the hope of ending French privateering in the West Indies, but he met with the opposition not only of his own council of state but also of John III. The latter considered that the privilege of trading, granted by the clause, would forthwith be abused by the French. One phrase in his objection indicates that he had Guinea in mind as well as the East Indies. He declared that, if the right to trade " in the lands beyond the sea " were conceded, the French would sail there in armed ships to rob as well as to traffic.[1] Accordingly, in the result, a clause, which might have legalised the position of the interlopers in 1544, was never actually ratified. It is not generally realised that the exclusive oversea privileges of the Portuguese so nearly disappeared before the middle of the sixteenth century.

Thus, John III and Charles V in their discussion of the terms of the Treaty of Crespy, differed about the way to check the French corsairs. But their collaboration was in no way undermined. Prince Philip wrote to his father, the emperor, on 28 September to tell him that the King of Portugal had ordered the commander of the Malagueta fleet, on his return home, to protect any of the Emperor's ships, which he might encounter.[2] Nevertheless, the French interlopers still sailed to Guinea. The Venetian ambassador referred to the maritime rivalry as a " silent war " between Portugal and France, which never ceased, and he asserted that it had driven King John III into the arms of the emperor (1546).[3] A slight improvement in Franco-Portuguese relations occurred in the following year, when an agreement was reached for the settlement of mutual losses at sea and for the revocation of all letters of marque, counter-marque and reprisal.[4] After this, various efforts were made to settle outstanding differences.[5]

Yet Frenchmen still sailed to the forbidden seas. One ship, *la Bonne Aventure*, sailed to Cape Threepoints in 1546 and reaped nearly 150 per cent in profits. Another French trader visited Cape Verde in 1549.[6] But after 1546 there would seem

---

[1] *Quadro Elementar*, iii. 306–9.
[2] *Cal. S. P. Span.*, 1544, p. 375.
[3] Tommaseo, *op. cit.*, i. 292–5.
[4] Almeida, *Historia de Portugal*, iii. 586 ; *Quadro Elementar*, iii. 320–1.
[5] *Ibid.*, iii. 330–3.
[6] Gosselin, *op. cit.*, p. 146.

to have been far more privateering than peaceful traffic. Portuguese shipping suffered heavily. One of the royal ships was burnt in Guinea in 1550. Many Portuguese ships were captured, especially caravels from São Thomé bringing sugar cargoes to Europe. The *Retenta*, when on its way back from São Thomé, was seized in 1550. The galleon *São João* appears to have been captured, when transporting a cargo of slaves and gold from the Gambia in 1551, and, in that same year, at least three other caravels fell victims to French corsairs. Unfortunately, we cannot be sure that these piracies were committed in Guinea. Some undoubtedly occurred near the Azores, which were the general rendezvous for returning ships. But the Cape Verde Islands were also one of the favourite resorts of the corsairs, and so we may be sure that some of the seizures were made near the archipelago.[1]

From the Portuguese point of view, diplomatic pressure was not very successful between 1530 and 1553. Regular French intervention in Guinea had begun in 1530 with the grant of a letter of marque to Jean Ango. Negotiations between the envoys of John III and the French government had led to various half-hearted embargoes, which were raised after the bribing of admiral Chabot had been disclosed. Then, John III began to co-operate with the Emperor Charles V in organising a convoy system for the defence of the trading fleets. Also he devoted both energy and money to the equipment of armed fleets and the building of forts around the coast of Guinea. But he failed to expel the French interlopers. Inspired by Jean Ango and guided mainly by renegade Portuguese pilots like João Affonso, these Frenchmen gradually spread the web of their commerce. They had trafficked chiefly on the Malagueta coast. The Cape Verde Islands they had frequented to rob and to plunder rather than to trade. Occasionally they had visited Mina. But they had not made any voyages to Benin.

All the schemes, devised by John III, to keep the interlopers out of Guinea virtually failed, and his imperial monopoly was seriously challenged. Although the Emperor Charles V had proposed to extend to Frenchmen the right of peaceful traffic to the Indies, the monopoly was theoretically still intact; in

---

[1] P. de Azevedo, " Defesa da navegacão de Portugal contra os franceses em 1552 ", (*Archivo Histórico Portuguez*, vi. 164–5).

practice, however, it was tottering, in spite of the armed caravels, the convoys and the Portuguese forts in Guinea. So the era of exclusive Portuguese trade in West Africa ended in 1553. No other power had questioned their monopoly for half a century, but now the French had intervened and the volume of illegal traffic had gradually increased. Thereafter, the enviable position, which Portugal had enjoyed in the reign of King Manuel the Fortunate, was never regained. It may be said that the years 1530–53 constituted the period when West Africa ceased to be the sole preserve of the Portuguese, and became the commercial playground of an ever-growing number of foreign pirates, filibusters and traders.

CHAPTER VII

TRIPLE RIVALRY IN WEST AFRICA, 1553-1559

WILLIAM HAWKINS of Plymouth had sent a few English ships to buy ivory on the coast of Sierra Leone after 1530, but this promising traffic did not survive the ensuing decade. For a time English commercial and maritime energies were diverted to other, and more fruitful channels. But Englishmen ventured to Guinea once more after 1553, and the international struggle in West Africa assumed hitherto unrivalled proportions. It was magnified because French interlopers did not abandon their operations in Guinea. Two swelling currents of interloping activity confounded the still waters of monopoly, and out of this there came a raging maelstrom. Portugal had to defend her oversea dominions against two sets of corsairs, who were often as bitterly opposed to one another as to the common enemy in possession. Taken as a whole, a sordid fight for trade resulted in which little mercy was given and none expected, while the interests of the negroes were entirely subordinated to those of the whites. Thus, the reappearance of the English in 1553 inaugurated an era of triple rivalry in West Africa.

For the most part, the Portuguese empire was in no very satisfactory condition at the opening of this period. Considerable native disturbances shook all the negro kingdoms on the coast between Sierra Leone and Benin in the middle of the century. These disturbances were caused by a vast migration of a black people called the Sumbas,[1] who appear to have left their original home in central Africa and to have marched slowly westwards. The Sumbas moved along a route behind Mina and Malagueta, overthrew some of the smaller settled negro kingdoms, destroyed numerous villages, and massacred and enslaved thousands of the natives. One horde of these

---

[1] Various spellings are *Sumbas, Cumbas, Zimbas,* and even *Manes.*

cannibals waged war against the peaceful Sapes of Sierra Leone, and eventually, after subjecting them, settled down and intermarried with them. Meanwhile, another horde of Sumbas separated from the main body and went into the interior to attack the Souzos. It so happened that this people possessed the most formidable native army in all West Africa and so, after securing help from their neighbours, the Foulos, they were able to defeat the invading Sumbas. Then the Souzos, in turn, overran part of Upper Guinea and established themselves on the banks of the Rio de Nuno.

Probably the migration and the wars lasted for a generation. Two quasi-contemporary writers assert that the invasion occurred in the middle of the century.[1] Moreover, João Bermudes, in a letter to King John III written before 1557, reported that the Sumbas were destroying all Guinea at that time.[2] The Sapes, disciplined and trained in the art of war under the tutelage of their conquerors, the Sumbas, had restored order in Sierra Leone by 1570, and were even helping the Portuguese against interloping slave-raiders like Bartholomew Bayão.[3] There is reason for believing, however, that the war in the interior against the Souzos was more protracted, and that peace was not concluded until after 1570.[4]

Portuguese trade along the coast was affected by these changes, though not altogether adversely. For this we have the evidence of captain André Alvares d'Almada and Father Fernão Guerreiro. Both relate that many negroes, fleeing from the invaders, were taken on board Portuguese sloops, which had been specially sent along the coast for that purpose. These negroes were afterwards sold as slaves. Even one of the native kings, named Bolulão, who was head of a Malagueta tribe, was obliged to surrender himself to the Portuguese for protection.[5] The slave trade, therefore, benefited from the negro wars. On the other hand, at least the coastal traffic near the Rio de Nuno declined. Captain Almada used the suggestive phrase that,

[1] Almada, *Tratado breve dos Rios de Guiné*, p. 83 ; Guerreiro, *Relaçaões Annuis*, ii. 139b.
[2] R. S. Whiteway, *The Portuguese Expedition to Abyssinia*, (Hakluyt Society), p. 299.
[3] Almada, *op. cit.*, p. 92.
[4] E. G. Ravenstein, *The strange adventures of Andrew Battell*, (Hakluyt Society), p. 150.
[5] Almada, *op. cit.*, p. 85 ; Guerreiro, *op. cit.*, ii. 139b.

when he navigated there, " trade had begun to revive because the Manes have abandoned their former habits of cannibalism and fighting " (c. 1580–94).[1] The implication is that trade profits had fallen during the period of the ravages of the Manes or Sumbas, and his evidence may be relied upon in this case, for he was well acquainted with the coast and lived for many years in the island of Santiago.

Besides the dislocation caused by the invasion of the Sumbas, in many districts of Guinea strained relations existed between the natives and the Portuguese. Among the reasons for this tension may be enumerated slavery and the slave trade, the activities of interlopers, and the methods used by the Portuguese to coerce the negroes into refusing to traffic with interlopers. These factors, which were operative from 1530 until the complete displacement of the Portuguese by the Dutch in the seventeenth century, served continually to estrange the negroes from their white rulers both on the mainland and in the island of São Thomé. This island was the scene of native unrest even at the height of its prosperity. Thus in 1536, John III had to send a special armed expedition to São Thomé, under Paulo Nunez, to suppress a negro revolt. Again, thirty-eight years later, a combined revolt of Angolares and slaves contributed partly to the decline of the sugar plantations.[2]

On the mainland, equal tension antagonised the Portuguese and the negroes in many places. The Portuguese government was unreal over most of the Guinea Coast. Their claim to conquest, dominion and tribute over all West Africa was not in accordance with the facts. They commanded the respect of negro tribes, who lived near their fortresses of Arguin, Axem, Samma, São Jorge and Accra, but not of other tribes. It may be that, formerly, they had established friendly relations with the inhabitants of the Kingdom of Benin. The factory of Gató, the slave traffic, and the proselytising work of various Portuguese missionaries had provided channels of contact in the early sixteenth century, and so, when the English trader, captain Wyndham, visited Benin in 1553, he found that the King of Benin spoke Portuguese and he noticed many other

---

[1] Almada, op. cit., p. 91.
[2] Ford, *The Letters of John III*, pp. 289–90 ; Rebello da Silva, *Historia de Portugal*, v. 115.

signs of Portuguese influence.[1] But he also found that the whites had to secure the permission of the native potentate before they were allowed to traffic,[2] which may be regarded as a correct diagnosis of the relationship between the Portuguese and the negroes. There was no element of servitude in the native attitude.

Nevertheless, the negroes seem to have displayed friendliness towards the inhabitants in the isolated civil establishments of the Portuguese in Upper Guinea. At this time, many Portuguese appear to have resided in Senegambia, and farther south they had created a small and prosperous settlement at Cacheo, on the banks of the Rio de S. Domingo. Here the residence of the chief factor of the trade of Upper Guinea was built. Here too, apparently, the Portuguese exacted a tribute from the natives.[3] Again, there were a few Portuguese settlements in Sierra Leone, one existing before 1545,[4] and another being founded shortly afterwards in the north of that province by Bento Corrêa da Silva, an emigrant from São Thomé, who left numerous descendants.[5] Generally, since the purpose of these settlements was mainly the promotion of peaceful trade, the negroes did not disturb them.

The Gold Coast remained the centre of Portuguese enterprise in West Africa. We have seen that a number of forts were situated near Cape Threepoints. But the position of the Portuguese was very insecure. They intimidated the negroes and rarely co-operated with them; and their white enemies, like the French and later the Hollanders, accused them of great arrogance. It is not surprising, therefore, to find that many of the Mina blacks were extremely discontented. One local prince, who bore the name Don John, copied probably from the white overlord king, repeatedly " had wars with the Portugals ".[6] The negroes also lived in great fear of the Portuguese. If they sometimes supported their masters against the interlopers, it was more for fear than for love; many were enslaved by the Portuguese; some were imprisoned and some put in irons; and

[1] Hakluyt, vi. 149.
[2] P.R.O., S.P. 69, 7, no. 449.
[3] Almada, op. cit., p. 54; P.R.O., S.P. 70, 99, f. 12.
[4] J. Fonteneau, La Cosmographie, p. 333.
[5] Almada, op. cit., p. 73.
[6] Hakluyt, vi. 200.

those, who escaped, did not scruple to conspire with the interlopers against the Portuguese.¹ A most unhealthy state of continual friction and occasional warfare was the general result.

Martin Frobisher, who was imprisoned in São Jorge in 1555–6, later asserted that no Portuguese dared to go more than a mile from the forts, without first obtaining the permission of the local rulers. He added that goods were always carried by sea, and not by land, from place to place on the Mina coast.² But a contemporary questioned the truth of Frobisher's declaration³, and, from intrinsic evidence, we know that he cannot be trusted absolutely. Sometimes, indeed, the Portuguese did venture among the natives. Two Portuguese accompanied the Sumbas during the invasion of Sierra Leone.⁴ As we saw, numerous Portuguese lived in negro villages in Senegambia though not on the Mina coast. Captain Diogo Carreiro, a bold pioneer, penetrated the interior as far as Timbuktu in 1565.⁵ Nevertheless, albeit exaggerated, Frobisher's statement contained a kernel of truth. The Portuguese were intensely unpopular among the Mina blacks.

Their economic situation in 1553 did not cause the Portuguese as much anxiety as their relations with the negroes. The Guinea trade was still comparatively prosperous, for the decline did not grow serious until the later part of the sixteenth century. Allowing that the invasion of the Sumbas caused some temporary and local disorder, we may yet produce evidence that commerce generally was profitable. The slave traffic benefited from the negro disturbances.⁶ The sugar plantations of the island of São Thomé and also of O Principe were flourishing.⁷ Furthermore, there are three indications of the prosperity of the gold trade. Roger Barlowe, writing of Guinea in 1540–1, said that near " the castle of the Myne ther be goodlie serras wher thei gather moche golde and carie it to the castle . . . and selle hit to the portugalles in truck of coper and clothes of colours ", and his other references to West Africa contain no

---

¹ Hakluyt, vi. 218.
² B.M., Lansdowne MS. 171, ff. 148–9 ; *Cal. S. P. For.*, 1562, p. 53.
³ B.M., Cotton MS. Nero B.1, f. 88b.
⁴ Almada, *op. cit.*, p. 83.
⁵ Viterbo, i. 322–4.
⁶ *Vide supra*, p. 139.
⁷ G. B. Ramusio, *Navigationi et Viaggi*, i. 126–7.

suggestion of any decline in the value of that traffic.[1] The same may be said of Jean Fonteneau's *La Cosmographie* (1545).[2] Thirdly, a letter of King John III reveals a further extension of the gold traffic in 1551, a fact which is confirmed by João de Barros in his *Da Asia*.[3] On the other hand, because the French had made a special objective of the Malagueta coast after 1530, it may be conjectured that some decline had occurred in the quantity of malagueta pepper annually transported by the Portuguese to Antwerp. This was certainly true in 1578.[4] Its significance for the Portuguese was that rival traders must be excluded.

Bearing in mind the political situation in West Africa, we may appreciate with what apprehension the Portuguese regarded the return of English interlopers. Their appearance in Guinea was foreshadowed by two voyages to Barbary in 1551 and 1552.[5] It was not a long step from Barbary to Guinea. The first English Guinea voyage, of which we have full evidence, appears to have been undertaken in the winter of 1553-4. It provides a suitable starting-point for this phase of triple rivalry, 1553-9. Our chief source is Richard Hakluyt's *Principal Navigations*. Hakluyt describes how a group of London merchants sent out three ships, the *Primrose*, the *Lion*, and a pinnace called the *Moon*, under the captaincy of Thomas Wyndham, a Norfolk gentleman, and with a Portuguese pilot, Antonio Anes Pinteado, who had been a captain in the Portuguese navy, to buy gold at Mina and pepper in Benin. The ships left Portsmouth on 12 August 1553 and, piloted by Pinteado, negotiated safely the passage to Mina and Benin. A great mortality depleted the ranks of the crew in Benin but, at length, two of the ships returned to England with a valuable cargo.[6]

Now it is possible that one or two unrecorded voyages were made to Guinea from England before that of captain Wyndham. The Venetian ambassador in London reported to the doge, on 21 October 1555, that a Portuguese envoy had been sent to England to request Queen Mary to forbid English ships from

[1] R. Barlowe, " *A Brief Summe of Geographie* ", (Hakluyt Society), p. 105.
[2] J. Fonteneau, *La Cosmographie*, pp. 329-38.
[3] Ford, *The Letters of John III*, pp. 376, 394 ; Barros, I. iii. 3.
[4] Azevedo, *Epocas Economico*, p. 81.
[5] Hakluyt, vi. 136-40.
[6] Hakluyt, vi. 141-52.

continuing their voyages to Guinea " as they have done for the last three years ".[1] This would place the first of the revived Guinea expeditions from England in the year 1552. Of course, the ambassador may have been wrong. But Camden's *Annals* confirm his statement.[2] More curious still is a letter, written by Braz d'Alvide, the Portuguese agent in France, to King John III on 25 August 1552, and printed in De Sousa's *Annals*. D'Alvide reported that Simão Pires, a pilot of Portugal who had a wife and children in Lisbon, had sailed to the north and then had been to Mina, where he had loaded 30 marks of gold and had purchased 18 tons of malagueta pepper, and had afterwards gone with his ships to England.[3] All this must have happened before August 1552. The fact that d'Alvide reported the voyage suggests that it was an unusual occurrence, and we are led to wonder whether Simão Pires acted under the orders of a group of English merchants. Did he pilot an English ship with an English crew ? There was a Simão Pires, who engaged in trade between São Thomé and Antwerp in 1550 and also in 1555, and upon each occasion he fell a victim to English pirates.[4] Service with Portugal in 1550 and 1555 and service with English merchants in 1551-2 would not be irreconcilable. Indeed, may he not have been forced to pilot an English ship to Guinea in the winter of 1551-2 after the capture of his own ship by English pirates in 1550 ?

Hakluyt does not mention any English voyage to Guinea, after the early ones of William Hawkins, before August 1553. But Hakluyt's evidence cannot be regarded as inclusive. For example, while we are told that Antonio Anes Pinteado sailed with captain Wyndham to Benin, we are not informed that another Portuguese pilot, Francisco Rodrigues, accompanied them, apart from a brief and vague reference to a Portuguese named Francisco. Nor are we told how the islanders of Madeira tried to persuade the English adventurers to surrender up the persons of Pinteado and Rodrigues. Nor, again, do we hear anything about a piratical attack by captain Wyndham's fleet upon a Portuguese ship on the Malagueta coast. Yet all these

[1] *Cal. S. P. Ven.*, 1555-6, no. 251.
[2] W. Camden, *Annales rerum Anglicarum et Hibernicarum regnante Elizabetha*, (Oxford, 1717, 3 vols.), ii. 243.
[3] M. de Sousa Coutinho, *op. cit.*, p. 438.
[4] P.R.O., S.P. 70, 95, ff. 244, 246, 252.

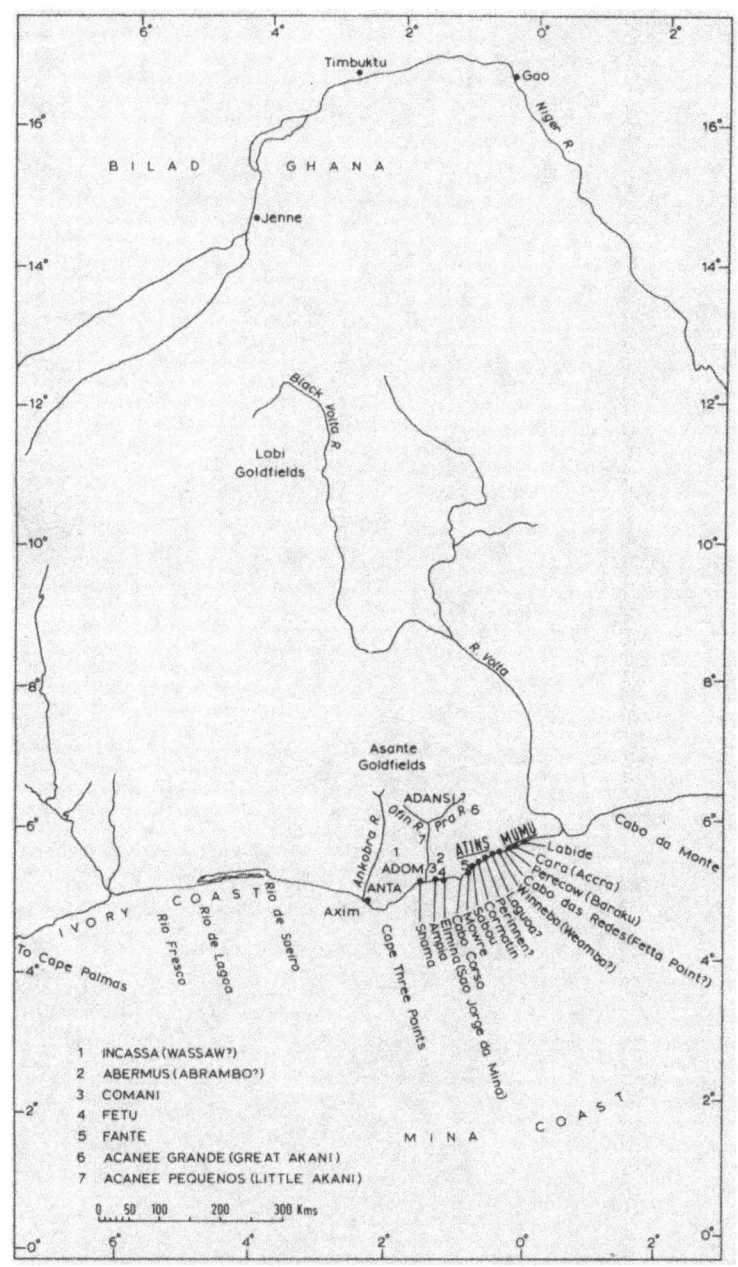

THE IVORY COAST AND THE MINA COAST
States shown in capital letters
Peoples shown in capitals underlined

events are described in Portuguese records.[1] Obviously there are many omissions in Hakluyt's version of the Wyndham voyage of 1553-4. One is thus led to suspect that, after the Hawkins voyage of 1540, that of Wyndham in 1553 was not the next English expedition to West Africa.

To the Portuguese, the intrusion of captain Wyndham was utterly objectionable. For twenty-three years King John III had tried repeatedly, by diplomatic pressure and coercive force, to exclude the French from Guinea. But the latter still made their voyages thither : thus, for example, in 1552 a royal ship loaded with sugar from São Thomé had been attacked and seized by French corsairs, and in August two French ships with cargoes of malagueta pepper had returned to Havre de Grace.[2] Force did not avail, for these ships had eluded the armed fleets of Portugal in West Africa. Equally unsuccessful had been diplomacy, for Braz d' Alvide had reported a new grant of letters of marque to French privateers in the same year.[3] In point of fact, the relations of France and Portugal had been gravely strained by the favour and indifference, alternately displayed by Francis I and Henry II, towards the exploits of their adventurous Breton and Norman subjects. The position was unchanged in 1553.

John III was not anxious to alienate England, as he had antagonised France. Yet, in his eyes, Thomas Wyndham was an interloper and a pirate, who had disregarded not only papal bulls but also the royal ordinances relating to the empire. If captain Wyndham had been caught, he would have received no mercy. He would have shared the fate of the accomplices of Eustache de la Fosse in 1480. His ships would have been sunk and he himself taken to Lisbon to be hanged. This English expedition, in fact, threatened a serious breach in the relations of his country with Portugal. If the English government should sympathise with their privateering subjects who voyaged to Guinea, the amicable relations of England and Portugal would disappear, as they did in 1569, and the resulting tension might culminate in war. When examined from the European angle, Wyndham's voyage raised grave issues.

[1] Letter from Madeira, 22 September 1553, printed in Viterbo, ii. 252-5 P.R.O., S.P. 70, 95, f. 255.
[2] M. de Sousa Coutinho, *op. cit.*, p. 438.
[3] *Ibid.*

Equally grave might be its repercussions in West Africa. English competition was likely to lead to a further reduction in Portuguese profits from the Guinea trade. The stability of the Portuguese traffic had already been shaken and undermined by the French corsairs, and it was doubtful whether it could survive the assault of a second group of interlopers. Moreover, the possible reaction of the negroes had to be considered, for many of the tribes, as we saw, hated the Portuguese. Native chieftains might combine with English privateers to attack the Portuguese stations. In fine, a situation already pregnant with danger was now aggravated by the coming of the English.

Consequently, John III, drawing upon the experience of twenty years, kept going a double set of negotiations at Paris and London respectively. No evidence of a Portuguese protest in 1554 against the Wyndham voyage has been found, but in Paris the dispute about the French voyages was certainly discussed. Proof is lacking of any French voyage to West Africa in 1553. But in 1554, the ship *Lamulle* departed for Guinea and Cape Threepoints;[1] at least two other French ships sailed for Guinea in the autumn and two ships were ready to weigh anchor;[2] while a manuscript journal of a gentleman of Gonneville records that the sailors of Harfleur freely made the traffic in malagueta pepper and ivory, which they sought in Guinea.[3] The Portuguese ambassador in Paris, perhaps João Pereira d'Amtas,[4] possibly objected to these illicit voyages in the course of his general protest against the activities of the French corsairs. But the only tangible result was a further alienation of France from Portugal. The Venetian ambassador reported to the doge that the King of Portugal was almost antagonised by Henry II, who refused to give him satisfaction.[5]

Actually, Henry II's attention was mainly concentrated upon his war with the Hapsburg empire, and perhaps for this reason, he endeavoured to shelve the dispute about Guinea. Unwilling to estrange Portugal at such a time, he consented to a cessation of the maritime struggle between his privateers and the subjects of John III. It was reported that a new letter

---

[1] Gosselin, *op. cit.*, p. 147.
[2] P.R.O., S.P. 69, 7, no. 449.
[3] P. Gaffarel, *Les Découvreurs Français*, p. 32.
[4] *Quadro Elementar*, iii. 340.
[5] Tommaseo, *op. cit.*, i. 383.

TRIPLE RIVALRY IN WEST AFRICA 147

of marque had been granted against Portuguese shipping in 1552, but Henry II now prolonged for five years the previous suspension of all letters of marque in order that mutual piracies could be adjudicated.[1] However, this did not settle the basic issue, which was the right of French corsairs to go to Guinea, Brazil and the Indies. Upon that question John III, like the Emperor Charles V, could get no satisfaction.

John Lok's voyage to Guinea in the following winter was the occasion of the first Portuguese protest to Queen Mary of England regarding the Guinea traffic (1554-5).[2] The Portuguese defenders of the castle of São Jorge soon learned about John Lok's exploits and, accordingly, the governor sent a report to his sovereign.[3] There was a fight at Samma, during which, as the Portuguese alleged, the English plundered the coast (11-12 January 1555).[4] Diogo Lopes de Sousa, the ambassador in London who may have been the governor of the castle of São Jorge in 1551, was instructed in the early summer of 1555 to protest to the queen. His formal reclamation pointed out that King John III could not allow foreigners to devastate the lands which, at great expense, had been acquired by the Portuguese. Indeed, he added, John III did not even permit his own subjects to traffic to Guinea without his licence. Accordingly, the king demanded reparations for the damage to his shipping, the restoration of all the merchandise which the interlopers had seized in Guinea, the punishment of the delinquent English traders, and a veto upon all future voyages from England.[5]

This protest to Queen Mary was similar to John III's representations in Paris more than twenty years before. It was equally ineffectual. Just as the influence of Jean Ango at the French court had been considerable (1530-40), so was that of the London group of merchants at the court of Queen Mary (1554-8). Indeed, certain members of the privy council were themselves actively interested in the Guinea traffic, and they did not wish to see it stopped.[6] Accordingly, a delay of several months ensued before John III received a reply. Those mer-

---
[1] *Quadro Elementar*, iii. 338-9.
[2] Hakluyt, vi. 154-77.
[3] Hakluyt, vi. 160.
[4] *Quadro Elementar*, xv. 102-4.
[5] *Ibid.*, xv. 102-4 ; J. A. Williamson, *John Hawkins*, pp. 44-5.
[6] *Cal. S. P. Span.*, 1558-67, p. 5.

chants, who had invested in the Guinea voyages, were summoned before the lord mayor of London in July to make answer to the Portuguese complaints.[1] They said, in their reply, that they had been moved by the common freedom enjoyed by all merchants to traffic to Guinea, and argued that the same liberty should be given to them as the French king gave his subjects; also they advanced a doctrine of effective occupation as against the Portuguese claim to monopoly by prescriptive right, declaring that they had only trafficked to those regions not effectively occupied by the Portuguese.[2]

Meanwhile, King John III resorted to a second diplomatic channel, opened for him by the marriage of King Philip II of Spain to Queen Mary of England. On 19 October 1555 he sent a letter to his ambassador in Castile, detailing the events of John Lok's voyage and instructing the ambassador to advise the King of Spain of this infringement of the Portuguese monopoly.[3] Now it was Philip's interest, as much as John III's, that neither French nor English corsairs should be allowed to sail beyond the Azores. Accordingly, he took the matter up with the English government. At the same time, João Rodrigues Correa, a new ambassador, was sent to London from Portugal to continue the negotiations,[4] though Diogo Lopes de Sousa did not leave England until May 1556.[5]

Not till December 1555 did the English government respond to John III's complaints. The intervening delay heightened the diplomatic tension. Apparently, as the winter approached, several expeditions to Guinea were planned in the ports of southern England. A London merchant, William Towerson, equipped two ships;[6] another group of merchants, including Edward Castlyn and Richard Stockbridge, projected a voyage which was forbidden in December;[7] and the organisers of a third expedition tried in vain to secure special permission for their enterprise directly from the Portuguese ambassador.[8] Of the ships, thus made ready for Guinea, at least the two

[1] *A. P. C.*, 1554–6, p. 162.
[2] P.R.O., S.P. 69, 7, no. 449.
[3] M. de Sousa Coutinho, *op. cit.*, p. 446.
[4] *Ibid.*
[5] *Quadro Elementar*, xv. 106.
[6] Hakluyt, vi. 177–211.
[7] *A. P. C.*, 1554–6, p. 214.
[8] *Cal. S. P. Ven.*, 1555–6, no. 327.

which Towerson commanded, slipped out of port. Others also left England, as may be inferred from the narrative of Towerson's voyage.[1] While these preparations were proceeding, a second Portuguese protest, made through João Rodrigues Correa, was referred by Queen Mary first to her council and then to her royal husband.[2] Naturally, the King of Spain supported the Portuguese contention, but as yet an effective embargo, directed against all prospective traders, was not imposed. At length, Queen Mary replied personally to the King of Portugal on 18 December 1555. She told him that she had prohibited English voyages to Mina, and that King Philip would try to recompense the Portuguese for their losses. Unfortunately, she added, it was impossible to surrender to John III the persons of those Portuguese, who had accompanied her subjects to Guinea, because some were dead and the rest had fled the country.[3] The privy council, following the queen's orders, began meanwhile to execute the embargo.[4]

The story of these Anglo-Portuguese negotiations of 1555 was probably repeated in 1556, though in this year the number of prohibitions relating to the Guinea traffic, issued by the English privy council, was much higher.[5] To a degree, therefore, King John III's protests were successful. Yet, as in the winter of 1555–6, so now some English ships eluded the net of the port authorities. The winter of 1556–7, indeed, appears to have been a particularly disastrous one for Portugal. William Towerson sailed again to Mina, and there were at least eleven other interloping vessels making the traffic, though most of them were French. For this there is the inherent evidence of Hakluyt's narrative of Towerson's second voyage; yet the documents, collected and printed by Edouard Gosselin from local records in the archives of the ports of Normandy, do not contain a single reference to a voyage to Guinea in this winter.[6] Thus, it is clear that the absence of evidence is not always a proof of the absence of voyages. Probably, many more ships sailed to Guinea at this time than is revealed in discovered records.

[1] Hakluyt, vi. 210.
[2] *Cal. S. P. Ven.*, 1555–6.
[3] M. de Sousa Coutinho, *op. cit.*, p. 447.
[4] *A. P. C.*, 1554–6, p. 214.
[5] *Quadro Elementar*, xv. 106; *Cal. S. P. Ven.*, 1555–6, no. 493; *A. P. C.*, 1554–6, pp. 305, 315, 322, 348, 358.
[6] Hakluyt, vi. 213; Gosselin, *op. cit.*, *passim*.

Let us now leave the course of diplomatic relations in Europe, and turn for a time to Guinea. Commercial rivalry there was keener, and embraced a far wider field, than during the preceding phase of 1530–53. After 1553, Malagueta ceased to be the main objective. The ensuing era witnessed a more varied attack upon the Portuguese monopoly. Ships from London and Plymouth, Dieppe, Havre and La Rochelle were to be found in all parts of Guinea. At least fifteen interloping ships, of which nine were certainly French, bartered for gold at Mina in the winter of 1556–7.[1]

The following Guinea season saw French ships trading on the Mina coast, at Sierra Leone, and one, *la Bonne-Aventure*, trafficking to Malagueta.[2] The Englishman, William Towerson, took a third expedition to Mina in the same winter.[3]

Many French raids on Portuguese shipping were carried out near the Cape Verde Islands, which became a special field for French piracy. French captains also trafficked to the adjacent mainland, for Towerson recorded " a great trade of the Frenchmen at Cape Verde " in January 1558.[4] Both Sierra Leone and Malagueta were also favoured trading resorts for pepper and ivory, though these traffics were now regarded by the interlopers as only supplementary to those of Mina and Benin. Indeed, Mina now held the priority, formerly enjoyed by Malagueta, as a place of traffic. Apparently, it was the gold more than the malagueta pepper which now attracted foreign merchants. This change in the general destination of the majority of the interlopers is indicated, not only in the narratives of voyages, but also in contemporary diplomatic negotiations. Whereas in 1538 Francis I had forbidden his subjects to go to " Brazil and Malagueta ",[5] the prohibitions of Queen Mary now referred to " Guynie, Bynnie or the Mina ".[6] It is not easy to interpret the significance of this change. Perhaps more renegade pilots were available, and the interlopers, having become more familiar with the trade and navigation of Guinea, were not satisfied with expeditions, which did not go beyond Mala-

---

[1] Hakluyt, vi. 212–30.
[2] Hakluyt, vi. 238, 240 ; Gosselin, *op. cit.*, p. 153.
[3] Hakluyt, vi. 231–52.
[4] Hakluyt, vi. 237.
[5] " *Bresy, ny a la Malaguete*", B.M., Cotton MS. Nero B.1, f. 88.
[6] B.M., Cotton MS. Nero B.1, f. 75.

gueta. So the Gold Coast instead was now the most popular destination.

Moreover, interloping ships, frequently rounding Cape Threepoints as they trafficked along the Mina coast, began to make their way further east to the coast of Benin. Pepper cargoes were to be had in the Kingdom of Benin, which now became an occasional objective. Thus Benin sometimes figured in contemporary diplomatic negotiations.[1] But the voyage to Benin was not often undertaken. True, a French ship visited that kingdom in 1554-5,[2] but it was a hazardous enterprise. The Portuguese had abandoned the factory at Gató because of the inclement climate, and English interlopers received a warning lesson about the dangers of the Benin voyage, when captain Wyndham insisted that his ships should sail on from Mina to Benin : 140 men had left Portsmouth in August and fewer than 40 returned to Plymouth in the following spring.[3] Nevertheless, valuable quantities of pepper awaited the bold trader, for the Portuguese crown had prohibited its importation ever since 1506. This fact aroused the interest of Jean Nicot, the French ambassador in Lisbon in 1559. Reporting what he had learned about the pepper to the Cardinal of Lorraine, he suggested that, if the French could secure the right to traffic to Mina and Benin, they would be released from their commercial dependence upon Antwerp, would no longer have to " bend the knee " to Portugal to get their pepper, and would make considerable profits.[4] Pepper attracted the interlopers to Benin.

Because three rivals competed now, the commercial struggle in West Africa was keener, and the interlopers attained a considerable measure of success. The Portuguese claimed, if they did not hold, the entire commodity market ; French and English traders wished to share its advantages. Logically then, the two groups of enemies of Portugal could better pursue their objective in co-operation. Sometimes they did collaborate. Thus, when William Towerson sailed to Guinea a second time in the winter of 1556-7, he encountered three French ships with two pinnaces off the Rio dos Sestos. Now a Portuguese armada had " gone to the Mina to defend it ", and so William Towerson

---
[1] *Ibid.* ; *A. P. C.*, 1554-6, pp. 305, 315 ; E. Falgairolle, *Jean Nicot*, p. 39.
[2] Roncière, iv. 77, note (1).
[3] Hakluyt, vi. 141-52.
[4] E. Falgairolle, *Jean Nicot*, p. 39.

made a working alliance with captain Blundell, the commander of the French fleet, to sail in company to the Gold Coast for mutual protection against the Portuguese.¹ All the interlopers then navigated together along the Malagueta and Mina coasts.

But a spirit of friendliness did not always govern the relations between the interlopers. After 1557, the English government supported Spain in war against France and this affected, to some extent, the situation in West Africa. William Towerson, who made a third voyage to Guinea in 1558, learned from a negro at the Rio dos Sestos that several French ships had sailed to Mina. Accordingly, he ordered his ships to make all speed for Cape Threepoints. Upon rounding the cape, they found four French ships buying gold and, without further ado, they attacked them. In the ensuing fight, the Englishmen managed to capture one of the Frenchmen, and they found over fifty pounds weight of gold on board their prize. They sank the ship, which had sprung a leak, and took the unfortunate French crew into their own ships.²

However, the situation in Europe did not determine without exception the alignment of friendships in Guinea. Those, who were allies in Europe, were sometimes rivals in West Africa, for the differentiation was small between the trader and the pirate. Towerson's second voyage illustrates this. The alliance between captain Blundell and Towerson, which was concluded on 30 December 1556, only lasted for just over one month. Admittedly the allies fought a combined action against five Portuguese ships at the end of January. But the English then charged the French with deserting them during the fight. Partly as a result, disputes about the trade began and the combination broke up.³

Commercial rivalry lay at the root of the collapse of the December alliance. The captains of the two interloping fleets had allied, not so much because England and France were at peace in Europe in 1556, but rather because of the need for protection against the more powerful Portuguese. Though very profitable, the Guinea voyage was very dangerous. Men were wont to make their wills before leaving their homes, lest they

---

¹ Hakluyt, vi. 213.
² Hakluyt, vi. 241.
³ Hakluyt, vi. 225.

TRIPLE RIVALRY IN WEST AFRICA 153

should never return.[1] Accordingly, when in Guinea, every action was calculated in purely material terms. Captain Towerson had accepted the French offer only after a careful examination of his position. He had argued with his men that the proposed alliance would give them added security at Mina, where the Portuguese would have armed ships patrolling the coast. Moreover, by sailing in company, they would also avoid competition. On the other hand, if the French went on ahead, not only might they ruin the gold market for the Englishmen, but one of their ships might fall into the hands of the Portuguese ; the latter would find out from the captive crew that English interlopers might be expected shortly at Mina, and would therefore collect their forces in order to attack Towerson's fleet. Accordingly Towerson, after a banquet on board the French admiral-ship, accepted captain Blundell's terms. The ships, thus united, fared well against a Portuguese armada at Mina. It had been agreed also that French and English should demand equal prices and should traffic at specified places, and in this way they eliminated competition. But the English found that the French cloth was more highly valued by the negro merchants than their own, and the price agreement worked against them. One of the French captains, for his part, complained that no gold was obtainable at his allotted place of traffic and suggested, therefore, that he should sail further eastwards. However, since this would have destroyed the market for the English, captain Towerson forbade it and, ultimately, was obliged to fire upon a French pinnace to prevent it.[2] In practice, the alliance was terminated from that moment. Both parties found it unsatisfactory and so it was ignored. The Anglo-French peace in Europe was conveniently forgotten. This commercial war in Guinea, in fact, did not take much notice of national policies ; it was private warfare for individual profit.

The first and third expeditions of William Towerson elucidate how the struggle for trade involved a race for markets. This was characteristic of Gold Coast rivalry. Each year only a limited quantity of gold appears to have been available at Mina. The native merchants from the uplands brought the

[1] J. W. Clay, *North Country Wills*, (Surtees Society, vol. cxxi, 1912), i. 1–2.
[2] Hakluyt, vi. 225.

gold dust down to the coast, and the first trading fleet to reach Mina generally reaped the full harvest of such gold as chanced not to be sold to the Portuguese in their castles and their ' strong houses '. Later fleets often found a flat market. Consequently, interlopers would speed up the voyage to the Gold Coast, even regardless of possible bargains on the Malagueta and Ivory Coasts. Captain Towerson's first voyage was thus hastened. He had heard that the pepper traffic on the Grain Coast was likely to prove profitable. But he did not " tary there, least the other ships should get before ".[1] He did the same in the beginning of 1558. A negro at the Rio dos Sestos told him that six French ships had " gone before " to Mina, and therefore he neglected the ivory, known to be for sale at the river-mouth, and sped on to the Gold Coast.[2] When he arrived, he found the French already bartering for gold, but he engaged their ships and drove them from the shore. It was exceedingly desirable to get a clear market.

Another feature of trade rivalry was the 'gift system'. Extant narratives show how this was operated at Mina. The natives were good business men, wary and circumspect.[3] Before business could proceed, the negro chiefs would demand small gifts such as one lateen basin, or one white basin and six manilla, or even a bottle of Malmoisie wine—so that the gin traffic was already pursued![4] There can be little doubt that rival captains employed the system in order to induce the natives to trade.

Moreover, interloping traffic was always hazardous. Thus, it was far too dangerous to trade right under the guns of the castle of São Jorge. Instead, " not attempting to come near the castle ", the interlopers were obliged to make " sale of their ware only on this side and beyond it ".[5] They traded where the Portuguese had no stations, not out of respect for the legal rights of the Lusitanian monarchy, but because the Portuguese were too strong for them. It may have been for this reason that various schemes were mooted and devised for the establishing of permanent forts on the West African coast. The French and

[1] Hakluyt, vi. 188.
[2] Hakluyt, vi. 238.
[3] Hakluyt, vi. 173.
[4] Hakluyt, vi. 208.
[5] Hakluyt, vi. 147-8.

English traders began to realise that they could not hope to compete with the Portuguese on equal terms, unless they held their own coastal forts like those of Axem and São Jorge, and they may have exchanged ideas upon the subject, because the earliest projects were considered almost simultaneously in England and in France.

The first proposal to build a fort, of which evidence has been found, was discussed in the winter of 1554–5. A native prince offered ground to build a castle on the Mina coast to the crew of the *Trinity*, one of the ships which sailed to Guinea under the command of John Lok.[1] This at least was the English version of the incident, but we may suspect that the initiative came from the interlopers. The negroes would scarcely have approved the building of a new fort on their territory; all white fortresses represented oppression to them. Yet the idea of an English fort, whose garrison might help them against the tyrannical Portuguese, would have appealed to most of the Mina chieftains. It was not difficult, then, for the English to plant a seed which, after a little delicate cultivation, sprouted and blossomed in the form of a definite offer from the natives to the white interloper. Unfortunately, when the English under Towerson returned to the same village in the following winter, they found that the natives were in league with the Portuguese, and the earlier offer held good no longer.[2]

A second negro prince made a similar offer in February 1557. Some of captain Towerson's men went ashore east of the castle of São Jorge where the King of Habaan welcomed them and, as the English alleged, " willed our men at their comming home to speake to our King to send men and provisions into his country to build a castle ".[3] Again, we may surmise that the account of the interview between the interlopers and the King of Habaan is biassed. Probably, the initiative once more came from the English rather than from the natives.

Meanwhile, French merchants were planning a more ambitious undertaking. Presumably, the natives had made offers to them, voluntarily or by inducement, similar to those proposed

---

[1] Hakluyt, vi. 147–8 ; P.R.O., S.P. 69, 7, no. 449.
[2] Hakluyt, vi. 207.
[3] Hakluyt, vi. 226. Sir Julian Corbett says that in 1556 some Englishmen "obtained a definite proposal from a native chief to establish a fort at Benin ", (*Drake and the Tudor Navy*, i. 79). So far, I have failed to verify this.

to the men of captains Lok and Towerson. Accordingly, in 1558, a bold huguenot captain was commissioned to establish a colony in the Gulf of Guinea. The project was organised upon a large scale. The King of Navarre gave his support and a sum of 10,000 crowns was invested in it. Michel Boileau, one of the Norman privateers, who had secured a concession from the King of Benin, now set out to occupy an island near that kingdom. He was to settle a colony of Frenchmen on the island which, as may be inferred from one of Jean Nicot's letters to the Cardinal of Lorraine, was to be used as a commercial base for the Benin pepper traffic.[1] But, soon after leaving France, he was overtaken by a Spanish warship at La Ferrol, his ship was seized and his men were put in irons. Thus, the project collapsed.[2] Yet this was the first interloping attempt to found a permanent station in Guinea and, in this respect, is worthy of more attention than it has received.

The Portuguese did not submit with indifference to the alarming growth of unlicensed trade. They proceeded to employ various expedients to ruin the traffic of their rivals. They took advantage of certain convenient geographical factors. There were very few good harbours on the West African coast and interloping captains, who wished to buy the various available commodities, were obliged to anchor their ships one mile or more from the shore. Then, they would either await the arrival of negro merchants, who would generally fill their canoes with their saleable goods and swarm out from the strand to the ships, or they would lower armed boats to go to the land. When the Portuguese in the castle saw this happen, they would often send swift galleys along the coast to attack and to destroy the interloping boats and to arrest the white crews and, if the negroes chanced to be trafficking in the canoes, they would drive them back to land and sometimes even burn the canoes.[3] Another method of interrupting the traffic was to send a body of Portuguese along the coast from the castle and to repulse the armed traders from the shore, or to catch the interlopers unawares on the land, while they were trading, and to imprison them. Even the ability on the part of the Portuguese to reveal their presence in the neighbourhood was sometimes a deterrent

[1] E. Falgairolle, *Jean Nicot*, p. 39.
[2] Roncière, iv. 78.
[3] Hakluyt, vi. 196; T. Astley, *Voyages*, ii. 568–9.

to the illicit traders.¹ They would also forbid the natives to trade either with the English or the French, and the negroes on the Mina coast, since they lived in great fear of the Portuguese, would often refuse interloping offers of trade on this ground alone.² The Portuguese, further, took ample advantage of the subservience of the blacks. When they heard or discovered that their rivals were making traffic, they would send a small armed party to the place of trade and cause the negroes to cease bargaining by firing a few rounds of ammunition. When Towerson made his first voyage to Guinea, the Portuguese sent a brigantine to pursue his ships wherever they went, and " to give warning to the people of the country that they should not deale with " the interloper.³

The wiles of the Portuguese exasperated the ruthless interlopers, who sometimes took a frightful revenge. Three French interlopers, chancing to encounter a Portuguese caravel at the Rio dos Sestos in 1557, engaged it and burnt it, and killed the entire crew save one negro whom they set on shore.⁴ English interlopers, who happened to be in great want of food on their return from Mina in 1558, burnt Samma to the ground out of sheer spite against the natives, because the latter would not trade.⁵

Land fortifications and naval forces were now the chief foundations of the Portuguese monopoly. Unfortunately, we have only scanty evidence about them. The Portuguese government does not appear to have made any drastic changes or radical improvements in the system of forts. Possibly Accra was built in this period.⁶ It may also be that the garrison of Mina was increased : whereas the number may have been down to thirty in 1545, its usual quota of sixty men had been restored by 1556.⁷ Perhaps too, an extension in the defences of Santiago was undertaken, because, while they were insignificant in 1540, they were considerable in 1566–7.⁸

We can be no surer of the arrangement of naval forces.

[1] Hakluyt, vi. 203.
[2] Hakluyt, vi. 247.
[3] Hakluyt, vi. 208.
[4] Hakluyt, vi. 238.
[5] Hakluyt, vi. 247.
[6] *Vide supra*, p. 102.
[7] G. B. Ramusio, *Navigationi et Viaggi*, iii. 429 ; Hakluyt, vi. 200.
[8] Barcellos, p. 159 ; Hakluyt, vi. 276–8.

Possibly the convoy system, inaugurated on a basis of Hispano-Portuguese co-operation in 1552, obtained throughout this period. In 1557 King Sebastian ordered all ships to go armed when they left Portugal, and instructed his captains to observe certain general rules when they navigated the West African coast.[1] This law, whose details, if known, might shed some light on the contemporary organisation of the Guinea convoys, probably regularised the empirical convoy system which King John III had founded. Moreover, every year the gold fleet sailed to Mina, but it is not known whether a fleet was still sent annually to Malagueta.[2]

Besides the trading fleets, the Portuguese also sent armed squadrons to patrol the coast of Guinea, as in the reign of John III. Now, however, they were more concerned to defend Mina than Malagueta. Furthermore, a higher tonnage of warships now ranged the African shores. The English traders frequently encountered these Portuguese armadas, and a large number of French prisoners in the castle of São Jorge, albeit corresponding to the greater volume of interloping traffic, also testified to the strengthening of the naval forces of Portugal.[3] The armadas were not sent out, as formerly, only on receipt of news in Lisbon about the departure of unlicensed fleets: the Portuguese ambassador asserted in 1562 that they now sailed every year from Lisbon to expel all interlopers from the traffic.[4] Moreover, the Portuguese attempted to combine their land and naval defence arms, for several galleys and caravels were attached to the castle of São Jorge, while two brigantines may have been attached to Santiago Island. These fleets co-operated with the forts in coastal defence, and when an interloping ship was sighted from the watch-tower of one of the castles, the galleys or the brigantines would go out to attack it.[5]

Diplomatic pressure was still applied in Paris and in London. King John III died in June 1557. His grandson and heir, Sebastian, was a minor, and the government passed into the hands of a regent, Queen Catherine, the widow of the late king.

[1] *Leys e Provisões del Rei D. Sebastião*, p. 166.
[2] Hakluyt, vi. 200, 229.
[3] Hakluyt, vi. 146, 215, 221, 229; E. Falgairolle, *Jean Nicot*, pp. 6, 15, 43.
[4] *Cal. S. P. For.*, 1562, p. 42.
[5] Hakluyt, vi. 220, 276-8.

At her instance, João Pereira was sent to England to protest against the third voyage of William Towerson (January 1559).[1] Meanwhile, the representations of cardinal Pole and King Philip II on the behalf of Portugal had already smoothed the way for him,[2] and so the embargo on English voyages to Guinea was gradually made effective. The close of the reign of Queen Mary seemed to witness a temporary victory for Portugal.

In Paris, however, the same good fortune did not attend the Portuguese. King Philip II could not play the rôle of mediator, as he had between England and Portugal, for France was at war with Spain. At this time, indeed, French opposition to Portugal was stronger than that of England. Jean Nicot, who was sent on a special mission to Portugal in 1559, vigorously championed the privateers in the contemporary negotiations. It would seem, from Nicot's correspondence that John III and, after his death, Queen Catherine tried hard through their agents in Paris to secure a renewal of the earlier French prohibitions upon the Guinea trade. But Nicot's letters also suggest that the French government was unsympathetic and adamant.[3]

Meanwhile, Frenchmen were claiming the right to traffic to the West Indies in the negotiations, which had been instituted to end the Franco-Spanish war. Queen Catherine of Portugal followed the course of these exchanges very closely. She opposed concession to France, because she believed that a rupture in the Spanish oversea monopoly would lead, sooner or later, to a similar breach in her own monopoly. She appears to have made representations to the Spanish government in the autumn of 1558, urging that the French demand for freedom of navigation to the Indies should be firmly rejected, and in the following March her agents sent a draft solution to the dispute, worded in such a way that it would not have endangered her own empire.[4] At Cercamp, which was the centre of the negotiations from October to January, the Spanish diplomats, though anxious to satisfy the Portuguese, found that the French would not relinquish their claim. Yet Philip II desired to end the war, and moreover, as the Bishop of Arras declared, the controversy about

[1] *Quadro Elementar*, xv. 111.
[2] *Cal. S. P. Ven.*, 1555–6, no. 493.
[3] E. Falgairolle, *Jean Nicot*, pp. 17–18.
[4] *Papiers d'Etat du Cardinal de Granvelle*, v. 285–6, 346.

the Indies was only a secondary issue and ought not to be allowed to stand in the way of peace.[1] Accordingly, both sides agreed to shelve the problem, and so no clause relating to navigation and trade to the Indies was included in the Treaty of Cateau-Cambrésis.

However, an interesting oral agreement was reached. Treaties between France and Spain were to lose their force west of the prime meridian and south of the Tropic of Cancer, and breaches of the peace beyond these " lines of amity " were not to affect the relations of the two states in Europe.[2]

This temporary settlement was not a satisfactory one from the Portuguese point of view. Of course, the Portuguese government was not a party to the verbal agreement, and therefore her empire was not bound by it. Yet the interlopers might use it as an argument to support their claims to trade to Guinea, for the whole of West Africa lay south of the Tropic of Cancer. The omens were bad for monopoly.

[1] *Ibid.*, v. 286 ; L. P. Gachard, *Relations des Ambassadeurs Vénetiens sur Charles-Quint et Philippe II*, pp. 314-5.
[2] Davenport, i. 219-21.

CHAPTER VIII

MONOPOLY ON THE WANE, 1559-78

THE West African monopoly of Portugal was further undermined after 1559 by certain important changes in Europe, which reacted upon the maritime balance of power. Events in France, England, Portugal and Spain contributed, in varying degrees, to this result. The growth of the huguenot movement in France stimulated interloping activity in Guinea. But this was partially counteracted by the increasing bitterness of the French religious wars, especially after the assassination of admiral Coligny, when the energy of the huguenots was concentrated more intensively upon the domestic conflict. The situation in England, where protestantism was finally accepted and guaranteed by the state, inspired more vigorous efforts to break down the monopoly. London merchants and Plymouth sailors now advanced religious arguments, as well as the argument of force, to support their clandestine operations in Guinea. Indeed, their operations ceased to be clandestine, when Queen Elizabeth took the crown which Mary had worn so uneasily. They openly attacked the papal division of the world and declared a holy war for the liberation of the seas. Meantime, Portugal's decline from the status of a leading imperial power encouraged illicit voyages; while Spain's championship of the cause of her weaker neighbour led the protestant corsairs to believe that a blow at the Portuguese empire was *ipso facto* also a blow at Spain.

Nor can we ignore the effect of the Counter-Reformation. The holy maritime war grew more bitter. The catholic states in Europe were drawn together and their imperial policies co-ordinated. Naval co-operation against the piratical marauders, first planned in the reign of John III, was continued. In 1567 the Kings of Spain and Portugal renewed their determination to sink without mercy all French and other ships which might be encountered beyond the Azores.[1] They were really confirming the principle laid down in the oral agreement of 1559 : there was to be no peace beyond the " lines of amity ".[2] Portuguese captains in Guinea might continue, with impunity, to sink at sight all interloping craft. Moreover, Hispano-Portuguese co-operation now extended over a wider field. Besides the convoy system and the use of force beyond the Azores, each sovereign helped the other in preventing the flight from the peninsula of subjects who might possess knowledge of the navigation to the Indies. Apparently, Castile now followed the lead given by her smaller neighbour in the policy of secrecy. Like Portugal, she feared the consequence to her oversea empire of any leakage of information. Accordingly, in 1567, the frontier guards of both states were empowered to put to death without process all those who would give no satisfactory explanation of their departure from the peninsula.[3] At the same time, both diplomatic corps acted generally in harmony and pooled such information as they could gather about intended or actual voyages to the forbidden seas. On their side, the protestant forces of north-western Europe were driven by the threat of a catholic revival to a more vigorous assault upon the two imperial monopolies. England, as was perhaps natural for the paramount protestant state, took the lead in Guinea enterprises from 1559 to 1571 ; while huguenots played the rôle of chief Guinea interloper from 1571 to the end of our period. Political and religious exiles from Portugal were welcomed in England and in the huguenot ports of France.[4]

It is obvious that after 1559 a close connection existed between religious strife in Europe and white enterprise in West Africa. One of the salient features of this interaction was the association of those in high places with many of the illegal voyages to Guinea. In France, admiral Coligny was the inspiration of the huguenot privateers, and his hand may be discerned at this time behind most of the French operations in Guinea. Thus, when two rowbarges were equipped at Newhaven for a voyage to Mina, one-fourth of the profits was

[1] " *Au dela des Isles Terceres ou Acores* " : M. de Fourquevaux to Charles IX, King of France, 13 Nov. 1567, L'Abbé Douais, *Dépêches de M. de Fourquevaux*, p. 288,
[2] *Vide supra*, p. 160,
[3] Douais, *op. cit.*, pp. 300-1.
[4] *Cal. S. P. Span.*, 1558-67, nos. 144, 260, 423, 431.

to go to him (December 1559).¹ He was always championing his co-religious friends, and in 1566 he pleaded the cause of captain Bontemps and recommended that Catherine de Medici should grant the captain the loan of two cannons for a new enterprise to Mina.² Sometimes he even won over the King of France to his own point of view. We find Charles IX assuring him that the crown would not resent hearing how the men of Rouen, should they meet armed Portuguese fleets overseas, had acquitted themselves with honour.³

Generally, the official attitude of the French government was studiously correct. It is true that Charles IX was sometimes as vague as Francis I in his replies to the protests of Portuguese ambassadors.⁴ It is also true that Jean Nicot, the representative of France at Lisbon, proclaimed the freedom of the seas and championed the cause of French prisoners at Mina in the years 1559-61.⁵ It is even true that Catherine de Medici was indirectly connected with French voyages to Benin (1560) and to Guinea (1566).⁶ For the most part, however, the government cautiously steered clear of anything suggestive of partisanship. Its members might wink at interloping expeditions, but they dissembled, and even refused to accept responsibility for the consequences.⁷

An examination of the personnel of those associated with the English voyages to Guinea reveals many highly-placed officials, and demonstrates that the English government was, more than the French, definitely and openly sympathetic towards these enterprises. We may turn for evidence to a project for the building of a fort in Guinea in 1561. The chief public adventurers in the scheme were a group of influential merchants, some of whom had been interested in the Guinea traffic during the reign of Queen Mary: Sir William Chester, Sir William Garrard, Sir Thomas Lodge, William Winter, Benjamin Gonson, Anthony Hickman and Edward Castlyn. Lodge was the lord mayor of the city of London; Benjamin Gonson was the treasurer of the navy; Winter was subsequently surveyor of

¹ *Cal. S. P. For.*, 1559–60, no. 408.
² Le Comte Jules Delaborde, *Gaspard de Coligny*, ii. 457–60.
³ Roncière, iv. 82–3.
⁴ *Cal. S. P. For.*, 1561–2, nos. 103, 124, 125.
⁵ E. Falgairolle, *Jean Nicot*, p. 44 *et passim*.
⁶ *Lettres de Catherine de Médicis*, i. 210–11; Roncière, iv. 83.
⁷ L. Paris, *Négociations, Lettres et Pièces Diverses relatives au Règne de Francois II*, p. 866; *Lettres de Catherine de Médicis*, ii. 450.

the navy. Even the queen and the cautious Sir William Cecil, the chief secretary of state, were favourably inclined towards the adventurers to Guinea. Whatever she might pretend, Queen Elizabeth cared little for nice legal points. Her primary criterion was the welfare of her country, and from the beginning, therefore, she questioned the monopolistic claims of Portugal and Spain. She refused to acknowledge Sebastian's right to forbid the subjects of another prince from trading where they liked (April 1560).[1] In June she actually ordered the lord admiral to deliver four of her ships to the Guinea syndicate to make the voyage to Africa, and the treasurer of the navy was to receive one-third of the profits.[2] In reality, though she declared that the four ships were sold to the interested merchants, she lent them upon conditions to the Guinea syndicate. The queen upon this occasion, as upon many others, was an active participant in the trade to Guinea.[3]

Cecil, for his part, was more cautious and even more subtle. He refused to adventure in the project of 1561, for he did not desire to be directly involved. But, during the Anglo-Portuguese negotiations regarding traffic to West Africa, his aim seems to have been to preserve friendship with Portugal, and yet to leave a loophole for his fellow-countrymen. For this reason he drew upon French experience. He knew that the French had a generation of accumulated wisdom behind their replies to the Portuguese protests. He knew that the huguenots were still troubling the Portuguese in Guinea at least as much as the English. He knew, too, that this was in spite of formal patents of prohibition, issued twenty years earlier by King Francis I. Accordingly, through Sir Nicholas Throckmorton, his ambassador in Paris, he closely followed the course of Franco-Portuguese negotiations, hoping, apparently, to model his own replies upon those of the French government.[4] This is not the place to raise the subject of Anglo-French co-operation in the struggle to break the Iberian world monopoly, but Cecil's correspondence with Throckmorton throws an interesting sidelight upon its scope. It demonstrates the chief secretary's sympathy for his seafaring countrymen.

[1] *Cal. S. P. For.*, 1561–2, no. 98.
[2] *Cal. S. P. Dom.*, 1547–80, p. 178 ; *Cal. S. P. Span.*, 1558–67, no. 144.
[3] J. A. Williamson, *John Hawkins*, pp. 54–5.
[4] *Cal. S. P. For.*, 1561–2, nos. 103, 124, 125.

The association of huguenot leaders and the government of England with the small merchants and navigators, who lived in the English and French ports, must have alarmed the Portuguese. From their point of view, an equally serious feature of the "silent war" in West Africa was the great increase in the number of interloping voyages between 1559 and 1571. The Treaty of Cateau-Cambrésis did not materially affect the situation beyond Cape Bojador. When the curtain is raised on the play of European activity there in 1559, we find Frenchmen and Englishmen busily trading in the forbidden seas. There is substantial evidence of the French enterprises. Reprisals against Villegagnon seem to have stirred the French to greater deeds, so that even those, who otherwise might not have interested themselves, took a hand. Catherine de Medici, who was certainly not a huguenot, and the Cardinal of Lorraine, who was nothing if not a catholic, seem to have been implicated. The ambassadors of both Spain and Portugal suspected the Cardinal of Lorraine, when four large ships left Newhaven for Guinea under captain Souris in November 1559. Two other ships were equipped for Mina in December. It was probably one of these six which returned home at the beginning of February, having lost its captain and fourteen men, but with a cargo of pepper, ivory and gold.[1] Captain Boileau, despite the disaster which befel his intended voyage to Benin in the winter of 1558-9, appears to have left for that same region in the spring of 1560, and Catherine de Medici was at least cognisant of his enterprise.[2] Three ships from Rouen were sunk in Guinea at this time.[3] Two French ships were destroyed off the Mina coast by the Portuguese in the following winter,[4] while admiral Coligny was responsible for the equipment of four or five armed vessels for Mina (1560-1).[5] Another five accompanied an English fleet, which left Portsmouth harbour for Mina in the first week of November 1561,[6] and at least one French ship and a pinnace were upon the Guinea Coast in the winter months of 1562-3.[7]

[1] *Cal. S. P. For.*, 1559-60, nos. 337, 408, 684.
[2] *Lettres de Catherine de Médicis*, i. 211.
[3] *Cal. S. P. For.*, 1560-1, no. 648.
[4] E. Falgairolle, *Jean Nicot*, pp. 66-7.
[5] *Cal. S. P. For.*, 1560-1, no. 716.
[6] *Cal. S. P. Span.*, 1558-67, no. 144.
[7] Hakluyt, vi. 258.

A lull followed in the winter of 1563-4. Probably the indignation, which the Portuguese had roused against themselves by their brutal treatment of Villegagnon and his men, had died down. Moreover, the outbreak of civil war between the huguenots and the catholics in 1562 must have limited the scope of maritime enterprise, for Dieppe, Rouen and especially Havre were hotbeds of protestantism, and therefore came to be among the chief theatres of war. Thus, the energies of the bold navigators of the seaports were exhausted at home in the defence of their religion and there was little surplus for oversea voyages. No evidence has been disclosed of any French ships in Guinea during the season of 1563-4.

But Frenchmen resorted to their old haunts of trade and piracy again after 1564. Captain Bontemps, a man as courageous as Jacques de Sores, set out from Newhaven in the *Green Dragon*, was driven from Mina by Portuguese galleys, and in April 1565 encountered the fleet of John Hawkins in the West Indies.[1] His misfortunes, however, did not deter him from a second voyage with two ships and a pinnace in the following winter (1565-6), when he also met with disaster.[2] The same winter another French ship was sunk in Guinea.[3] In the next trading season, Bontemps set out boldly upon a third venture from Rouen,[4] and Jean Honguière, another of the French privateering captains, was furnished with the *Greyhound*, insured in London, for an enterprise to Mina, the Slave Coast and the West Indies.[5] However, the chief interests of the French in this renewed burst of activity seem to have been the trade and the fisheries of Cape Verde and the opportunities for piracy, provided by the confluence of maritime highways at the islands of Cape Verde and the Canaries. Frenchmen were very " welcome to the Negros " at Cape Verde ;[6] John Hawkins met a fleet of five French ships under captain Bland trading with the negroes at the cape in the winter of 1567-8 ; and they had nearly two hundred sail at the Canaries in May 1567, many of which probably frequented the waters hard by Cape Verde.[7]

[1] Hakluyt, vi. 265.
[2] Roncière, iv. 82 ; P.R.O., H.C.A. 24, 39, nos. 19, 20.
[3] Roncière, iv. 83.
[4] *Ibid.*, Delaborde, *op. cit.*, ii. 457-60.
[5] P.R.O., H.C.A., 24, 39, no. 16.
[6] Hakluyt, vi. 273-4.
[7] Hakluyt, vi. 337 ; P.R.O., S.P. 70, 90, f. 81b.

After 1568 a second gap ensues in the evidence, and may possibly be attributed to similar causes. Huguenot attention was concentrated upon the second and third religious wars, and all available ships were needed for fighting nearer home. It is not until 1571 that we hear of other French ships making the Guinea voyage. Then we learn that twenty warships departed from Havre for Guinea, Brazil, and the West Indies.[1]

Meanwhile, the English adventurers were taking a more important part in the interloping descent upon the Portuguese empire beyond Barbary. The evidence for English voyages to Guinea between 1559 and 1561 is mainly circumstantial. Martin Frobisher was mixed up with the notorious pirate, Henry Strangewyse, in a project for a voyage to Mina. Strangewyse intended, apparently, to take three ships with him on the " Enterprise to the Castle of Mina ". He had the backing of forty gentlemen of consequence and his associates included Frobisher, John Lok and possibly Francis Lambert, all three of whom had been connected with voyages to Guinea and Barbary in the reign of Queen Mary. But there was some irregularity about the scheme and so, upon information from James Aldaye, Sir William Cecil overthrew it. Possibly the preparations of Strangewyse, who was already under suspicion of piracy in respect of certain Spanish ships, alarmed Cecil at a time when he was anxious not to antagonise Philip II. The pirate was arrested and, during the subsequent enquiry before the High Court of Admiralty, part of the inner story of the adventure was disclosed. Strangewyse was imprisoned but later released (December 1560).[2]

This episode is the only certain example of an English Guinea project during the first three years of the reign of Queen Elizabeth. Whether Strangewyse was involved in any other undertakings at this time we do not know. His life story, were it written, would make interesting reading. We know that he was in the eye of the government, as a man experienced in West African navigation and possessing unusual qualities of seamanship : when a Portuguese exile in France, captain Melchior, offered to pilot an English expedition to a secret

[1] *Cal. S. P. Span.*, 1568–79, no. 291.
[2] K. M. Eliot, " The First Voyages of Martin Frobisher ", (*E.H.R.*, xxxii. 89–92) ; P.R.O., S.P. 12, 4, nos. 64, 65 ; S.P. 12, 14, no. 60 ; H.C.A. 1, 35, 13-16 August 1559.

destination up one of the creeks of the Barbary coast, where rumour spoke of fabulous wealth to be had for the asking, Strangewyse's name was mentioned by the English ambassador in Paris as a suitable man to send (1561).[1] It would seem that the project failed to mature. Yet King Sebastian apparently wrote to Elizabeth in October 1560 regarding English voyages to Guinea, and a Portuguese envoy, Emanuel d'Aranjo, came to London in the spring of 1561 to follow up the protest.[2] Here is strong circumstantial evidence of unrecorded traffic. We may, therefore, accept without hesitation the conclusion of Dr. J. A. Williamson that the trade was being " actively pursued " from 1558 to 1561.[3]

During the ten years after 1561 our evidence suggests a greater volume of English than of French traffic to Guinea. Moreover, the stream of traffic was steady, for contemporary records show that not a single winter passed without one or more voyages having been made from English ports. It is impossible to estimate how many voyages were made because of the unreliability of our evidence. The vigorous protests of the Portuguese government, culminating in a grave threat of war in 1569, suggest that more ships actually sailed than extant records reveal.[4]

The scope of English enterprise was threefold : first, there was direct traffic between England and Guinea ; secondly, John Hawkins inaugurated the transatlantic slave trade ; and thirdly, several attempts were made to establish a permanent station as a base for trade and military operations in West Africa. As for direct traffic, two profitable expeditions to the region of the Mine were undertaken, one in the winter of 1561-2 and the other in the early months of 1563. The second voyage was a financial success in spite of armed resistance from the Portuguese near the castle of São Jorge. Some of the men, who sailed upon this occasion, were old hands at the game, like William Rutter, and doubtless they were not unduly embarrassed by their several running fights with the galleys of the castle. Indeed, they may even have confronted their enemies with a

---

[1] *Cal. S. P. For.*, 1561-2, no. 279.
[2] *Ibid.*, nos. 136, 137.
[3] J. A. Williamson, *John Hawkins*, p. 53.
[4] For an expert account of many of these voyages, see J. A. Williamson, *John Hawkins*, pp. 53-8, 78-165, 231.

kind of scornful bravado. Time was to show, however, that the Portuguese could not always be despised. The Guinea syndicate in London, pleased with the success of the two earlier voyages, planned a third for the following winter. Captain David Carlet set out for Guinea in October 1564, but he was betrayed by the negroes of the Mina coast, and he and some of his crew were imprisoned in the castle. Even so, the voyage was not without its compensations, for, while one ship was captured by the Portuguese, a second, the *Minion*, at length reached London and its cargo was rumoured to be worth 20,000 gold crowns.[1] It was in July that the *Minion* was reported to be back in the Thames. Her condition, and the frightful tale which her crew must have told, after their exhausting adventure, cannot have provided any special inducement for others to repeat the voyage. Yet vice-admiral Winter sent out the *Mary Fortune* to Guinea when the ensuing season began, and George Fenner captained a trading enterprise to the archipelago and mainland of Cape Verde in 1566–7.[2] The *Mary Fortune* was ill-named. She was sunk by a Portuguese flotilla near the Rio dos Sestos, most of her crew were drowned, and the survivors went to augment the English contingent of prisoners at the castle of São Jorge. Captain Fenner's well-armed fleet of three ships and a pinnace did not sail further south than Cape Verde. Apparently, his original intention was to purchase gold at Mina, but the reception, which he encountered at Santiago, was so hot, and the reports of Portuguese galleys off the Mina coast so alarming, that he decided to return to England. As the years passed, the gold traffic was proving less lucrative and more dangerous.[3]

One reason for Fenner's return may have been the unfriendly attitude of the natives at Cape Verde. Two Englishmen, who had been handed over to the negroes as hostages, were made captive, and a ransom demanded for them, whereupon captain Fenner solicited on their behalf the help of a French ship, which happened to arrive opportunely at the cape. For the animus of the negroes was not directed against the French in the same manner. The English adventurers were generally unpopular

[1] *Ibid.*, pp. 54–9.
[2] *Cal. S. P. Span.*, 1558–67, nos. 316, 327, 428 ; B.M., Royal MS. 13 B.1, f. 188 ; Hakluyt, vi. 266–84.
[3] J. A. Williamson, *John Hawkins*, pp. 158–61.

there, because, three weeks before Fenner dropped anchor, another English ship had visited the cape, and its crew had incurred the hatred of the inhabitants by seizing three negroes.[1]

Thus, English participation in the slave trade was spoiling peaceful commerce. The French, on the contrary, generally eschewed the slave trade in the sixteenth century, and for this earned the gratitude of the natives and were more welcome than either the English or the Portuguese at Cape Verde. We do not know the identity of the English interloper, who thus roused a hornet's nest for the unlucky captain Fenner, but it has been suggested that captain Lovell was responsible.[2] With the backing of John Hawkins, a fleet of four ships under Lovell's command set out from Plymouth in November 1566 to trade to Guinea, and three of the four ships subsequently made their way to the West Indies. Lovell was later accused of piracy by the Portuguese, and the case was tried before the High Court of Admiralty in 1568. The captain was charged with having seized a number of Portuguese ships with their cargoes. Near Santiago he captured two large ships, loaded with negroes, and two other ships were taken at the islands of Fogo and Maio. His object, then, was evidently to load as many blacks as possible before sailing to the West Indies. But he did not merely plunder Portuguese vessels, for, as we saw, he organised at least one raid for slaves upon the mainland.[3]

Hawkins's association with the enterprise of John Lovell helps to explain its character. It was John Hawkins who first put into operation the idea of English participation in the Africo-Caribbean slave trade, when he made the celebrated voyages of 1562–3 and 1564–5.[4] His inspiration was behind the slaving voyage of captain Lovell, and he probably inspired other voyages about which to-day we know nothing. We hear of at least one other English ship which loaded 125 negroes at Cape Verde in the winter of 1564–5 and, what would appear more significant, its commander was Bartholomew Bayão, a Portuguese renegade.[5] Bayão was well known to the Portuguese, who invoked the help of the tribe of the Sapes in Sierra

[1] Hakluyt, vi. 273.
[2] J. A. Williamson, *John Hawkins*, pp. 121–6.
[3] P.R.O., S.P. 70, 99, ff. 1–49. I have accepted Dr. Williamson's view that " Cobel " read " Lovell " in the original MS.
[4] J. A. Williamson, *John Hawkins*, pp. 78–116.
[5] P.R.O., S.P. 70, 95, ff. 260, 260 b.

MONOPOLY ON THE WANE

Leone to expel him from the coast.[1] Was this man one of the Portuguese who regularly aided the English in their interloping activities? And did he suggest the slaving voyage to John Hawkins? Unfortunately, the voyage of 1564–5 is the earliest notice of him, so that these questions cannot be answered. Yet Bayão was a clever cosmographer, well acquainted with the African navigation, and he was engaged in more than one enterprise for England. It would seem that his voyage to Cape Verde and the Spanish Indies ended disastrously, for in 1570 he was a prisoner at Seville. In this year he escaped and fled back to England, where he was welcomed by the merchants and some of the councillors, because " no one could have come more apt for their designs ". A scheme was immediately set on foot for a plantation in South America from which the traffic of Guinea, the Spanish Indies and the Pacific might be controlled. Bayão was to lead the necessary expedition. It so alarmed the Spanish authorities that the ambassador, Guerau de Spes, tried to bribe Bartholomew Bayão to enter the service of King Philip II. But Bartholomew was a difficult man with whom to deal and perhaps set his price too high, for he remained in England. Nothing came of the scheme of colonisation, but Bayão returned to the slave trade. In the spring of 1571 he equipped three ships and a pinnace for the Senegal, from whence he intended to carry slaves to Hispaniola. He was evidently held up for a time by an embargo, but efforts were made for his release. We do not know whether he did actually sail.[2]

Profits from the slave trade must have been very considerable. Unless this be accepted, it is difficult to explain the continued participation of men like Hawkins and Bayão. It is well known that the former undertook a large-scale operation in the winter of 1567–8 and was the victim of a fearful massacre in the bay of San Juan de Ulua (23 September 1568). Yet his interest in the slave trade did not sag. Dr. Williamson has pointed out that his subsequent prestige and close connection with the English government barred him from an active part in the slave commerce after 1569. But he seems to have been the owner of certain ships which were equipped for it in the winter of 1570–1. Nor was his friend, vice-admiral Winter, deterred

[1] Almada, *Tratado breve dos Rios de Guiné*, p. 92.
[2] *Cal. S. P. Span.*, 1568–79, nos. 186, 238, 242.

by San Juan de Ulua. Soon after, two fleets belonging to him sailed from England for Guinea and the West Indies, one in the February following that fateful September day, and the other during the winter and spring of 1570–1. A few unknown vessels left England for Guinea and the West Indies in December 1569, and two others for Cape Arguin in February 1570.[1] We know very little of these enterprises, for Hakluyt does not chronicle them. But the evidence which remains suggests that their conception was in every way similar to the first slaving voyage of Hawkins.

The character of English enterprise in Guinea thus began to change. During the early years of English traffic to West Africa, gold, pepper and ivory were the primary attractions for the syndicate of merchants who adventured in it. However, as trading beyond Cape Palmas grew more dangerous, so did the gold trade tend to decline. John Hawkins then projected a new type of commerce, wherein the Guinea voyage itself ceased to form a complete cycle. This new trade did not necessitate facing the guns or the galleys of Portugal on the Mina coast, for plenty of negro slaves were procurable between the Senegal and Sierra Leone. Nor did it involve the greater risk of fever, which attached to the farther voyage. It did not even mean that the other commodities of Guinea, apart from slaves, need be ignored. Hawkins found it convenient in 1563, when about to leave Sierra Leone for the West Indies, to send one of his ships straight back to England with the pepper and the ivory, which he had purchased. His plan was copied by those who came after him. Captain Lovell seems to have sent one of his ships back from Guinea in the spring of 1567;[2] and we have reliable evidence that one of a fleet of three ships, owned by William Winter and sent to Guinea to participate in the transatlantic slave trade, returned to England without visiting the Caribbean (1570).[3] The slave trade was thus gradually preferred, particularly after the failure of the expedition of captain Fenner. Nearly all the ships, sent to Guinea during the Anglo-Portuguese crisis of 1569–71, were potential slavers.

[1] *Cal. S. P. Span.*, 1568–79, nos. 161, 180, 192, 238, 242, 291.
[2] J. A. Williamson, *John Hawkins*, p. 125.
[3] *Cal. S. P. Span.*, 1568–79, no. 192.

The men, who were interested in Guinea clearly saw that trade, whatever its character, could be greatly facilitated by a permanent station in West Africa. We have noted in the preceding chapter that this idea had already been considered between 1554 and 1558. A keener interest in trade now led to correspondingly more thorough efforts to plant settlements, but no greater success was achieved than before 1559. The pre-eminence of Englishmen among the interlopers in the period from 1559 to 1571 is indicated by the fact that nearly all the contemporary projects of colonisation in Guinea were of English origin. The first elaborate plan for such a settlement was unfolded by the London Guinea syndicate to John Lok in September 1561. They had decided to send out an expedition to build a fort " upon the coast of Mina in the king of Habaan's country". This prince was the one who, four years earlier, had made the " offer " of a place for a factory. Captain Lok was now commissioned to reconnoitre the coast and to choose a convenient site. He was instructed to pay special attention to anchorage, the fertility of the soil, and the question of supplies of timber, victuals, and above all fresh water. He was also to select a place " naturally strong ", such as would require only a few men to defend it, and he was to consider the possibilities of native aid both for the building and the subsequent defence of the fort. Finally, the attitude of the King of Habaan was to be sounded again, without giving him explicit information about the future plans of the merchants.[1] Perhaps the organisers of the enterprise feared lest he should divulge the scheme to the Portuguese.

The instructions thus issued to John Lok show that those, who drafted them, were familiar with many of the problems involved in the construction and the upkeep of a fort in West Africa. Certain Portuguese renegades were evidently consulted, and the queen seems to have favoured the project.[2] Yet there is no evidence that it was ever executed; nor did John Lok command the expedition when it sailed.[3] No reference to any repetition of this scheme occurs for three years. The idea was temporarily abandoned.

[1] Hakluyt, vi. 253–4.
[2] *Cal. S. P. Dom.*, 1547–80, vol. xix, no. 21 ; vol. xvii, no. 43.
[3] Hakluyt, vi. 255–7.

The Portuguese were alive to the danger that their enemies might build forts in Guinea. Doubtless they obtained information, not only through their agents in France and England, but also from the natives of the Mina coast. The Spanish ambassadors in Paris and London sent news when they were able to get it. So did patriotic Portuguese, who chanced to be engaged in trade between England and Portugal. Thus, when the expedition of 1561 set sail, the fact that the English ships carried out timber and victuals for a year " in greater quantity than is required for their own use " did not escape the vigilant eye of bishop Quadra, who was then the Spanish ambassador in London. We may be sure that King Philip II passed this information on to the Portuguese government as he did upon many other occasions.[1] The Portuguese were very alarmed by the new development in the activity of the interlopers, and they began to suspect every expedition of colonising intentions. They regarded with special apprehension the preparations of John Hawkins. Ayres Cardoso, their ambassador in London, was instructed to discover whether, in the ships being equipped for Guinea, were loaded any materials for the building of fortresses (September 1564).[2] This is plainly a reference to Hawkins's second voyage. When he sailed a third time, it was rumoured in Portugal that his object was to capture the castle of São Jorge da Mina. Botolph Holder, an English merchant in Lisbon, wrote home that certain Portuguese from England had reported that the fleet of John Hawkins was bound for Mina. The report seems to have spread a panic among those interested, for, in May, a wholly unfounded rumour got abroad in the Portuguese capital that Hawkins had taken and spoiled the castle.[3] This was not the English captain's intention, as we now know, but the fact of the rumour indicates the temper of the times. The situation was both delicate and dangerous for Portugal. If the castle of São Jorge fell into either English or French hands, what would happen to the Portuguese dominions and Portuguese trade there? Moreover, such fears were not entirely unjustified. Nine years before, as we have related, the pirate Strangewyse had planned to

---

[1] *Cal. S. P. Span.*, 1558–67, no. 144.
[2] *Quadro Elementar*, xv. 168–9.
[3] P.R.O., S.P. 70, 98, ff. 43–4.

attack Mina.¹ Only two years earlier Martin Frobisher had fitted out what would seem to have been a piratical expedition to Guinea.² John Hawkins certainly considered the possibility of establishing a fort in Guinea, as is proved by an extant document in the English Public Record Office entitled *A proposition of ordenance, powder, armour and municion for the fort in genoia yf there shalbe nede of fortificacon* (24 June 1567).³ And in 1567 the Portuguese in Guinea suffered one of their deepest humiliations, when French corsairs sacked the island of São Thomé. It is no wonder that the third voyage of John Hawkins was regarded with such apprehension.

Three further projects remain to be mentioned. In October 1566 captain Monluc sacked Madeira Island. Considerable speculation about his destination preceded his voyage. One view put forward was that Monluc would try to found a fortress in the Portuguese dominions and perhaps in Guinea.⁴ The French had not abandoned the idea of a permanent station in West Africa. Two Portuguese exiles, Antonio Luiz and André Homem, accompanied Monluc, and their association with him suggests that the idea of building a fort in Guinea was taken quite seriously by the leaders of the French enterprise. Moreover, these two men crossed to England after the Madeira enterprise and approached captain Winter. They offered to take him to a part of 'Ethiopia', where a flourishing trade in gold might be pursued, and a secure and defensible harbour obtained.⁵ The offer, which was based apparently upon the idea of a permanent settlement, was not accepted.

A third and final project for a settlement in Guinea occurs in 1570. One, Duckett, writing to Cecil in that year, outlined a plan for the erection of a fort at Habaan ('Abane') on the Mina coast.⁶ Evidently mindful of the 'offer' made to the English more than ten years before, but conscious of the difficulty of building a fort in West Africa, Duckett proposed that " the frame of a house " should be made in England, and then taken out in sections. Aware also of the problem of

¹ *Vide supra*, p. 167.
² *Cal. S. P. Dom.*, 1547–80, vol. xxxix, no. 86; vol. xl, no. 7.
³ P.R.O., S.P. 12, 43, no. 12.
⁴ *Cal. S. P. For.*, 1566–8, no. 719; De Thou, *Histoire de France* (1734), vol. v, bk. 44, p. 501
⁵ B.M., Cotton MS. Nero B.1, f. 154.
⁶ *Cal. S. P. Dom., Addenda*, 1566–79, vol. xvii, no. 115.

manning the fort, he suggested, following the Portuguese policy, that forty or fifty " condemned men " should remain behind in Guinea until the next expedition. It was at this time, moreover, that the council were conferring with Bartholomew Bayão about the colonisation of a region from which the traffic of Guinea might be controlled.[1] We are tempted to associate the two schemes, and to believe that Duckett and Bayão exchanged ideas. Yet nothing appears to have issued from the discussions. Perhaps Cecil was unfavourable because of the strained political relations of England and Spain.

The intrusion of so many interlopers into West Africa came at an unhappy moment for Portugal. The sovereign was a minor. Sebastian did not assume the reigns of government until 1567. The regency of Queen Catherine was replaced in 1561 by that of cardinal Henry, Sebastian's uncle, but internal quarrels were robbing Portugal of that solidarity which the earlier members of the House of Aviz had fashioned. Moreover, the menace of Spanish invasion was beginning to threaten Portuguese independence. Portuguese finance, too, was in a parlous condition, for the government could not pay its debts,[2] and the burden of imperial defence was too heavy.

The situation in Guinea was not calculated to encourage Sebastian's subjects in their fight against the corsairs. The natives were as restless as in the previous generation. It is probable that the sense of insecurity, engendered by the invasion of the Sumbas, had not yet been dissipated. Nor were the Portuguese any more popular. Negroes who lived around the castle of São Jorge hated its defenders. Stark warfare broke out in 1570. It seems that the Portuguese were engaged in a campaign against the native tribes of the Comani and the Fetu, possibly one of reprisal or intimidation because of English or French trade with them. The tribes responded by assembling in considerable numbers and laying siege to the castle. Our record of the episode comes from a Netherlander, Pieter de Marees, and is, therefore, probably biassed in favour of the blacks, but he leads us to believe that São Jorge would have fallen had it not been for the artillery of its white garrison.[3]

[1] *Cal. S. P. Span.*, 1568–79, no. 186.
[2] *Cal. S. P. Ven.*, 1558–80, no. 133.
[3] P. D. Marees, *Beschryvinge van het Gout-custe*, pp. 94–5.

Disaster was just averted upon this occasion, but six years later a serious catastrophe did befall the Portuguese a little further along the coast at Accra. We cannot say whether this fort was already standing before 1576. The Portuguese were either building or repairing its defences at the time when they were attacked. The local negroes objected to a work of fortification, which represented to them the mechanism of tyranny. Accordingly, they planned an assault. Native merchants from the interior were induced to approach the fort under the pretence of wishing to trade, while armed warriors lay concealed nearby, ready to attack when the gates were opened. The ruse evidently succeeded, for the Portuguese were slain and the fort burnt. When the news was taken to Portuguese headquarters, an expedition was despatched by sea to the site of the ruined Accra, but the natives seem to have prevented a successful landing. So did the region of Accra pass out of Portuguese control.[1]

Another problem which troubled the Portuguese was the discontent of the Angolares in the island of São Thomé. We have referred to a native revolt on the plantations during the reign of King John III. Now occurred a far more serious rising. The Angolares were slaves brought from Angola to work in the sugar mills. Many of them escaped to the hills in the south of the island, from where they began to ravage the northern plains. In 1574, co-operating with plantation slaves, they rose against the whites, and thereafter the Portuguese enjoyed little peace.[2] São Thomé declined and the planters began to drift from the island to Brazil.

The uncertain position of the Portuguese was not due entirely to circumstances over which they had no control. There were untrustworthy officials in the Portuguese service. The castle of São Jorge and the other isolated habitations of whites upon the Guinea Coast were a long sea-journey from Portugal. The home government could not exercise a minute day to day control over the actions of its servants while they lived so far away, even though the force of law might ultimately prevail. Officials in Guinea, as in other parts of the Portuguese empire, were thus guilty of occasional neglect of their duty. Scanty evidence does

---

[1] *Ibid.*, pp; 88–9. T. Astley, *Voyages*, ii. 568–9.
[2] Rebello da Silva, *Historia de Portugal*, v. 115.

not allow the reconstruction of a very vivid picture, nor does it permit us to generalise. But the case of Manuel de Mesquita Perestrello, captain of the castle of São Jorge during the year 1562-3, throws light upon the moral poverty of some of the servants of Portugal in the age of Sebastian. This man was appointed chief captain of the Mina fleet in 1562, but, when he arrived at the castle, he found that its captain, Ruy Gomez d'Azevedo, had died. Manuel therefore remained as chief captain and, as he subsequently declared, duly conformed to all the conditions of that office. Yet he was arrested the following year, brought home and imprisoned in Lisbon. A royal letter of 1569 suggests that he suffered a long imprisonment. Among the charges brought against him were those of unpaid debts, private trading—a common fault with the officials at São Jorge—and neglect of the obligation of defending the coast from interlopers. It appears that on his way out to Mina he encountered some English ships and, instead of attacking them, he retreated. Manuel de Mesquita's reply seems to have been that, knowing of the death of captain d'Azevedo and hearing the sound of guns, he felt it incumbent upon himself to land and to take charge of São Jorge for fear of an assault upon that castle.

We know that the Portuguese did fear that their chief station in West Africa might fall into English hands, so that perhaps de Mesquita was truthful in this, if not in any other respect. At any rate, he was pardoned in 1569.[1] But the charge of running from English ships and neglecting to head them off from the coastal trade was a particularly grave one. It would scarcely have been levelled against this captain, except it could be supported by incriminating evidence. Moreover, the alternative is not a pleasant one. If the charge were faked, then it can only have been the fabrication of a bitter enemy of de Mesquita, who was able to enlist the help of witnesses from Mina. This being so, there were men at the castle, while de Mesquita was there, unfriendly towards him. The alternative to his guilt is a hypothetical schism among the officials at the castle of São Jorge. Our evidence, in fact, suggests that this Portuguese navigator was really guilty, for the royal letter of pardon contains no reference to compensation. But no matter

[1] Viterbo, ii. 235-40.

which solution be accepted, everything points to an unhappy situation at the castle. A corrupt administration like this could not hope to exclude the corsairs for very long.

We may speculate that there were others in Guinea, besides the officials at São Jorge, who failed in their duty towards their country. Many of the native merchants, theoretically the subjects of King Sebastian, ignored their due allegiance and traded with English and French interlopers. Some of the mulattoes, especially those who dwelt on the banks of the rivers Gambia and Senegal, probably acted as agents for the white trespassers. We know that French and English corsairs sometimes carried natives home in order that they might learn their languages, and it is known that Portuguese renegades and mulattoes served as intermediaries between the unlicensed traders and the natives after 1580.[1] Probably, half-breed factors aided the interlopers onwards from 1559.

A fall in the value of Guinea profits aggravated the political discomfort of the Portuguese. We have already remarked the effect of interloping commerce: not only was the Lisbon government obliged to spend more money on defences, but the market in West Africa yielded the contractors a decreasing harvest of gold, slaves, ivory and pepper. The financial problem waxed very grave in Sebastian's reign, and probably a great deal of thought was given to it. Eventually, the king decided to free himself from the cost of a direct pursuit of the gold trade. M. de Fourquevaux, the French ambassador in Spain, reported that the King of Portugal or his council had leased the 'Mine' to a number of his subjects, on condition that these gentlemen built fortresses, settled the region and protected it from French depredations (13 November 1567). The ambassador sent an explanatory report at the end of November. It appeared, he wrote, that the king did not wish to pursue the traffic any longer himself, but he was to provide the new merchant group with ships for the voyage to Mina. He was also to receive one-tenth of all exports to Mina and one-fifth of all imports. In that way, it was estimated, he would collect more revenue than by directing the traffic personally or through his factors.[2]

[1] Almada, *Tratado breve dos Rios de Guiné*, pp. 14-15.
[2] L'Abbé Douais, *Dépêches de M. de Fourquevaux, 1565-72*, pp. 288, 301.

We cannot rely absolutely upon these reports, for they do not represent first-hand information. Yet we may interpret them as proof of the fall in profits. It had ceased to be worth the while of the Portuguese monarchy to pursue the gold traffic directly. Now, therefore, the Mina trade was to remain in permanent farm. A record of 1591-2 alludes to the " Renters of the Mine " and thus confirms this view.[1] Yet it may be added that King Sebastian was more interested in rebuilding his north African empire. He desired to reverse the policy of withdrawing from some of the north African outposts, which his grandfather had followed. Accordingly, he was not very interested in the Guinea traffic, and was glad to shift the responsibility from himself. Finance was not, then, the sole motive behind the change.

Presumably, a company of Portuguese merchants now took over the administration of the gold traffic. Profits might yet be made, for in the winter of 1562-3, according to the allegation of a prejudiced contemporary, at least 27 cwt. of gold was delivered by the King of Samma to the King of Portugal.[2] This is almost certainly an exaggerated statement. The yield in the 'sixties cannot have been so high or so certain as in the days of King Manuel for, apart from customs, the merchants who leased the contract were no longer required, apparently, to pay an annual rent. This stands in striking contrast to the grant of 1469. Yet they were expected to undertake a programme of colonial expansion. Possibly, we may attribute the wars between the negroes and the Portuguese in 1570 and 1576 to efforts of the new company of merchants to extend their political sway. Possibly, too, the building of Accra fort was their work. Still, we have no evidence of any attempt to settle people upon the Mina coast.

The episode of 1567, together with its consequences, are interesting because they demonstrate that the Portuguese did not accept defeat without resistance. They refused to despair in spite of a falling revenue, native discontent, corruption among some of the Guinea officials, uncertainty in regard to the home government and a great increase in the number of interloping voyages. Their never-ceasing aim was to re-establish in practice

[1] Hakluyt, vii. 98.
[2] *Cal. S. P. Dom., Addenda*, 1566-79, p. 247 ; the dating of this is based upon the arguable assumption that Duckett's reference was to the voyage of William Rutter, *vide* J. A. Williamson, *John Hawkins*, p. 57.

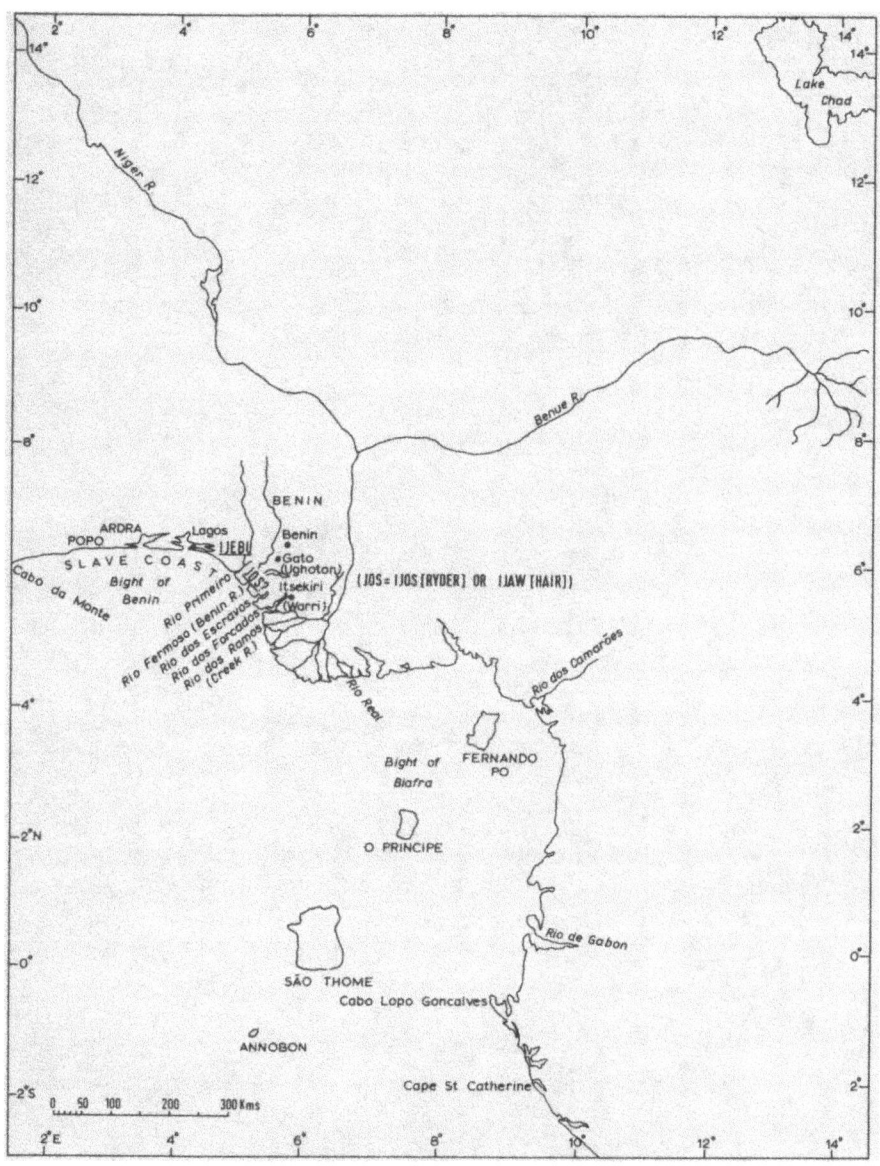

THE SLAVE COAST AND THE NIGER DELTA
States shown in capital letters
Peoples shown in capitals underlined

the monopoly which they still theoretically enjoyed. The methods, which they used, differed only in degree from those they had practised in the reign of King John III. In Europe the diplomatic game was played to a stalemate, but in Guinea a ding-dong battle raged.

Let us first consider the struggle in West Africa. As might have been expected, steps were taken to strengthen the forts. One of the chief strategic centres in the triangular struggle was the region of Cape Verde. It is, therefore, remarkable that no efforts were made apparently to fortify the mainland of Senegambia. Here the French were popular and the English habitually seized slaves. Those Portuguese, who lived in the region or navigated its rivers, were fully aware of the need of defending it. We may cite, in support of this, a letter from Diogo Carreiro to King Sebastian. Carreiro had boldly explored the upper reaches of the river Senegal as far as Timbuktu in the later months of 1565, and had made his way back to the coast in the following spring. He reported his success, recounting how he had inflicted defeat upon a French fleet, but he lamented the vulnerability of the estuary of the river. A small fort and a single brigantine would, he believed, suffice to protect the coast.[1] He did not pretend that his idea was new, for he mentioned that, long before, King John II had projected such a fort. Nothing had then been achieved and nothing was now attempted. Nearly a generation later captain Almada was to voice the same opinion with equal futility.

However, Santiago Island was now well-fortified. It would seem that there were no less than four forts, three at Ribeira Grande and one on the west side of the island.[2] Its importance necessitated this strong protection. It was not only an important *point d'appui* in the imperial communications of Portugal and a base for commerce on the mainland nearby, but at this time, it boasted a flourishing civil life of its own, was the centre of a prosperous fishing industry and—ill-omen for its inhabitants—a popular resort for the corsairs. Auxiliary to the forts were caravels and two brigantines,[3] the latter being employed to patrol the trade-routes between Santiago and the

[1] Viterbo, i. 322–4.
[2] Hakluyt, x. 269–71.
[3] Hakluyt, vi. 277–8.

mainland. As at Mina, this combination of land and sea forces was often successful. The evidence of witnesses before the High Court of Admiralty in London shows that the *Flower de Luce*, one of four English ships which sailed for Mina late in 1561, was driven from Cape Verde by Portuguese ships. Contrary to the general belief, this ship seems to have gone beyond the Canaries. John Wallet, the master, testified that he sailed as far as Cape Verde, where one ship of Portugal and a pinnace attacked his ship and obliged him to return home.[1] A more serious English disaster at Cape Verde was that experienced by captain Fenner in 1567, when an ugly encounter ensued between the interlopers and the brigantines, caravels and land forces of the governor of Santiago Island.[2] But the French seem to have fared even worse than the English in the archipelago, possibly because their ships frequented that region in greater numbers. The victory of Diogo Carreiro over a French fleet, already mentioned, was very probably a consequence of support from the island (1565). Five years later captain Gosselin lost thirty of the crew of his ship *l'Auge* in a one-sided battle in the river Gambia. Yet, as a list of spoils of 1567 shows, there were times when the trade between the mainland and the islands suffered heavily from the depredatory activities of the interlopers.[3]

Many settlements of Portuguese dotted the coast and the river valleys from the river Gambia to Sierra Leone. Indeed, the tendency at this time was for the trade between the islands and the mainland to be diverted southwards and for Cacheo on the Rio de S. Domingo to become its base. Yet no forts were built. When John Hawkins razed Cacheo to the ground in 1567, he does not appear to have encountered any substantial resistance. Neither was Sierra Leone given protection, nor the Rio dos Sestos, favoured resort for the interlopers though it was.

Apart from fort Accra, we cannot say whether any other extensions in the defence-works of the mainland were executed in this period. The Portuguese gentlemen, who took over the control of the Mina coast in 1567, were presumably responsible for the

---

[1] P.R.O., H.C.A. 1, 35, 13–16 August 1559 ; J. A. Williamson, *John Hawkins*, pp. 54–6.
[2] Hakluyt, vi. 276–8.
[3] P.R.O., S.P. 70, 95, ff. 261–6.

building or the improvements at Accra. Possibly, too, they fulfilled the conditions of the lease by strengthening fort São Jorge. A town called Dondou thrived adjacent to the castle, and from this side, apparently, it was most vulnerable.[1] This may be deduced from the evidence of the pirate Strangewyse. He had, he said, consulted with the captain of a Portuguese caravel, which he had seized, about the situation of São Jorge, and he had decided " ffirste to have taken ye towne and efftsoones ye castle " (1559).[2] Illuminating descriptions of the organisation of the native town may be found in seventeenth-century records, but this is one of the earliest references to it. Perhaps, then, the new Portuguese Guinea company took steps to counter the danger of an assault upon the castle from the town side. It may also have been upon their initiative that the chapel, which crowned a nearby hill, outside and commanding the town, was removed to a site within the walls.

We can write more confidently about the island of São Thomé. King Sebastian feared an attack upon this island. Many a sugar-laden hulk, plying between São Thomé and Antwerp, was the victim of piracy in the middle of the sixteenth century, and the corsairs doubtless extracted much valuable information relating to the situation and defence of the island from the unfortunate crews. Plans for raids on São Thomé, of which no vestige of evidence remains, must often have been drafted. In 1567 a French fleet did actually ravage the sugar plantations, dealing a heavy blow at the prosperity of the island. The Portuguese government had sent a caravel loaded with arms and munitions in the previous year, and Francisco de Gouvea, the governor, had been ordered to take a general muster of all the islanders who could bear arms. But these preparations came too late to avert the ensuing catastrophe. Yet de Gouvea continued his work undismayed so that, before the end of his ten years of office, the foundations of a fortress had been laid. His successor, Diogo Salema, completed this, the fort of Sebastian, in 1575.[3]

The Portuguese, besides repairing and strengthening their forts, also increased considerably the number of armed fleets which they sent to Guinea. It would seem that the popularity

[1] Hakluyt, vi. 216.
[2] P.R.O., H.C.A., 1, 35, 13–16 August 1559.
[3] *Ensaios*, II. i. 44–5.

of the African adventure among English seamen drove the Lisbon government to even greater exertions than had formerly been customary against the French. Thus in October 1567, fearing lest John Hawkins might besiege the castle of São Jorge, the government sent four galleys and four triremes to Guinea. But the name of ' de Canes ' inspired such dread in Portuguese hearts that a second armada of ten ships sailed from Lisbon in the following February.[1] In other ways, too, the government followed old lines of policy, convoying the annual fleets, intimidating the negroes, sending their fast oar-propelled galleys along the coast from the castle of São Jorge to head off interlopers from the traffic and, occasionally, burning the native canoes.

But the Portuguese discovered two things : while you could convoy an annual fleet from Lisbon to Mina, you could not give adequate protection to a large number of small ships engaged in local or casual trade ; and while you could intimidate the natives who lived just under the walls of the forts, you could not subject the more remote tribes who were often in feud with the black subjects of Portugal, as were the Fetu and the Conrani. The results were that local shipping was victimised by pirates, and the Portuguese were unable to hinder those traders, who trafficked, like captain Wyndham, " on this side and beyond " but not under the guns of the fort of São Jorge. The menace to local shipping was frightful : caravels with cargoes of slaves, ivory, hides and wax were frequently seized, when describing the course from Senegambia and the Rio de S. Domingo to Santiago Island, and so were sugar-laden hulks *en route* from São Thomé to Flanders. Indeed, many of the interlopers were what we of the twentieth century would call pirates, though they might flourish before their contemporaries letters of authority, marque and reprisal, secured from the Prince of Condé, the King of Navarre and the Prince of Denmark, and so salve their sixteenth-century consciences. Such a one was Tristram Maynard, who departed with two ships from England to make a voyage to Guinea and, being forced by a storm into the Road of St. Mary in the Scilly Isles, raided a Spanish hulk which was likewise driven to shelter there, and returned at once

---

[1] B.M., Cotton MS. Nero B.1, f. 156 ; P.R.O., S.P. 70, 98, ff. 43-4.

to Plymouth with his plunder. Fortune so favoured Tristram that he did not have to plunder as far afield as Guinea (1570–1).[1]

King Sebastian, wishing to protect casual as well as regular shipping in Guinea, issued elaborate instructions in November 1571, which provided for a further extension of the existing system of armed convoys. In future, no ship of more than thirty tons was to leave Portugal unless it carried artillery, arms and men according to certain prescribed quotas ; and all ships, which sailed beyond the Barbary coast, were to be armed. Shipwrights were to be subsidised for each large galley which they built, and men, who took these galleys to Guinea and Brazil at their own expense, were to keep such prizes as they might make of interloping foreign ships. Moreover, Sebastian empowered his subjects, if they so desired, to patrol the islands and coasts of Africa with armed vessels and to seize interlopers. Then followed the new arrangements for the convoys. Ships for São Thomé might leave Portugal in any month between August and March, but they were to sail in fleets of not fewer than four ships, under a chief-captain who was to swear to do all in his power to safeguard his fleet. Again, should two or more fleets leave for São Thomé or Brazil at the same time, they were all to sail together, and ships for the islands of Cape Verde and the rivers of Guinea were to sail with them. All these fleets were to go in company as far as Santiago Island. Single merchant ships or warships for Guinea were forbidden to weigh anchor, except they should sail with the East Indies armada. Similar convoy arrangements were to hold for the homeward journeys, and any fleet from São Thomé and Guinea, which happened to meet a returning Portuguese squadron, was to sail with it and under the orders of its chief-captain. Whenever a great concourse of interlopers threatened shipping near the African coast, returning ships were to await the arrival of the armadas from Mina and the East Indies.[2] Thus, by amplifying earlier regulations, Sebastian tried to counter the assault of the scheming corsairs.

Meanwhile, his agents scrutinised events in England and France with great care. His envoys sent regular reports to Lisbon about the departure of ships from the ports, while the

[1] P.R.O., H.C.A. 1, 39, 24 February 1571.
[2] *Leys e Provisões del Rei D. Sebastião*, Law of 3 November 1571.

ambassadors of Spain gave what help they could. Traders and travellers, returning to Lisbon from the danger-zones, revealed to the government whatever they had learnt.[1] The progress of an interloping fleet would be closely followed and attempts made to discover its strength and destination. Thus fishing caravels, which sailed into Lisbon harbour from the Barbary coast, brought news of Hawkins's fleet in 1568.[2] Then, armed fleets would be sent to anticipate the enemy and, if possible, to destroy him. Success did not always grace these efforts, for the interlopers met guile with guile. Just as the French corsairs had often concealed their intentions in the days of Jean Ango, so now the English privateers sometimes tried to throw the Portuguese off the scent. Strangewyse in 1559 pretended a voyage to La Rochelle, Barbary or Benin, but intended an attack on the castle of São Jorge da Mina.[3] It would seem from the records that even the mariners on board believed that they were to go to La Rochelle. Probably, it was easier to persuade seamen to take ship for La Rochelle than for Guinea, but we may ascribe another motive to Strangewyse in thus hiding the truth from his crew. He would not endanger the success of his venture by giving scope for gossip at the ports, where wandered spies in the pay of Portugal.

Some of the bigger men of the Elizabethan Age, like John Hawkins, might make known the true object of their adventures, but lesser men could not afford to risk the dangerous consequences of publicity. It is likely that many expeditions, nominally destined for La Rochelle, were in reality directed farther afield. La Rochelle was a favourite resort for privateers and pirates, and a valuable half-way house on the route to the Azores, the Cape Verde archipelago and Guinea. To quote one hitherto unpublished example: Thomas Fenner who, together with a notorious pirate, Edward Cook of Southampton, set out in the autumn of 1564 to make a voyage to Guinea, stopped at La Rochelle on the way.[4] Duplicity on the part of the corsairs often misled the Portuguese so that their precautions proved vain. The story of the struggle in the second quarter of the century was being repeated in the third. But now, in

[1] P.R.O., S.P. 70, 98, ff. 43–4.
[2] Ibid.
[3] P.R.O., H.C.A., 1, 35, 13–16 August 1559.
[4] P.R.O., H.C.A. 1, 36, 26 December 1564.

addition, the invention of the Portuguese failed. They seem to have been unable to devise new expedients to counter the old cunning of the interlopers.

Meanwhile, the European negotiations dragged on. In 1559 Jean Nicot, representing France in Lisbon, opposed any concession to the Portuguese demands. But his firmness did not stop João Pereira d'Amtas, the Portuguese ambassador, from protesting vigorously in Paris : Queen Catherine, in September, sent him the letters patent relating to Mina, which King Francis I had issued more than twenty years earlier.[1] However, the government of France preferred the advice of Jean Nicot and so gave d'Amtas very little satisfaction. Reply appears to have been made in April 1561 to the effect that, since the French had long been wont to go to the fisheries about Cape Verde and other places, they were minded to continue their visits.[2] Subsequently, however, the Portuguese took advantage of a project for a marriage between King Sebastian and Marguerite, the Duchess of Valois and sister of King Charles IX. As the Austrians were also angling for the hand of Sebastian, he was able to impose terms. He made it a condition of accepting the French princess that her countrymen should cease voyaging to Guinea and the Indies. Negotiations, begun in 1563, were still running on these lines in 1572.[3] The French king, for his part, could disclaim responsibility for the illicit expeditions and point out that they were the work of a rebel faction, the huguenots. This fact and the marriage project tended to alleviate the tension between France and Portugal, but neither led to a satisfactory solution of the Guinea problem.

Anglo-Portuguese negotiations during this period were equally unsuccessful, but of a far graver character. The great concourse of English mariners to West Africa rendered the task of Portuguese ambassadors in London a heavier and more important one than that of their compatriots in Paris. A succession of Lusitanian diplomats advanced all the old arguments about priority of discovery, the cost in men and money formerly entailed in conquering Guinea, and the papal division of the world. But Queen Elizabeth was even less impressed than the

---

[1] E. Falgairolle, *Jean Nicot*, pp. 17-18, 38-9 ; *Quadro Elementar*, iii. 367.
[2] *Cal. S. P. For.*, 1561-2, no. 124.
[3] *Quadro Elementar*, iii. 383, 395-6, 399, 427, 445, 451-3.

former King of France by the lengthy verbiage of the diplomatic agents of her " well-beloved brother ", King Sebastian. Admittedly, a royal edict of May 1561 obliged the English adventurers to observe certain formalities before embarking for the Guinea Coast, but this was tantamount to official recognition of the validity of their activities.[1] Sir William Cecil, with his usual caution, tried to adopt the same tone in his replies as the French, and instructed his ambassador to follow closely the Franco-Portuguese discussions.[2] But, in effect, the queen responded to the Portuguese protests by reaffirming the principle of effective occupation as a basis for possession. There was no reason, she declared, why her subjects should be prevented from going to those parts of Africa or Ethiopia, where the King of Portugal had no dominion, collected no tribute and exacted no obedience.[3]

However, after the depredations of John Hawkins on the Guinea Coast (1567–8), and especially after the issue of letters of marque and reprisal to the brothers Winter against Portuguese shipping, the Lisbon government came to regard the situation as intolerable. They had threatened war in May 1568. Nine months later they confiscated all English property in Portugal, and began military preparations. Tension between the two nations rose to fever-pitch and did not relax for two years. There was a complete stoppage of Anglo-Portuguese trade. It was not until 1571 that friendly relations were restored. During the interim period, a large number of Englishmen made the voyage to Guinea.[4] But Queen Elizabeth, facing what professor Pollard has called the gravest crisis of her reign, did not wish to alienate King Sebastian along with the pope, Philip of Spain, Mary Queen of Scots and the Northern Earls. Moreover, an influential group of merchants, interested in Anglo-Portuguese trade, pressed for peace. Accordingly, a concession of a vague and temporary kind appears to have been made to Portugal. When Hector Nunez and William Curtis thought to make a voyage from London to Guinea, their scheme was forbidden (March 1571);[5] that same month, John Garratt, master of the

---

[1] *Cal. S. P. For.*, 1561–2, no. 157.
[2] *Ibid.*, nos. 103, 124, 125.
[3] *Ibid.*, no. 820 ; J. A. Williamson, *John Hawkins*, pp.58–62.
[4] *Vide supra*, pp. 171–2.
[5] *A. P. C.*, 1571–5, p. 20 ; B.M., Cotton MS. Galba C. iv, f. 22.

Castle of Comfort, was lying off Harwich ready with his ship to go to Cape Verde and the coast of Barbary, but letters of the council were brought to him vetoing his adventure and, with an ill-grace, he was compelled to obey;[1] while Bartholomew Bayão, planning to sail to the Senegal and to transport slaves thence to the West Indies, was delayed by the order of the government.[2] Meantime, the terms of a treaty between England and Portugal were drafted and considered (February 1572).[3]

There is little more to tell of European enterprise in Guinea during the remaining years of the reign of King Sebastian. After ten years of considerable anxiety, the Portuguese in West Africa were not again exceedingly troubled until the Spanish annexation of their country and their empire. John Hawkins sent three English ships to Guinea in the autumn of 1572 and, even yet, our records may reveal evidence of a few who copied this pioneer.[4] But it would seem, for the most part, that, except for an occasional visit to the Cape Verde Islands *en route* for the Caribbean like that of Andrew Barker in 1576–7,[5] English seamen avoided the Guinea navigation after 1571. Possibly the closing of the slave market in the West Indies to Englishmen was partly responsible for this; so perhaps was the willingness of certain English merchants to forgo the Guinea trade in order to preserve that with Barbary.[6] The negotiations between England and Portugal were very protracted. At length, a treaty was signed whereby Englishmen were allowed to trade to the Madeiras and the Azores (1576).[7] No mention was made of either Barbary or Guinea in the treaty, so that the real dispute remained unsettled. The Portuguese seem to have interpreted these omissions as implying *inter alia* that the Mina traffic was closed to their rivals.[8] Probably, they regarded the treaty as a confirmation of the principle laid down in the oral agreement of 1559 in respect of the " lines of amity ": the Madeiras and the Azores provided the limits beyond which

---

[1] P.R.O., H.C.A., 13, 18, 1 April 1571.
[2] *Cal. S. P. Span.*, 1568–79, nos. 238, 242.
[3] B.M., Cotton MS. Nero B.1, f. 155.
[4] B.M., Add. MS. 26,056. B, f. 291b.
[5] Hakluyt, x. 82–8.
[6] V. M. Shillington and A. B. W. Chapman, *The Commercial Relations of England and Portugal*, pp. 143–4.
[7] B.M., Cotton MS. Nero B.1, f. 180.
[8] *Cal. S. P. Span.*, 1580–6, p. 3.

traffic was forbidden, except by the special licence of the King of Portugal. Yet the real position was vague and remained so, because, under the existing circumstances, the English government found it paid to refrain from interpreting the clauses of the treaty.

The stalemate after 1571 was not so marked where the French interlopers were concerned. As we have seen, they probably eschewed the slave trade from West Africa, and so were not affected by the closing of the Caribbean to all but the legal contractors. Consequently, a steady trickle of French ships to Guinea marked this last phase in our story. Most of these went to Senegambia and Sierra Leone and set a course thence for the West Indies.[1] Huguenot warfare against the Catholic League in France helps to explain the continuity of French Guinea enterprise. La Rochelle remained a hotbed of piracy, so much so that King Sebastian promised to support Henry III in its reduction (1575).[2] Moreover, a group of Rouen merchants, who had formerly been interested in the Barbary and Guinea trades, now associated themselves in the Hallé-Le Seigneur company, founded nominally to trade with the Canary Islands and the Barbary coast. But three of the leading confederates were interested in the Guinea traffic, Laurent Hallé, Eustache Travache and Adrien Le Seigneur. Indeed, the Le Seigneurs created a family tradition of French trade with Guinea: Adrien Le Seigneur helped to finance a voyage to Guinea in 1546; Alfonse Le Seigneur invested in the Benin trade in 1554; Adrien was associated with another Rouen merchant in a project for a voyage to the Mina coast (1566); another member of the family, Jacques by name, who had trafficked to Lisbon, Andalusia and Madeira in 1549, busied himself in the Guinea trade along with Adrien in 1580; while as late as 1595 Adrien seems still to have been interested.[3] It is not surprising, therefore, that the Hallé-Le Seigneur company should have extended its operations to Cape Verde (c. 1573).

Probably a number of enterprises, *prima facie* for Barbary, were actually more ambitious. A phrase in the testimony of an

---

[1] C. et P. Bréard, *Documents relatifs à la marine normande*, pp. 148-54.
[2] *Quadro Elementar*, iii, 460-1.
[3] Roncière, iv. 91-4; Address by C. de la Beaurepaire in the *Bulletin de la Société de l'Histoire de Normandie*, 1887-90, pp. 255-6; P.R.O., H.C.A., 24, 39, no. 16; Gosselin, *op. cit.*, pp. 91, 151, 154.

examinee before the English High Court of Admiralty suggests this : one, John Garrett, stated in April 1571 that his ship was bound upon a voyage " unto Caput Viride & soe unto the Quoast of Barbarye ".[1] He implies thereby that Barbary was at least as far, if not beyond, Cape Verde ! We may deduce that the word ' Barbary ', like the phrase " being at the seas ", concealed many secrets from sixteenth century courts of law. Is it not natural, then, that the Rouen company should have traded beyond Barbary ?

This company was chiefly interested in the trade of Senegambia. Cargoes of amber, wax, ivory, gum, hides and civet were purchased from the Jalofos, through the agency of Portuguese half-breeds and exiles, and taken home to France. For over thirty years the French trade with this region seems to have been unbroken. Occasionally the ships of the company were attacked by Portuguese brigantines from Santiago, but, in that event, they would take refuge in Beziguiche harbour, a few miles south of Cape Verde. Indeed, the Portuguese seem to have abandoned the local trade partly because of the intensity of French rivalry and the danger of piracy, and partly because one at least of the native princes, Boudomel Bixirim, though he welcomed the French interlopers, was hostile to the Portuguese.[2] As we have remarked before, the Santiagians now traded mainly with the mainland settlements around the rivers Grande and S. Domingo. However, there were other Frenchmen who traded to Sierra Leone and to Mina, as a perusal of contemporary documents would reveal.[3] It appears from what is, unfortunately, unreliable evidence that the destruction of Fort Accra encouraged French interlopers to return to the Mina coast. They reduced their prices and thus, in spite of Portuguese threats, won the favour of the negroes. The Portuguese burnt the native canoes, but the blacks built new ones and trafficked with the French.[4] And so a little drama, similar in every detail to a much greater one between Portuguese and Hollanders which began twenty years later, was played out in 1576–8.

[1] P.R.O., H.C.A. 13, 18, 1 April 1571.
[2] Almada, *Tratado breve dos Rios de Guiné*, pp. 13–15 ; Guerreiro, *Relações Annuis*, ii. 130b ; P.R.O., H.C.A. 24, 59.
[3] Bréard, *op. cit.*, pp. 148–76, *passim*.
[4] T. Astley, *Voyages*, ii. 568–9 ; P. D. Marees, *Beschryvinge van het Goutcuste*, pp. 88–9.

Yet, around the castle of São Jorge and the forts of Axem and Samma the original white colonisers preserved their hegemony. Twice a year, in the autumn and the spring, fleets still left Lisbon for the Mina coast to load the gold which was stored in the warehouse at São Jorge; the contractors of Mina still maintained their factors at the forts; tribute for the right to fish was still exacted from the natives in those few places where the arm of Portugal yet stretched; the personnel of the Guinea officials was still changed every three years; and still the guns of São Jorge and its smaller sisters threatened death to all who ignored the monopoly.[1] Beyond the Mina coast monopoly was more real, for a flourishing and expanding slave trade was pursued around the coast of Benin.[2] But São Thomé Island was slowly and imperceptibly declining, though its function as a base for the slave traffic gave it prolonged life until Loanda began to displace it after 1578.

. . . .

It was just at this time that King Sebastian led his ill-fated expedition against the Moors in northern Africa. His death in 1578 completely altered the situation in Guinea. Within two years Portugal passed under the sway of Spain and, not many months after that, the Portuguese empire overseas was also reduced to submission. West Africa, though not without resistance, submitted with the rest. The result of the change was that a position of uncertain stalemate gave way to one of acute rivalry. On the one hand the bitter enemies of Spain at once attacked her new imperial possessions. On the other hand, Philip II was able to draw upon the wealth of his older empire in the new world to defend his newer empire in Africa. Philip called in the new world to redress the balance in West Africa, but his enemies invoked the New Religion to redress the territorial balance overseas. The protestants of England and the huguenots of France soon found new allies in the calvanistic zealots of Holland for the mortal struggle over trade and territory in Guinea. Enterprise in Guinea ceased to be a story of beginnings and became one of acute rivalry. Spain sought to prop up a decaying empire with obsolete theories; the protestant powers looked forward to a future partition. Monopoly had waxed and waned.

[1] P. D. Marees, *op. cit.*, pp. 220–2.   [2] *Ibid.*, pp. 230–1.

APPENDIX TO THE SECOND EDITION

1. Professor R. Mauny confirms the view of de la Roncière in ' Les prétendues navigations dieppoises à la côte occidentale d'Afrique au xive siècle ' in *Bulletin de l'I.F.A.N.*, xii (1950).

2. This background summary of the situation in Portugal on the eve of the voyages of exploration needs modifying at least in the following respects: (1) It is probably significant that the vigorous house of Aviz came to power with the support of the rising merchant bourgoisie. Although Livermore contends (*New history of Portugal* [1969], p. 107) that the influence of mercantile families has been exaggerated, and though Boxer (*Portuguese seaborne empire* [1969], p. 25) argues that the merchants and shipowners of Lisbon and Oporto displayed little interest in maritime exploration until the trade in gold, slaves and ivory at Arguin opened up the prospect of profit, it remains true that the positive enthusiasm of the royal dynasty for trade and discovery, from the reign of John I to that of Manuel the Fortunate, the Pepper King, was reinforced by the backing of the merchant class as well as of the papacy, the church and the aristocracy.

(2) Aviz leadership in overseas expansion was facilitated by the strength of the monarchy at home, and this contributed to the relative advantages which Portugal enjoyed at this time over other possible maritime rivals. Notwithstanding the prominence given by the chroniclers, especially Ruy de Pina, to the protracted struggle between the monarchy and the feudal factions associated with the Bragança family, the crown had effectively destroyed the power of the old nobility before the accession of King John I.

(3) The motives of Prince Henry ' the Navigator', however, are still as controversial as his personality is enigmatic. This is so, despite the very thorough review of all the evidence by scholars from many parts of the world before, during and since the Congress of the Portuguese World, held in Lisbon in 1960 to commemorate the quincentennial anniversary of his death, and despite the documenta-

tion in fourteen volumes (to date) of *Monumenta Henricina* (Coimbra, 1960-72). Henry's dedication to discovery is not in dispute; nor is his primacy in its initiation and promotion. Some modern scholars, however, attach importance to the part played by his elder brother, Dom Pedro, especially during the regency of the years 1438-47. Furthermore, recent scholarship inclines to the view that the geographical knowledge available to the prince, and to the members of his school of navigation at Cape Sagres, may have been substantially greater than the surviving records explicitly state. The Henrician circle may have known much more about the ancient transaharan gold trade, more about 'Bilad Ghana' (Land of Ghana) or 'Bilad al-Sudan' (Land of the Blacks), and more about the negro peoples of the Sudanic empires. These Portuguese, who " had known so much and told so little " (R. Hallett, *Penetration of Africa to* 1815 [1965], p. xvi), whether traders, officials or chroniclers, were much too discreet, and much too loyal to the policy of national secrecy, to give anything away to their rivals. It is possible, therefore, that the prince was not unaware of the feasibility of a direct sea-route to the Orient south round Africa; or at least that, as the frontier of discovery along the West African coast was advanced, the possibility dawned upon him. But this must remain an open question. One last point requires comment. What were Henry's real motives? Recent scholarship gives priority to the economic urge. As Bovill argued, in his *Golden trade of the Moors* (1958), it makes more sense to attribute to the prince the desire to tap by sea the old transaharan gold trade than to interpret his work in terms of scientific curiosity, or the crusading ideal, or " the incessant war on Islam ". Other scholars stress the shortage of gold and silver bullion in Europe, arguing that output, notably of Hungarian silver, was failing to keep pace with rising demand. It is suggested that in Portugal in particular the royal treasury was denuded, not only by coinage debasement but also because of the long-drawn-out struggles with Castile. The dream of exchanging ' baser merchandise for nobler ' (i.e., beads or cloth for gold), by the opening up of direct seaborne trade with subsaharan Africa, dazzled the eyes of knowledgeable contemporaries. It is reflected in the project of the Englishmen, Tintam and Fabian, described in this book on pages 60-62. The lure of the gold trade, so the argument goes, was irresistible. One version of this as the spur to discovery is that "religion supplied the pretext and gold the

APPENDIX

motive" (C. Cipolla, *Guns and sails* [1965], pp. 132-6). I myself have reservations. Each generation is apt to reinterpret its history in the light of its own hypotheses; and in the twentieth century it is modish to explain human actions in economic or materialistic terms. But was this so in pre-Reformation Europe? Religion (and the crusading spirit) would seem to have been as powerful a factor in the life-pattern of fifteenth-century Western Christendom as profit is today, and the motivation behind the work of Prince Henry must surely be seen and understood in terms of the century in which he lived.

3. The name 'Guinea' (Portuguese 'Guiné') is probably derived, not from 'Ghana', but from the Berber word for 'negro', namely 'aguinaou'. Medieval Arab knowledge filtered slowly into Europe: a Genoese map of *c*. 1320 shows 'Gunuia'; and on the Catalan map of 1375 the legend 'Ginyia' appears (Delafosse, *Haut-Sénégal-Niger*, ii [1912], 277-8; Bovill, *op. cit.*, p. 116, footnote). To the Portuguese by the mid-fifteenth century 'Guinee . . . is the land of the negroes'; it is a vaguely-defined but vast region lying to the south of the Sahara desert; its capital city or chief trade mart is known to them as Djene (Jenne) or Gine. Consequent upon maritime discovery, they applied the name also to the coastal regions of West Africa, as the chronicle of Azurara repeatedly shows; then, in 1455, the papal bull *Romanus pontifex* granted to the rulers of Portugal all the lands 'from the capes of Bojador and Nam through all Guinea and beyond'; and the climax to this misuse of the name came, after the building of fort St. George (Elmina) in 1482, when King John II of Portugal adopted the style and title of 'Lord of Guinea'. It was a particular misuse of the name, because the rulers of Portugal never at any time exercised any authority over the interior of West Africa. Later writers from Europe, concerned to describe the coastal trades, came to distinguish between 'Upper Guinea' and 'Lower Guinea'. As indicated in the text, sixteenth-century Portuguese regularly used the term 'Guinea of Cape Verde' to describe the coast from the Senegal to Sierra Leone, and they referred to the region south of the Gambia as 'the rivers of Guinea'. The French, having their main base (later, St. Louis fort) in Senegal, came to describe this region south of the Gambia as 'the rivers of the South'. Seventeenth-century writers, not least Barbot, drew a very clear distinction between the 'Upper Coast' or 'Upper Guinea' (i.e., from the Senegal to Cape Mount) and the 'Lower

APPENDIX

Coast' or 'Lower Guinea' (i.e., from Cape Mount to Cape Lopo Gonçalves).

4. This brief account of some of the coastal and inland peoples between the Senegal and Sierra Leone, which was based on some of the contemporary Portuguese records, needs to be revised in the light of much recent research. Race classification is a controversial issue in modern African studies, but the reader may care to consult the relevant sections of J. H. Greenberg, *Languages of Africa* (The Hague, 1970) and G. P. Murdock, *Africa: its peoples and their culture history* (New York, 1959). A useful summary of what is now known about the peoples of Upper Guinea may be found in Ajayi, vol. i, chs. 4, 6, 11 and 12. Bovill, *op. cit.*, has described the rise and fall of the interior empires of the Western Sudan. Rodney in his *History of Upper Guinea* (pp. 6-16, 38-70, and map 3 on p. 57) surveys the shifting distribution of the peoples on or near the coastal region, and his map shows their locations around 1545. The peoples named here in my book have been identified as follows: the 'Jalofos' were the Wolof, the term 'Jolof' being the name of the chiefdom; the 'Barbacini' (or Barbacijs) people of Serer stock living along the Salum valley; the 'Serreri' Serer; the 'Mandiguas' Mandingos, occupying the interior but reaching down to the Gambia estuary; the 'Beafares' the Biafada, living on and south of the Jeba river; the 'Guogoliis' (or Cocolin) probably Landuma-Tyapi: Tyapi from the interior still call themselves 'Cocoli'; the 'Naluns' (or Nanuus) the Nalu, north of the river Nunez; the 'Teymenes' (or Teminis) the Temne, inland but also on the coast at the mouth of the Scarcies river; the 'Bouloees' (or Bolones) the Bullom, on the coast from the Scarcies to the Kittam; the 'Jaalunguas' (or Jalungas) probably of Susu stock; and the 'Souzos' the Susu. By collating early records (e.g., Gomes, Cadomosto, Pereira, Fernandes) with later sixteenth-century accounts (e.g., d'Almada), it is now possible to reconstruct fairly accurately the names and locations of virtually all the more important peoples known to the Portuguese, and this is precisely what such scholars as Dr. P. E. H. Hair have done so well (see Hair in *JAH*, viii.2[1967],249-56; J. Suret-Canale in Ajayi, i.434-38; and A. Teixeira da Mota, *Guiné portuguesa* [2v, Lisbon, 1954].).

5. In fact, Pacheco Pereira makes several derogatory references to the negroes of the Malagueta (and Ivory) Coasts: they are " evil people [who] attack our ships in great canoes ", " idolators "

without "religion or goodness", and "vicious people and seldom at peace". However, since he was a patriot and a christian, since he deplores the decline or ruination of the former trade along this part of the Guinea coast partly because the shrewd local merchants had begun to ask higher prices, and above all since his text records the active involvement of his countrymen here in slave trading, his strictures on the local peoples can scarcely be regarded as objective.

6. Ryder (pp. 26–8) has identified the rivers and peoples along the Slave Coast mentioned in the *Esmeraldo*. In particular, he identifies the 'Jos' as the Ijo. But see also Hair in *JAH*, viii.2 [1967], 261–5.

7. On fort Arguin and its trade, see Blake, i.22–27.

8. The date of the second voyage of Diogo Gomes is uncertain. Most scholars agree that it was undertaken between 1458 and 1460, probably in 1460.

9. Part of the contemporary evidence, on which this account of the first phase of Castilian rivalry with Portugal for the developing trade of Guinea is based, is translated and printed in Blake, i.185–92, 200–03. For the wider background to Castilo-Portuguese rivalry, see Livermore, *op. cit.*, pp. 111–19. Boxer (*op. cit.*, pp. 20–23) makes an important analysis of the papal bulls, particularly in the context of the motives for Portuguese discovery. He argues that an earlier bull—*Dum diversas* of 18 June 1452—though explicitly concerned only with the Portuguese in Morocco, was implicitly designed to provide papal backing also for Portuguese action in Senegambia. He confirms that the words used in the papal bulls "closely follow(s) that of the preliminary requests for their promulgation made by the Portuguese Crown". In addition, he emphasizes the significance of the bull *Romanus pontifex*—the "charter of Portuguese imperialism"—as the papal authority for the Portuguese monopoly in Guinea, by referring to the fact that the terms of the relevant clause in the bull were solemnly proclaimed in Lisbon cathedral on 3 October 1455 in the presence of foreign representatives including those of Castile.

10. See a full and detailed analysis of the progress of Portuguese discovery from Cape Bojador to Cape St. Catherine in A. Teixeira da Mota, *Topónimos de origem portuguesa na costa ocidental de Africa* (Bissau, 1950). This work lists all the capes, bays, rivers, creeks, points, islands, etc., known to have been named by the Portuguese as they advanced along the coast or soon afterwards, and gives the

written historical sources from which the information is derived. The section dealing with the coast from Cape Palmas to Cape St. Catherine may be found on pp. 247-338. See also, Blake, i. 3-18.

11. Jean Barbot seems to have made two voyages to West Africa, one in 1678-9 and another in 1681-2, and his *Description* must be seen as mostly of late seventeenth-century derivation, though some parts of his work were borrowed from other writers. The outcome of meticulous research by a group of scholars, and especially of Dr. P. E. H. Hair, is that we now know that the work, as translated and published by Awnsham and J. Churchill in 1732, contains some additional material not contained in the original versions which were written in French between *c*. 1683 and 1688. MS. 63, in the Admiralty Library, London, which I have consulted by kind permission of the Librarian, comprises the substance of Barbot's writings, taking the form of a series of letters, and includes the engravings. There is also a version of his journal of his voyage of 1678-9 in B.M., Add. MS. 28, 788, and I understand from Professor John D. Fage that this manuscript is being prepared for publication.

12. Most of the more important Castilian records about this first challenge to Portugal in West Africa, and also some other source material, have been translated and printed in Blake, i. 185-246.

13. Eustache de la Fosse's account of his Mina voyage in 1479-80 has come to be recognised as a record of unique value for the historian. It is the only surviving, direct and personal description of a fifteenth-century trading voyage to the Gold Coast. Other accounts of other voyages may—indeed, surely must—have been written in his generation; if so, they are not known to exist today. His alone has come down to us. Internal evidence suggests that the extant narrative was written down long afterwards, and not before 1516. Therefore, it may contain information about Guinea picked up subsequent to the voyage, and so it must be used with caution. It is nevertheless a remarkable record. It shows Eustache himself as a merchant of consequence and a link in a wide Flemish-Castilian network interested in Guinea and particularly the Mina gold trade; and this confirms other evidence that reports and rumours of the discovery of 'the Mine' by the captains of Fernão Gomes had caused unusual excitement in Europe. Eustache, like others including his financial backers, clearly hoped to take advantage of the war between Castile and Portugal to challenge

the latter's attempt to monopolise the Mina gold trade. He strikes one as the Towerson of the fifteenth century: he was curious as well as knowledgeable; he kept a careful record of prices prevailing on the Mina coast; he conversed with his captors about navigational aids for the Mina voyage; and, again like Towerson, he wrote down a brief (Akan) vocabulary, which is unique for its time and has recently been thoroughly analysed for the purpose of tribal identification (see P. E. H. Hair, ' A note on de la Fosse's " Mina " vocabulary ' in *Journal of West African Languages*, iii [1966], 55–7; also *ibid.*, v [1968], 129–32). Eustache was also familiar with trading conditions on the Mina coast: he knew, for example, that ' Chama ' (Shama or Samma) and ' L'aldee duos partz ' (the Village of Two Parts) were the two main ports for getting gold. We know from Pacheco Pereira's *Esmeraldo* that Shama was the place " where the first gold was obtained in barter ', and it would seem that gold was being traded at the Village of Two Parts well before the time when Diogo d'Azambuja chose it as the site for the fortress of São Jorge da Mina. Eustache's record is also the earliest to describe the preliminary negotiations (which had to precede trade) with the local Mina rulers, whom he describes as the ' manse ' and ' caramanse' (see new note 28). Furthermore, he explains how the opening of the gold barter at Mina had to await the arrival of the merchants who " came down from the mountains to buy their goods ". The failure of his expedition tells us even more. As explained in the text, the Portuguese intervened, captured his ship, confiscated its cargo, and obliged Eustache himself to take part in the sale of the goods ashore. His two captors bore famous names: Fernão do Po, who was, writes Eustache, a gentleman who treated his captive with the courtesy befitting his rank; and Diogo Cão, ' *un bien rebelle furs* ', as Eustache comments, and we must presume that Cão was more ruthless than Fernão do Po in dealing with interlopers! We are told, too, how Fernão do Po, with two caravels detached from the annual Mina fleet, was sent east 200 leagues to the ' Rio dos Esclavos ' to obtain slaves for sale at Mina, and in due course returned with 400 slaves. This is the first, direct evidence we have that, by this time, the slave trade between the ' five (slave) rivers of Benin ' and Mina was well organised; it is the earliest indication that, every year on the arrival from Portugal of the Mina fleet, part of it was immediately despatched east to the Benin coast for this purpose (see Ryder, pp. 24–7; Blake, i. 17-18). Pereira

APPENDIX

in his *Esmeraldo* (p. 121) affords later confirmation of this. The slaves were sold at Mina as load-bearers for the Dyula merchants who came down from the interior bringing gold for sale to the Portuguese (see Ivor Wilks, 'A medieval trade-route from the Niger to the Gulf of Guinea' in *JAH*, iii. 2 [1962], 337–41; *Ghana Notes and Queries*, no. 12 [June 1972], 3–8; and for the identification of the merchants from 'distant lands', named by Pacheco Pereira, see P. E. H. Hair in *JAH*, viii. 2 [1967], 259).

14. But see new note 2.

15. For an analysis of the evidence of English interest in Guinea, 1480–88, and the documentation, see Blake, ii. 263–9, 295–8.

16. It is desirable to see this problem in the perspective of the interplay of papal and dynastic politics of the late fifteenth century. The papal bulls *Inter caetera* (4 May 1493) and specifically *Dudum siquidem* (26 September 1493) were contrary to previous grants to Portugal, certainly since 1454: *Dudum siquidem* literally revoked previous grants. John II's concern is reflected in the fact that he used every possible method, including bribery, to reverse the situation. The Treaty of Tordesillas of 1494 effectively restored the balance in favour of Portugal in her struggle with Castile for the newly-discovered lands and particularly ensured afterwards that Brazil would fall within her sphere. The controversial bulls of 1493, of course, were the work of pope Alexander VI, an Aragonese and a Borgia, and generally accounted the most corrupt of all renaissance popes. In these circumstances, it is unlikely that the rulers of France and England attached much (if any) importance to so extraordinary an example of papal arbitration. See A. Da Silva Rego, *Portuguese colonisation in the sixteenth century: a study of the royal ordinances* (Johannesburg, 1959), pp. 13–21.

17. Much more is known today about the farming out of the 'trades of Guinea' than was the case when this section of my book was first written. Some of the 'contracts' are documented and explained in Blake, i. 22, 36–9, 57–63. They include the contracts of 'Arguim', 'Senegal', 'Gambia' (or 'Gambia and Cantor'), the 'rivers of Guinea', 'Sierra Leone', 'Mina', and the 'five rivers of Benin' (sometimes described as 'Rios dos Escravos' and in at least one instance as 'Rio Primeiro', i.e., the 'first' of the 'five rivers'. See Ryder, pp. 26–7). Some contracts authorised the farmers to trade in particular regions, e.g., Gambia and Cantor, or the 'rivers of Guinea'; others related to commodities, such as

the 'pepper' contract which, I suspect, entitled the farmers to purchase 'pepper' wherever it could be got in Guinea. Much the most prized of the several 'contracts' was the gold trade of the Mina coast. If we accept the statement of João de Barros that control of the gold trade reverted from Fernão Gomes to the crown in 1475—and correspondence between King Manuel and the officers of the Casa da Mina appears to confirm this (Blake, i. 99–108 and *passim*)—, there are hints in the records that at least from the reign of King Sebastian and possibly earlier, this trade was regularly auctioned to contractors. I now question the statement in the text that Affonso de Torres was a Mina contractor in 1541: certainly he traded to Mina but not necessarily in the role of a contractor. It is established, however, that the Mina trade was farmed in 1567 (see p. 179). Long afterwards, an anonymous writer, in listing the officers at Axim fort and the castle of São Jorge da Mina and stating their salaries, recorded (*c.* 1607) that the Mina trade was sometimes farmed out, and that " the last farm, which was leased to João Baptista Revelasques, was valued at 60,000 cruzados . . . beyond which he had to pay all the costs and the officers " (L. Cordeiro, *Memorias do Ultramar* [Lisbon, 1881], no. IV, pp. 13–14). If the Portuguese records of this farm of the Mina trade perished in the Lisbon earthquake of 1755, a chance dispute in the English high court of admiralty has preserved part of the story of the involvement of the wealthy Revelasco family. The brothers Revelasco, João Baptista and Francisco, Italian-born but naturalised citizens of Portugal resident in Lisbon, bankers to Philip II of Spain, farmers of the Lisbon customs and of the East Indies 'pepper contract'— João was alleged to have enough pepper in his Lisbon house to load 30 ships—were also farmers of the Mina gold trade. Antonio de Sousa, a witness in the court dispute, testified in 1591 as follows (spelling and punctuation modernised): " That there was in the ship when she was taken [the *Francis*, returning from Elmina and seized by English privateers] 8 chests of grains [Guinea pepper], one chest of gold containing the value of 15,700 ducats [*c.* £4,000 at the exchange rate then prevailing], and nothing else but 8 negroes; which was [*sic*] laden in the same *Francis* by one, Simon Ffaraoesto, . . . for the proper use and account of Francisco Revelasco . . . Ffaraoesto is deputy general for the said Francisco Revelasco for all Genney and the domains subject to the castle de Mayne, which contains 200 leagues in length, that is to say, from Caput de Palma unto Rio de Volta. Which castle de Mayne and the domains thereof the said Francisco Revelasco doth rent and farm of the king for some 60,000 ducats by the year and 6 muskattes [civet cats], he the said Revelasco bearing and defraying all charges of war and otherwise for the defence of the said castle and coast . . . He [Antonio de Sousa] has seen the contract passed between the now king of Spain and the said Francisco Revelasco, and likewise he has seen the ordinances set down by . . . Revelasco to be observed and kept in . . . castle de Mayne and places aforesaid. . . . He was hired to serve . . . Revelasco at the castle de Mayne to see and view what goods were carried and recarried from and to the same place, and that no mariners or other persons should carry any gold or other goods from thence but that which was marked with the mark of the said Revelasco, for the space of three years, and was to have 150 ducats by the year for his wages. Of which time he served but 9 months there [he became sick and returned home], and for his coming and going he was to have his meat and drink and no more ". This is the most detailed account of any of the Guinea ' contracts ' known to me (see P.R.O., H.C.A. 13. 29: 27 Feb. and 12, 13, 16, 27 March 1591).

18. By now, as stated in the Preface, a substantial amount of additional archival material has been unearthed.

19. The four main areas in West Africa from which gold was formerly obtained were: (1) Bambuk, along the upper reaches of the Faleme river; (2) Bure, where the Tinkisso joins the river Niger; (3) the middle Black Volta river basin, known as the ' Lobi ' fields; and (4) the ' Akan ' fields in Ashanti (Asante). ' Wangara ', known to medieval Arab writers as the principal source of transaharan gold, was possibly a mis-spelling of Gangara which is in the Bure ' field '; but it is also the name by which Dyula merchants, active in promoting and controlling the gold trade, knew themselves. The gold was everywhere extracted from alluvial deposits. Shallow mining, as well as washing and sifting, was practised. There is a vivid description of the methods used today to extract gold in Bure in *Ghana Notes and Queries*, no. 1 [1961]. 4–5; and it is generally accepted that the methods so described are unlikely to have changed much over the past five centuries. It is also generally accepted that most, if not all, of the gold obtained by the Portuguese along the Mina coast came from Ashanti; the gold obtained by them in Upper Guinea came from Bambuk and perhaps some from Bure.

The 'trade war', which developed as a result of Portuguese efforts to divert by sea the much older commerce north across the Sahara, may be seen as one facet of the long struggle between the Cross and the Crescent, with the evangelising Portuguese taking the initiative; and, in this context, it is significant that King John III of Portugal forbade the Benin-Mina slave trade, on the grounds that the slaves were taken into the interior by their moslem Dyula masters to become converts, thereby strengthening the Islamic world. As Bovill pointed out (*op. cit.*, pp. 120–31), the Portuguese did not win this 'trade war': much of the gold dust continued to be carried overland to North African ports, especially from Bambuk, Bure and the Black Volta. Cloth of many varieties (hambels, burnouses, caps, etc.), much of it, as with the transaharan trade, from North Africa, linen, metalware and beads were among the inducements offered by the Portuguese traders to African merchants to bring the gold southwards down to the Mina coast. But if stocks warehoused in their fortress of São Jorge ran low, because of the failure of fresh supplies to arrive from Portugal, the Mina gold trade could be gravely damaged. Indeed, the supply position was a constant anxiety to governors of the fortress who were keen to promote a flourishing trade; and one of them, Antonio Froes, in a letter of 19 August 1513, referred directly to the trade war when he wrote of the "Mandinga leak, which was never so gaping as at present": Africans were taking the gold north instead of bringing it southwards to Mina! See A. Teixeira da Mota, 'The Mande trade in Costa da Mina according to Portuguese documents until the mid-sixteenth century', a paper read at the Conference on Mandingo Studies, School of Oriental and African Studies, London, 1972; also R. Mauny, *Tableau géographique*, pp. 293–9; Ajayi, i. 354–62; P. D. Curtin, 'The lure of Bambuk gold' in *JAH*, xiv. 4 (1973). 625–31.

20. As hinted here and elsewhere, a perennial issue in the sixteenth-century Portuguese colonial service was the maintenance of standards of integrity. Royal ordinances, however drastic or severe, did not necessarily win obedience. The greater problem was that of enforcement, especially because of corruption at all levels in the overseas service. The temptation to ignore, evade or deliberately flout royal regulations was strong because the private pickings in all branches of trade on the Mina coast were so high. How difficult this problem was is nicely reflected in the royal Manueline correspondence: the unreliability of the guards appointed

at Lisbon to oversee the loading and discharge of Mina cargo; the very strict control over trade at the Mina markets or ' fairs ', so as to check smuggling or illegal private trade, and the logistical problems which this posed; etc. (Blake, i. 99-106). Indeed, the record of corruption, real or alleged, among some of the governors of the castle at Mina, though by no means all, tells its own tale. Duarte Pacheco Pereira, governor from 1519 to 1522, holding the post as a reward for distinguished service to the crown, was brought home a royal prisoner from Elmina and accused of defrauding the royal treasury and seeking an illegal fortune in gold while there. Afterwards pardoned, he died apparently in mean circumstances. Much more revealing is the case, some forty years later, of Manuel de Mesquita Perestrello (see above, p. 178). Appointed governor in 1562, he was within the year, apparently by the instigation of merchants whom he had defrauded, brought home, tried and found guilty, and imprisoned; in 1569, he was pardoned. Among the charges made against him were that he: (1) failed to press home attacks upon interloping English ships trading on the Mina coast; (2) engaged secretly in private trade, selling bonded merchandise and buying prohibited Guinea pepper; (3) failed to pay over monies due to various Portuguese merchants adventuring in the Mina trade; and (4) manipulated prices at Mina to his own advantage. It was claimed by the prosecution that by devious and unlawful means he had amassed a fortune worth more than 30,000 cruzados. His prosecutors declared: " That he set the prices of the merchandise of other parties very low and that he took it at the said prices, and these being much lower than the current prices, they had no possibility of selling their goods, since he had not declared them lost to your highness . . . That, likewise, there were in the said caravel up to 20,000 bracelets and 100 cauldrons and close to 200 basins, beyond those included in your highness' goods; and that he . . . had them landed by Diogo Delgado, who was his overseer and managed his business, and by his orders and on his account had them landed and taken to the village [Mina town] by the guards, his servants, and had them placed in the houses of the negro chieftains, and they were sold on his account, and both by day and by night there came merchants to buy the said merchandise; and these transactions were public and generally known, so that during this time no bracelets, cauldrons or basins were sold at the *feitoria* [factory at Mina]. And that, by thus ordering the said bracelets,

APPENDIX

basins and cauldrons to be sold, he consented to the said Diogo Delgado and his servants to go by night to the village and stay out, when the gates of the fortress were closed, which was against the law. And that he did use strong language against the *meirinho* [police officer] for having gone to the village to find out where the bracelet was [*sic*]. And that from his window he did signal with fire to the said caravel to advise it when it was time to land the merchandise; and that many goods, chests and wicker baskets were introduced by the window into the house of the governor, which objects were hauled in by rope, since the fortress gates were already locked. And that on one night, at this time, there landed a boat from the said caravel, which was seen by a person who shouted out, and that he [the governor] came to the summons in most leisurely manner so as to give time to the crew to escape " (*THSG*, iii. 3 [1958]. 196-9, 206-10). This delightful and human, if wicked, story has all the drama of *Jamaica Inn*. It suggests a fluctuating situation on the Mina coast which from time to time the royal house of Aviz found most difficult to control. Not that it was always quite as anarchic, but it could be bad enough under a venal governor to allow the interlopers to exploit it. One possible remedy was to raise the salary of the governor ' to take the profit out of smuggling '; and a hint of this occurs in the comment of one scholar (1778) that Mina " which at that time [governorship of João de Barros, 1522-5], though it yielded more to the Kings, was not so profitable to the Captains as it was later to be " (*Ibid*. iii. 3 [1958]. 202). The salary of the governor of Mina at the end of the sixteenth century stood at 2,000 cruzados (Cordiero, *op. cit.*, no. IV, p. 13). But see also *THSG*, xv. 1 (1974), 104-5.

21. No new evidence about the annual value of gold imported from Mina to Portugal at the end of the fifteenth century has been found, but efforts have been made to interpret it. Fage and Magalhães-Godinho agree in computing the figure at some 24,000 oz, which Fage values at *c*. £100,000, representing roughly one-tenth of the annual world production at that time (Fage, *Ghana*, pp. 43, 100). Magalhães-Godinho, working from mint records, argues that Mina gold released Portugal from dependence upon the supply of transaharan gold, and gave her monetary independence: King John II and his immediate successors became the ' kings of gold ' (*L'économie de l'empire portugais, passim*). See also Ajayi, i. 360. It is interesting to note that, in the mid-sixteenth century, successful

English and French traders, though interlopers on the Mina coast, were able to obtain gold in relatively large quantities: Wyndham's haul (1553-4) was reportedly around 2,400 oz.; Lok's (1554-5) 6,400 oz.; and according to a report, perhaps exaggerated, that of a French trader (1558) 11,200 oz. Suret-Canale (in Ajayi, i. 388), quoting estimates published in 1879 of the sources of gold used in Europe, and taking into account gold obtained elsewhere in Guinea, accepts that over half of Europe's gold came from Africa between the years 1493 and 1520, and, indeed, that "until the middle of the sixteenth century, the traffic in [West African] gold was on the same vast scale as that of America". João de Barros, writing c. 1552, had this to say of the value of the Mina gold trade to Portugal: "As far as the increase of the royal patrimony is concerned, I do not know in Portugal of any land-tax, toll, tithe, transfer-tax or any corn tax more certain or one which yields more regular annual revenue . . . than what is yielded by the trade of Guinea" (Quoted in C. R. Boxer, *Four centuries of Portuguese expansion, 1415-1825* [Johannesburg, 1961], pp. 26-7). In all calculations as to the volume of the gold trade, one factor remains unknown, namely, the extent of illegal private trade!

22. Ryder (pp. 30-41) describes this Benin pepper trade, the story of the factory of Gató (Ughoton), and the reaction of the warlike and powerful Oba of Benin (Ozolua?), in whose territory the factory stood, to the arrival of the whites. It should be emphasized that the African peppers, both malagueta and Benin 'tailed' pepper (hence the latter's name *pimento del rabo*, see Blake, i. 151), though important to spice-starved Western Christendom, did not prove in any way as profitable an investment for the Portuguese as Mina gold or, later, the slave trade. Ryder points out that the Gató factory was built (c. 1486-7) primarily to regulate the Benin pepper trade as an exclusive royal monopoly in the expectation of riches. In fact, when Indian pepper became available in large quantities following the opening of the direct sea-route to the Orient, the significance of Benin pepper was abruptly dwarfed: indeed, already by 1504 the amount of Benin pepper being annually delivered to the Portuguese factory at Antwerp had fallen to a mere fraction (0.04%) of the comparable quantity of Indian pepper! Though other merchandise doubtless figured in the accounts of the factory of Gató (e.g., slaves, beads, ivory, cotton cloth), the essential *raison d'être* had gone. Thereupon, King Manuel, often called the 'Pepper

King', forebade the Benin pepper trade, and the factory was abandoned in 1506.

23. Incomplete records still do not allow very reliable estimates to be made of the scale of the slave trade up to the end of the sixteenth century. Scholars are agreed, however, that in this period most of those who were sold into slavery came from Upper Guinea (Ajayi, i. 260–1). Rodney (pp. 95–121) analyses in detail the conduct of the slave trade in Upper Guinea. He argues that the great majority of slaves were bought, not seized, by European traders, that slave raids by whites (e.g. John Hawkins) were rare, and were harmful to good relations with the African élite who by and large "engaged in partnership with the European slavers all along the coast" (p. 117) in the common pursuit of profit in the trade. He concludes that local wars were "the most prolific agency for the recruitment of captives" (p. 102), citing in support of this such examples as the Mane invasions and the organised attacks upon the mainland of the Bijagos islanders.

24. The kinds of goods exchanged in the Capverdian trade are indicated in Blake, i. 86–7. For a more recent analysis of Portuguese trade in Upper Guinea, see Rodney, ch. III and *passim*. He emphasizes the crucial intermediary role of the *lançados* and *tangosmaos* (here in my text partly inaccurately called 'half-breeds), whose activities figure so prominently in the writings of later, sixteenth-century contemporaries, such as captain d'Almada. These traders, mostly of Portuguese or Capverdian origin, appear to have become very widely scattered very soon after the opening up of trade by the Portuguese, at tiny trading posts up the numerous estuaries and creeks, some far upstream and inland, as at Farim, Geba, Cantor, and even briefly in the gold-bearing region of Bambuk (see Ajayi, i. 388–9). They especially concentrated around the important trading centres of Cacheu and Guinala. The Portuguese authorities, concerned to enforce the commercial regulations, were quite unable to control them and before long gave up trying. Rodney's definition of these men (p. 74), drawn from contemporary sources, runs: "The bogey of the Portuguese authorities was the *lançado* or *tango mao*, terms used to describe the private trader on the coast. The former takes its origin from *lançar*, 'to throw', and refers to the fact that these white residents had 'thrown themselves' among the Africans. A *tango mao* was defined as a white trader who had gone to the extreme of adopting the local

religion and customs, and who had his body covered with tribal taboos ". It would seem that they were at first welcomed by most of the African rulers, who were eager to encourage trade. They lived as guests of their African hosts and often took African wives. However, as time passed, the standing and influence of their descendants declined in African eyes; acceptance of African authority and African customary law became increasingly irksome to them; and towards the end of the sixteenth century, as captain d'Almada affirms, some of them are to be found withdrawing into the relative security of fortified posts, as at Cacheu (c. 1590) and at Porto da Cruz, near Guinala (c. 1583). See new note 39.

25. This, as shown elsewhere (new note 22), is incorrect: Ryder has argued that the Gató (Ughoton) factory was abandoned in 1506. However, the Benin-Mina slave trade did continue until the reign of King John III (see new note 19). Ryder, drawing upon documents in the Portuguese archives, has also shown that, although the royal factor was withdrawn from Gató (1506), white traders, mostly from São Thomé island, continued to use this port, and some trading was also done in Benin city itself, where from time to time Portuguese merchants hired buildings for storage. He describes (pp. 42–65) the part played by the islanders of São Thomé in the Benin-Mina slave trade; the contract held for a brief period by the island's captain, Fernão de Mello, to supply Mina with slaves; the transfer of this contract to Antonio Carreiro of the island of O Principe (1514–18); and the resumption of direct control of this trade by the crown in 1519 and its canalisation through São Thomé where King Manuel placed his own factor. However, it would seem that the contract for the supply of slaves to Mina—at least 500 per year—was subsequently refarmed, for it was held by Georg Ebert between 1529 and 1532. The general character and commodities of the trade of São Thomé and O Principe with the Benin mainland are also described by Ryder, who then proceeds to explain how, following the failure of a second Portuguese mission to the Oba of Benin (Esigie?) in 1538, this trade came to an abrupt end in 1553 when Benin-Portuguese relations were ruptured (Ryder, pp. 63–75). Thereafter, the Portuguese turned elsewhere, and by the end of the century they had developed, in particular, a close working relationship with the Itsekiri kingdom of Warri (see also Ryder, ' Missionary activity in the Kingdom of Warri ' in *JHSN*, ii. 1 [1960]. 1–4). French traders, especially looking for Guinea pepper, were active

APPENDIX

in challenging the Portuguese in Benin in the 'thirties and 'forties, while Wyndham's voyage to Benin took place in 1553-4; and so it is not unlikely that the crisis in Benin-Portuguese affairs arose partly from the refusal of the Oba, no matter how hard-pressed by Portuguese emissaries, to abandon his consistent policy of trading openly with whom he wished. See also John L. Vogt, ' The early S. Thomé-Principe slave trade with Mina, 1500-1540 ' in *International Journal of African Historical Studies*, vi (1973). 453-67, and Jorge Faro, ' A organizão comercial de S. Jorge da Mina em 1529 e as suas relações com a ilha de S. Thomé ' in *Boletin Cultural da Guiné Portuguesa*, xiii (1958). 305-63.

26. This description of São Thomé is translated and printed in Blake, i. 145-66. Its date is uncertain: it was written after 1535 and before 1550.

27. Precisely why did Portugal embark on fort-building? The controversy about the European forts in West Africa, particularly those on the Gold Coast, lasted a very long time, through the seventeenth and into the eighteenth century. Was the cost of building, and especially of maintenance, justified by the monetary returns from the trade? Therefore, it is of interest to ask why the Portuguese, as the first Europeans to pursue a regular trade there, decided to invest in fortification; and particularly to ask why King John II decided, against the views of some members of his Council, to build a fort on the Mina coast. I do not now think that the argument advanced here in the text of the book was overriding. Scholars today, when more is known about the polities, wars and movements of West African peoples during the fifteenth and sixteenth centuries, would argue that my reference to the want of " stability . . . among the native tribes " is exaggerated. Admittedly, evidence of instability can be offered: e.g.: the Mane invasions (see new note 38); the Benin wars of Oba Ozolua and his successors (*Esmeraldo*, p. 126; J. U. Egharevba, *Short history of Benin* [Ibadan, 1960]): and war escalation allegedly resulting from the rising volume of the slave trade. But it is unlikely that conditions in general among African societies along the West Coast were so fluid and unstable that this more than all else influenced John II to resort to fortification. The chroniclers do not say so. Barros, perhaps having in mind the *padrão real* (royal patronage; see Boxer, *op. cit.*, pp. 228-32), comments that John II envisaged the fort to be built at Mina as " the first stone of the Oriental

Church". Both Pina and Barros stress the need for a 'strong house' to safeguard the merchandise on the Mina coast. It is probable, then, that financial and commercial motives predominated: the need was for secure storage on the coast for goods, supplies, water and provisions, especially to facilitate trading in the intervals between the departure of one annual Mina fleet and the arrival of the next; and officers and men had to be accommodated in safe lodgings. The advantages were obvious of a base ashore, not only for maritime defence against any challenge from Europe (which must be anticipated after the abortive Castilian assault), but also to serve, like a staple town, as a centre through which royal factors, having to account to the royal exchequer (see Blake, i. 107) could closely supervise all trade along the coast, watching over the royal interests like a hawk, and limiting, if not eliminating, all smuggling and illegal private trade. The protection of the royal monopoly was probably the primary consideration. Indeed, King John II's horizons were much wider, and his motives more complex, than simply defence against African attacks on the Mina gold trade, though this also could be important; and in this context the subsequent plans to fortify Senegal and Sierra Leone (Blake, i. 78, 80–86), no less than the building of the castle of St. George of the Mine, may be seen as different parts of one single, and inspired, imperial policy.

28. For more detail, see Blake, i. 40–57. But note that much discussion about the interpretation to be put upon the fragmentary historical evidence has ensued since this book was first published. For example, who was Caramansa? The chronicler, Pina, described him as " the lord of that place " (the Village of Two Parts); Barros as " lord of that village ". In contrast, Eustache de la Fosse (see new note 13) refers to " the manse and caramanse who were the king and viceroy " (ruler of Fetu and his deputy in the village?). His remark has been seen as (1) proof of a moslem (Dyula) presence at Mina, for ' mansa ' is the Mande title for ' ruler ', and (2) circumstantial support for the thesis of pre-colonial trade between Mina and Benin (*JAH*, iii. 2 [1962]. 339, 343–4). As against this, however, European writers from A. B. Ellis (*History of the Gold Coast*, p. 18) in 1893 to W. W. Claridge (*History of the Gold Coast and Ashanti*, i. 44–7) in 1915, identified Caramansa as Kwamina Ansa. Then, in 1921, J. S. Wartumberg, himself an Elminan, drawing upon Elminan oral traditions, described Kwamin Ansa as sixth *Omanhen* of

APPENDIX

Elmina, who ruled from c. 1475 to 1510 (see his *São Jorge da Mina*). This statement would seem to imply a claim that Elmina already enjoyed existence as an independent state prior to the coming of the Portuguese; in support of this, indeed, the Elminans, though Akan-speaking, claim to be distinct from their Fante neighbours (see H. M. Feinberg, 'Who are the Elmina?' in *Ghana Notes and Queries*, no. 11 [June 1970]. 20–25). But most writers today dispute this. They still prefer the older view, recorded, for example, by Olfert Dapper (*Déscription de l'Afrique*, p. 283) that the 'Village of Two Parts' was so-called because it was divided by the river Benya, land on tne one bank being claimed by the Comani (of Eguaso) and on the other by Fetu. Indeed, Dr. R. Henige in 'The problem of feedback in oral tradition' (*JAH*, xiv. 2 [1973]. 225–9) questions Wartumberg's 'oral tradition' as of relatively recent manufacture, derived *inter alia* from Ellis and produced as 'evidence' in a long-drawn-out dispute between the years 1899 and 1934 about claims to the Elmina stool. If Henige is right, then we can accept that Elmina was probably not independent in 1482 and we can prefer Daaku's opinion (pp. 52–4) that Caramansa was " the local ruler of Fetu ". It is necessary, however, to mention another bare possibility: that the 'Two Parts' of the village may have been, not parts separated politically by a river boundary, but the 'wards' of two rival *asafo* (miliary companies) (see A. K. Datta and R. Porter, 'The Asafo system' in *JAH*, xii. 2 [1971]. 279–97). This obscure and complex issue illustrates how sophisticated the minute study of the African past can become. For my part, the opinion of Barbot can stand, until and unless it comes to be proved false. Barbot (p. 156), writing long afterwards but probably drawing on earlier writers and the oral traditions of his own time, argued that Elmina won its independence of the Fetu and the Comani with Portuguese support: Elmina, he wrote, was a " little republic, ever since the Portuguese made it independent of . . . Commenda and of Fetu, who formerly were masters of it by equal halves ". The exact nature of the relationship, which developed between the Portuguese and the Elminans, is another uncertain issue which has provoked discussion. Whether the mysterious 'Elmina Note' ever existed is not proven: the original has not been found (*THSG*, iii. 3 [1958]. 180–93). But it is clear that Diogo d'Azambuja entered into " agreements with the negroes ", presumably the Elminans (Pina, ch. 2 in Blake, i. 77), that the Portuguese encouraged detribalisation among the Elminans (Daaku, p. 53), and that, having helped them to assert their independence, they had organised the Elminans as their " friends and allies " by 1523 (Blake, i. 44-7).

29. We now know, from documents in the royal chanceries in the Portuguese archives, found and transcribed by Commander A. Teixeira da Mota, summaries of which he kindly sent me, that in 1556 King John III entrusted Cristovão de Oliveira, captain of the Mina fleet, with the task of building a fort at Accra to be called the fortress of São Vicente. This was not done, possibly because of damage suffered in Oliveira's running fight with Towerson off Shama (see new note 44). Nevertheless, gifts were presented to the ' ruler of Cará ' (Accra) and a site for a fort chosen. Later, a fort was erected, evidently sometime during the 'sixties, but it was damaged or destroyed (by African attack?) before September 1572. See also, Letter from Mina, of 29 September 1572, in A. Brasio, *Monumenta Missionaria Africana*, ser. i, vol. 3, pp. 89–113.

30. Barbot's statement is of dubious value, but the presumption that fort construction was begun can stand. It also now seems clear that the expedition of Pero Vaz da Cunha sailed to Senegal in 1489. For a summary of all known evidence, see A. Teixeira da Mota, *D. João Bemoim e a expedição portuguesa ao Senegal em* 1489 (Lisbon, 1971).

31. See the survey of these forts in A. W. Lawrence, *Trade castles and forts of West Africa* (London, 1963). He makes it clear that the fort at Shama (Samma) was not built before 1558. See also Blake, i. 40–57; *THSG*, iv. 1 (1950). 57–67; *JAH*, viii. 1 (1967). 39–64. For tentative lists of the Portuguese governors of São Jorge da Mina, see *THSG*, ii. 2 (1956). 53–62 and iii. 3 (1958). 194–214. However, new evidence renders these lists incomplete; e.g., they omit Lopo Soares de Albergaria (1495–99), Fernão Lopes Correia (1499–?), Antonio Froes (?1513), Joao Vaz de Almada (1526–29) and Estavão da Gama (1529–32).

32. This was true, I think, of West African historiography in 1937. It is no longer true, as shown in the preface to this new edition of the book; the perspective on the history of Guinea has been radically altered. Study and research today concentrate, not on the Portuguese and their European rivals on the Guinea coast, nor on the Atlantic slave trade and the oriental empire of Portugal, but on the history of the indigenous peoples of West Africa; and in

APPENDIX 213

this context the impact of Europeans is seen to be as marginal as that of Islam.

33. In fact, this active French interest in the Guinea pepper trade at this time was not confined to the Malagueta coast but also extended into Benin waters. In 1533, French vessels seized Portuguese traders in the Bight of Benin, and by 1539 French ships, in search of Benin pepper, were trading directly with the merchants of Benin (Ryder, pp. 68–9). On the crucial importance of Antwerp in the control and distribution in northern Europe of the trade products of Guinea, see J. Denucé, *L'Afrique au xvie siècle et le commerce anversois* (Antwerp, 1937).

34. Extracts from the more important (relevant) letters of King John III, and the ' Description ' of the Dieppe captain, have been translated and printed in Blake, i. 137–79, *passim*. The " new mines of gold . . . about fifty leagues from Myna ", referred to here in the text as a " new gold mine ", presumably means another place on the Mina coast where gold could be obtained from the negro merchants in significant quantities. It is possible that this refers to the development of the gold trade in the Accra area. Later records refer to the discovery (*c.* 1570–73) of new ' mines ' in the Mansu (Ankobra) valley, presumably near Axim.

35. The whole of this section of the text (pp. 116–27), based as it was on very fragmentary records, needs revision, particularly in the light of what is now known of the naval operations of Duarte Coelho for the defence of Guinea, especially of the Malagueta trade, during the years 1531–33. These have been carefully investigated by Commander A. Teixeira da Mota in his *Duarte Coelho, capitão-mor de Armadas no Atlântico*, 1531–35 (Lisbon, 1972). Drawing upon newly-found evidence in Portuguese archives, he describes Coelho, as seen here, as the ' captain-major of the Atlantic fleets ' of Portugal. It is clear from all the evidence, both old and new, that King John III of Portugal and the Count of Castanheiro were so seriously disturbed by the scale of the French attack on their trade and their shipping, off Brazil, the African Islands and the Guinea coast, as to organise a system of maritime defence more elaborate and more systematic than heretofore. Da Mota shows that Duarte Coelho commanded two naval operations in Guinea waters during these years. His first command (*c.* August 1531–*c.* February 1532), in charge of the Mina fleet, was to Mina, thence to São Thomé, and so back to Lisbon, possibly to ensure the safe transport home to

Portugal of Mina gold. His second, which is the operation described here in the text, involved leaving Portugal in October 1532, cruising off the Malagueta coast where the plan " to build fortresses " was for reasons unknown not carried out, and then returning under new royal orders to the neighbourhood of the Azores to meet the ' India fleet ' to protect it on the last, and most vulnerable part of its homeward passage. Ceolho's ships reached the Azores (*c.* July 1533), where they made a successful rendezvous with the East Indies fleet of Antonio de Saldanha and that of Martim Afonso from Brazil. In the light of this new evidence, the various references in the text of the book to Mina and Malagueta fleets for the year 1543 appear to be incorrect (e.g., text pp. 119–22). This error arose, because the events described in the text are dated 1543 in the appendix to A. Herculano's edition of Sousa Coutinho's *Annaes* (p. 411), but the date 1543 appears to be an error for 1531 (see A. T. da Mota, *op. cit.*, p. 6, note 2). Commander A. Teixeira da Mota also (*op. cit.*, p. 9, note 9) questions the statement in the text (p. 126, ll. 10–12) that Duarte Coelho transported " convicts or political prisoners among the men who were to garrison the proposed fort ". I accept his argument, more particularly because he adds that records exist in the Portuguese archives of the appointment of various officers for the fort to be erected on the Malagueta coast. It remains true, however, that the charge was made by Englishmen and, much later, by Dutch writers, that the garrisons of the Portuguese forts in Guinea were partly recruited from among exiles and pardoned criminals. The main argument in the text (pp. 122–23) concerning a regular system of naval defence and ships sailing in convoy during the years following the fierce French assault on the Portuguese in West African waters, can stand. In general, as more new evidence is forthcoming and the new documentation is critically analysed, a more detailed and much more accurate picture of the tactics and strategy of naval defence by the Portuguese in Guinea waters is emerging.

36. The reader may well question this description of King John III of Portugal (1521–57), who is generally seen as a serious and conscientious man, interested in the fine arts, but of limited education and intelligence, and responsible for the introduction of the Inquisition into his country. During his reign, the real decline of the empire set in. Royal indebtedness grew, with high interest rates; the yield from oriental spices dwindled owing to falling prices

APPENDIX 215

in Europe; the Portuguese factory in Antwerp was closed (1549); and economy dictated withdrawal from four of the eight North African bases. Nevertheless, John III, as his correspondence shows, partly because of his financial difficulties, took a close personal interest in imperial affairs, and clearly attached importance to the security and promotion of the Guinea trades, especially that in Mina gold. In these circumstances, the French attack on his monopoly of the Mina trade, the Ango ' affaire ', and the subsequent intrusion of English interlopers, would appear to have been matters of national survival for John III.

37. This is now known to be incorrect. See new note 33.

38. This account of the Mane invasions and their results needs revision in the light of recent research. As indicated in the text, my initial version was based on quasi-contemporary evidence, notably on statements made by captain d'Almada (writing c. 1593-4 but active on the coast from c. 1560) and the Jesuit missionary, Baltezar Barreira (c. 1609). D'Almada, who in one passage seems to suspect a Mande origin for the Manes, describes in another passage the movement of these invaders from the northern Congo to behind Mina and the Malagueta coast westward to Sierra Leone. This version of the warring migration was embellished by later writers. Barreira possibly had his own, independent sources; but one of his references led to the subsequent (and misleading) identification of the Mane invaders of Guinea with the Jaga warring bands of the Congo. Later writers, repeating and elaborating a remarkable legend, included Francisco Coelho (c. 1669) and Francisco de Lemos (1684) (see D. Peres [ed.], *Duas descrições seiscentistas da Guiné* [Lisbon, 1953]); and the legend became current through the dubious repetitions of such well-known writers as Barbot down to our own time. During the last twenty years, scholars have critically analysed exactly what contemporaries wrote down, and they have collated all this with some newly-discovered, or rediscovered, evidence, such as the ' Relation of Sierra Leone ' of André Dornelas (c. 1625; MS. 51-VIII-25 in the Library de Ajuda, Lisbon) and the ' Description of Sierra Leone ' of Manuel Alvares (c. 1616; in the Library of the Geographical Society, Lisbon). Their general conclusions (subject to minor ambiguities) amount to the following: that the Manes were probably of Mande origin; that the Mane warriors raided southwards towards the Ivory or Malagueta coasts; that they then turned westwards towards Sierra Leone; that, as

they went, they recruited non-Mane peoples into their armies who were known as the 'Sumbas' (which is a Sape—strictly, Temne—term for 'man-eaters' and was applied by them generally to the armies of the invaders); and that a Mane raiding group may have hived off from, or arrived independently of, the main force to make its way towards the Mina coast. In point of fact, André Dornelas, having retired to Santiago after some fifty years on the Guinea coast, recorded (c. 1625) that the Manes had approached the Portuguese fortress at Mina, had engaged in a few skirmishes with the defenders, and then, because of the fire from the fort's guns, had withdrawn. The only contemporary confirmation of this is Barreira's story that he was told by Tora, a Mane king, still alive in 1606, that invading Manes had made contact with the Portuguese at Mina. Long afterwards (c. 1669), Coelho repeated this tale. But there is no known archival or documentary confirmation. However, to continue: scholars now also mostly accept that the main Mane force moved westwards behind the Ivory coast, in two (or possibly three) main formations; that one arm of this force attacked and conquered the Sapes (a culturally largely homogeneous group of coastal peoples, including the Bullom, Temne and Limba, see *JAH*, viii. 2 [1972]. 219); and that a second formation, advancing on a roughly parallel course further inland, attacked the Susu but were repulsed by a combined army of Susu and Fula (Fulani). Furthermore, it is generally agreed that the Mane invasions must have occurred roughly between the years 1545 and 1560; that the invaders were gradually assimilated, though a Mane ruling class survived in some of the invaded areas; that the slave trade with the Portuguese (and with other whites, including John Hawkins) flourished, because of the spate of captives issuing from the wars of conquest; but that other branches of commerce in the affected areas were, as captain d'Almada recorded, seriously dislocated for a generation or more, and recovery was taking place only slowly in his day. Trade routes from the interior down to the coast were diverted to avoid wartorn or troubled districts. Captain d'Almada, hinting at widespread devastation in Sierra Leone, describes how the Susu temporarily abandoned their former trade down to the coast here, diverting it northwards down the river Nunez. He also hints at the dispersion of refugees: in his time on the coast, such a group of Sape refugees were living in Papel country on the Cacheu river.

A clear, modern account of what is now known about the Mane

APPENDIX

invasions may be found in Rodney, ch. II. He mentions the more important source materials and assesses in detail the effects of the invasions upon the peoples and the trades of Guinea. It is desirable however, to consult on special points still in controversy such studies as P. E. H. Hair, 'An ethnolinguistic inventory of the Lower Guinea Coast before 1700' in *op. cit.*, and Y. Person, 'Les Kissi et leurs statuettes de pierre' in *Bulletin de l'I.F.A.N.*, ser. B, xxiii. 1–2 (1961). 1–59.

On the entirely separate Jaga wars in the Congo (*c.* 1568–72), see D. Birmingham, *Trade and conflict in Angola* (Oxford, 1966), chs. 3 and 4; and G. M. Childs, *Umbundu kingship and character* (London, 1949), pp. 181–90.

39. See new note 24. The coastal region of Upper Guinea, with its many estuaries, inlets, bays, islands and mangrove swamps, is an immense and varied habitat. It is probable, therefore, that during this period the individual fortunes of Portuguese residents, merchants and traders along its shores and also inland near or far up the rivers, varied much according to time, place and circumstance. Nevertheless, with this qualification, we can tentatively accept the generalisation (Rodney, p. 88) that " the latter half of the sixteenth century was a period of crisis . . ., during which the *lançados* made strenuous attempts to change the nature of the agreements [with local rulers, etc.], and to escape, in one way or another, from [African] authority ". Their difficulties arose, at least in part, because, as captain d'Almada recorded, Africans grew more contemptuous of them as time passed, and insisted on improved trading terms. But this was not the whole story. Their regulation of the trades as intermediaries, and indeed the commercial activities of men from Santiago, or direct from Portugal, were all alike adversely affected by at least two other factors, namely, the onset of local wars and the raiding attacks of interlopers from France and England. The dislocation resulting from the Mane invasions to the south in Sierra Leone spread far and wide, and there were local wars too, possibly the outcome of a kind of chain reaction. Hints of this emerge in the records. Thus, captain d'Almada tells how his countrymen had not been able to send any ships up the river Casamance for more than 25 years because of war up the river between the negroes, with one side blocking the entrance to the river and attacking Portuguese ships there, and thereby denying access to their enemy, the king of ' Casamanca" (*Tratado* [ed.

L. Silveiro, Lisbon, 1946], p. 39). Not less serious was the damage done by interlopers, particularly the English in the 'sixties. To quote two examples: captain John Lovell who, during the winter of 1566-7, inflicted heavy losses upon Portuguese shipping off the Cape Verde islands; and the more famous John Hawkins whose men in January 1568 actually burned down the Portuguese trading house on the river Cacheu. This disaster calls for comment. Hawkins had on his two previous voyages seized Portuguese ships in the waters of Sierra Leone. On this occasion, however, he took armed vessels up the Rio de S. Domingo (Cacheu river) and attacked the whites in their trading house on its (north?) bank. Witnesses in a Portuguese court of law alleged that Hawkins and his men, armed to the teeth, landed at Cacheo, slew many Portuguese residents, seized 30,000 ducats, and burned down the factory there. We know, from other evidence, that the white traders had a ' factory of São Domingos ' on the Cacheu river in 1535 and another further south in Biafada country at Guinala on the Ria Grande de Buba in 1558 (Rodney, p. 76). It would seem that in 1568 Hawkins destroyed the ' factory of São Domingos '. Witnesses are specific: this trading house was the place where " the royal dues and taxes are levied and collected by the servants and factors of Antonio Goncalves de Guzman and Duarte Leo, [the farmers or contractors of the trade of Cape Verde and the Rivers of Guinea] ". But one witness also insisted that on the Rio de S. Domingo " there are two settlements of Portuguese: one is in Chacheu port and the other is in Duguenguo [elsewhere ' Begundo ', presumably Buguendo] ". Did Hawkins burn Cacheo? Or did he burn Buguendo? (See P.R.O., S.P. 70: 95, ff. 242-67 and 96, ff. 1-49.

40. It is now established that Diogo Carreiro never reached Timbuktu, though this was his design. His letter to King Sebastian of Portugal was written on 29 March 1565 from the Senegal river. " I have pacified all the chief kings here," he wrote, " and in the name of your highness I was liberal in distributing gifts to them. I have a clear, open and full understanding of the river and the road to Tubuqutu, and—God willing—when this reaches your highness, I shall have arrived there and be on my way back ". But it was not to be. It appears that he was killed on land as he made his way upriver. For new evidence, and an analysis of the background to the plan, particularly the hope of diverting more of the overland, transaharan gold trade to the coastal parts of Guinea, see A. Teixeira

da Mota, *A malograda viagem de Diogo Carreiro a Tombuctu em* 1565 (Lisbon, 1970).

41. This is misleading. See new note 28. The 'Mina blacks' or Elminans, who lived in the African town near the fortress of São Jorge, came to be allies of the Portuguese whose direct interest it was to cultivate good relations with them. Indeed, if occasional differences could, and did, arise (Blake, i. 133-5), it is clear from the records that the officers and merchants of the fortress had easy and ready access into Mina town, and that detribalised Africans from the town were enrolled in a trained and armed force, which the Portuguese afterwards recruited for the defence both of the fort and also of the entire Mina coast (Blake, ii. 388). Nonetheless, their relations with other peoples along the Mina coast were often less than amicable and subject to the whims and fancies of local rulers. Evidence of their efforts to foster friendship with African rulers and their subjects is available. Indeed, it is probable that governors of the fortress of São Jorge were from the outset instructed, primarily for reasons of trade, to maintain peace and good relations with all African peoples: certainly chapter 13 of the *regimento* of 1529 was insistent on this point. To implement this policy, 'gifts' were customarily made to local rulers and other notables. Commander A. Teixeira da Mota informs me that he has analysed all the known, relevant evidence for the years 1517-22 in the draft of a new book on the governorship of Duarte Pacheco Pereira (1519-22) which he is preparing for publication. This evidence, generously made available to me, if collated with other evidence for the period from 1482 to 1530, confirms that the principal recipients of 'gifts' were the rulers of Fetu and Comani, whose lands were nearest to the fortress. It emerges that a new governor, on his arrival, would make such 'gifts', and likewise on the accession of a new ruler to the stool of Fetu or Comani. In addition, 'gifts' went to other African potentates exercising sway further along the coast— those of Ahanta, Shama (Samma), Ampia, Sabou, Cabo da Redes, Accra and 'newly-discovered' (1520) Labide; also to the rulers of those inland countries who controlled the merchants' 'roads' or trade-paths from the interior to the coast, and among these were the 'kings' of the 'Cacres' or 'Cateres' (Incassa), the 'Assans' (Wassaw), the 'Abermus' (Abrambo), the 'Atins', and the 'Acanes', 'Acanees' or 'Hacanys' (Akani, Great and Little; but known to the Portuguese in the first half of the sixteenth century

respectively as ' Acanes Castelhanos ' and ' Acanes Portugueses '). On the controversial location and identification of the Akan states, see A. Boahen in *THSG*, xiv. 1 (1973). 105-111, though he does not appear to have consulted the important Teixeira chart of 1602. Akan traders were the most active in the Mina gold trade. Their gold—' Akan sica ', the purest gold—was of high quality, and the vital importance of keeping open the ' roads ' to and from Akani seems to explain repeated Portuguese efforts to penetrate far inland during the sixteenth century and to maintain good relations with the Akani rulers. Some evidence of this survives: thus, in 1513 Gonçalo Valada was sent from São Jorge da Mina to visit Akani, particularly to restore peace between the rulers of Great and Little Akani and so get the trade routes opened; in 1517, another emissary, Nicolau Garcia, visited the lands of Akani and Abrambo, in 1518 Wassaw, and in 1519 Ahanta; while in 1520 João Vieira visited Wassaw, Akani and Abrambo. Disputes or wars between rival African rulers threatened, at times impeded, the free flow of trade, and some evidence survives to show how the Portuguese at São Jorge would sometimes intervene to get the ' roads ' reopened: thus, in 1520 a special ' gift ' was made to a Wassaw notable " for the agreement which he made between his brother, the king [of ' Asa ' (Wassaw)], and the ' Adus ' [of Adom] in the dispute they had whereby the merchants' road was interrupted ". As late as 1548, we have evidence, too, of " civil war among the Akans ". In the last resort, however, the basis of Portuguese power on the Mina coast was force or the threat of force. It is also likely that their influence with African rulers along the coast was weakened by the activities of French and English interlopers; and the fortification of Shama and Accra, undertaken in the 'sixties, reflected their determination to recover lost prestige and uphold their monopoly (see Blake, i. 43-57, 94-6, 112-14, 130-31).

42. Lopo de Sousa Coutinho (c. 1505-77), after distinguished service in India, was rewarded by King John III with the governorship of São Jorge da Mina. But the evidence is vague as to the time of his appointment (*THSG*, iii. 3 [1958]. 203). Ford's *Letters of John III* refer (p. 376) to a Lopo de Sousa as " captain of the city of São Jorge da Mina ". But a son bore the same name. Which (if either) was the ambassador in London in 1555?

43. But see new note 22.

44. This running fight, lasting through 27 January 1556/7,

took place off-shore from Shama. Towerson and his French allies did not have things all their own way. Captain Cristovão de Oliveira, apparently commanding the Portuguese fleet, as Portuguese records indicate, afterwards claimed two enemy ships sunk. Towerson himself admits the loss of a pinnace. The fact remains, however, according to the account in Hakluyt's *Principal Navigations*, that the Mina fleet failed to prevent Towerson from continuing a profitable trade for gold along the Mina coast for another five weeks. See Blake, i. 181. Commander A. Teixeira da Mota plans to publish new material drawn from Portuguese archives.

45. Hakluyt's record of the three Mina voyages of Towerson contains much valuable detail about social, economic and political conditions in the Gold Coast. It deserves thorough analysis. Dr. Danquah has drawn attention to Towerson's palaver with the chief of Shama (1556), for it is " the first reference in English literature of the Gold Coast symbol of a chief's power as a ' stool ' " (*THSG*, iii. 1 [1957]. 12–13). Much fascinating evidence is also preserved in this record of: (1) the places where gold could be traded (e.g., Ahanta, Shama, Weamba, Perinnen, Laguoa, Perecow, Egrand, Mowre and Cormatin); (2) the terms, conditions and commodities of the Mina coast trade; (3) the weights used by the African merchants (see A. Ott, ' Akan gold weights ' in *THSG*, ix. [1968]. 17–42); (4) the forceful and ruthless tactics used by the Portuguese on land and by sea against both Africans and Europeans to defeat the challenge to their monopoly of the gold trade; (5) the equally ruthless behaviour of English and French interlopers against the Portuguese and against Africans who refused to trade with them; and (6) the shrewd, hard-headed attitude of the Africans towards all European traders. They clearly resented Portuguese efforts to intimidate them. As one of them said: " the Portugales were bad men, and . . . they made them [the Africans] slaves if they could take them, and would put yrons upon their legges . . . and Don John of Shama had wars with the Portugals ". However, the Africans were all things to all comers, and they cleverly played off the Portuguese against the English and both against the French, adapting policy and tactics to circumstances and generally ensuring at least some advantage to themselves.

46. The Anglo-Portuguese negotiations are summarised in *THSG*, iii. 2 (1957), 137–50. On the English voyages to Guinea to the year 1560, see Blake, vol. ii. The English merchants' claim to

freedom of trade and navigation is printed in full in *Ibid.*, ii. 355-8. For a recent analysis of Hakluyt's record of these voyages, see vol. i, ch. 16 (by P. E. H. Hair) of D. B. Quinn (ed.), *The Hakluyt Handbook* (2 vols., London, 1974).

47. But on the 'Sapes', see new note 38.

48. More correctly, Sebastian took over the reins of government in 1568, and the rule of the Cardinal replaced that of the Regency in December 1562.

49. But see new note 29.

50. But see new note 20.

51. Incorrect, due to my misreading Carreiro's letter. See new note 40.

52. Not entirely correct. It is clear, for example, that in 1574 a Portuguese fleet, under Antonio Velho Tinoco, fought and defeated some French ships in Sierra Leone waters close to the present site of Freetown. See A. Teixeira da Mota, *Dois escritores quinhentistas de Cabo Verde* (Lisbon, 1971), p. 5.

53. But see Ryder (pp. 69–77) where it is argued that trade with Benin decayed, partly because of a rupture with Portugal. As against this, however, the Portuguese opened up new areas for the purchase of slaves, such as Ardra, Ijebu, Popo and especially Ode Itsekiri. The want of records does not allow a firm conclusion. Also, even if the total volume of legitimate trade shrank, that of private trade, particularly with the islanders of São Thomé, and perhaps of smuggling, may well have been considerable, not least because of the rising demand for slaves for Brazil and the West Indies.

54. The years immediately following the death of King Sebastian were years of much uncertainty, wild rumour and acute tension among Portuguese in Guinea, particularly for the officers of the crown in the castle of São Jorge da Mina. This partly resulted from the succession crisis at home, the intrigues of prince Dom Antonio, and the Spanish conquest of Portugal. In England and France, the weakness of Portugal at this time was exploited. In collusion with Dom Antonio, schemes for the seizure of Elmina were mooted, with some degree of official sanction. The various English projects came to nothing (see e.g., *Cal. S. P. Foreign*, 1581-2, nos. 176, 179, 180; 1583, nos. 142, 160, 175; *Cal. S. P. Domestic, Elizabeth*, vol. 167, no. 7). The efforts of the French were more fruitful. For the historian, perhaps the most significant episode

was, that one French scheme actually led to Rouen merchants gaining access within Elmina fort by the collaboration of the then governor, Vasco Fernandes Pimentel (1579-82).

It would seem that the crisis in Portugal prompted a group of Rouen merchants, some of whom (e.g. Jacques Le Seigneur) had an old family interest in the Guinea trade, to attempt once again to establish themselves strongly in the Mina gold trade. Their first effort failed. In 1581, one of their ships, the *Chérubin*, after a deadly, running fight with the Portuguese off Cormantin, was captured and taken to the castle. In the following year, however, this time with a licence to trade from Dom Antonio, they sent four ships to the Mina coast; and this time they were welcomed by governor Pimentel, allowed to ride their ships at anchor near the castle, invited into the fort, and permitted to use its facilities as a warehouse and a base for trade subject to the customary dues payable to the Mina contractors. How is this to be explained? It is likely that Pimentel had learned of the substantial support being offered to Dom Antonio by Catherine de Medici, a circumstance which may have influenced him, like some other patriots in the Portuguese overseas service, to rally to the cause of the Portuguese pretender to the throne. At any rate, he now entered into a formal agreement with the Rouen merchants, allowing *inter alia* two of their factors to stay in the castle to oversee the sale of the cloths and other goods, which the French had brought with them, in return for a cargo of gold which was computed at 20,000 ducats. The text of this agreement, dated 27 July 1582, together with a letter from the governor conveying a message of goodwill to France and an analysis of the French involvement at Mina, were printed in full by Charles de la Beaurepaire in ' La marine normande sur la côté de Guinée et particulièrement près du Castel de la Mine ' (*Bulletin de la société de l'histoire de Normandie* [Rouen, 1887-90], pp. 252-71, 294-7).

However, this advantage to the French was short-lived. Philip II of Spain reacted strongly. Following his conquest of Portugal and the rout of Philippe Strozzi's fleet at the Azores (July 1582), he sent a naval squadron to the Gold Coast; and this squadron took over the castle of São Jorge da Mina, seized the French goods in the warehouse there, killed the French factors, and took Pimentel a prisoner back to Lisbon. In 1583, a third French expedition to the Mina coast was repulsed! The former regime of a Portuguese monopoly on the Gold Coast was thus restored.

It should be stressed that the French did not temporarily ' occupy ' Elmina.   (See *THSG*, iv. 1 [1959], 60).   More accurately, French merchants, in league with prince Dom Antonio, were given the facilities of the fort for their trade by agreement with governor Pimentel, an arrangement which collapsed with the assertion of the authority of the new ruler of Portugal, Philip II of Spain.

SELECT BIBLIOGRAPHY
OF
MANUSCRIPTS AND PRINTED WORKS
ON EUROPEAN ENTERPRISE IN
WEST AFRICA TO 1578

I. DOCUMENTARY MATERIAL

A. *MANUSCRIPT*

There are numerous references to West Africa in the various collections of state papers, and in the records of the High Court of Admiralty preserved at the Public Record Office, London. Most of these references relate merely to interloping voyages to Guinea, and shed little, if any light upon white enterprise on the African coast in the sixteenth century. This is also true of the volumes of manuscripts preserved in the British Museum. Only the more valuable of existing records are selected for mention here, and it should not therefore be assumed that the list is exhaustive. The unsorted manuscript material in the Archivo Nacional da Torre do Tombo at Lisbon has not yet been fully explored. Some of these manuscripts, however, have been printed *in extenso* by Snres Senna Barcellos, J. J. Lopes de Lima and others.[1]

(1) PUBLIC RECORD OFFICE, LONDON

S.P. 12. STATE PAPERS DOMESTIC, ELIZABETH

Vol. 4, nos. 64, 65. James Aldaye to Sir William Cecil. Reports on a Guinea voyage, planned by the pirate Henry Strangewyse. 25 June 1559.

Vol. 14, no. 60. Queen Elizabeth orders release of Henry Strangewyse. 17 Dec. 1560.

Vol. 26, no. 43. Indenture and charter-party. The *Minion* and *Primrose* are made available for a voyage to West Africa. 1562 (?)

Vol. 26, nos. 44, 45 Covenants for the previous and the present voyages are compared. 15 Dec. 1562 (?)

[1] *Vide infra* various cited collections of Portuguese documents.

226   WEST AFRICA: QUEST FOR GOD AND GOLD

Vol. 39, no. 86. Examination of Walter Darby and Martin Frobisher *re* a Guinea voyage. 29 and 31 May 1566.
Vol. 40, no. 7. Examination of Martin Frobisher. 11 June 1566.
Vol. 43, no. 12. Ordnance and ammunition for a fort in Guinea. 24 June 1567.
Vol. 49, nos. 26, 27. Case of the *Mary Fortune*, belonging to the brothers Winter, which had been sunk by a Portuguese armada in Guinea. 16 Jan. 1569.

S.P. 69. STATE PAPERS FOREIGN, MARY
Vol. 7, no. 448. Allegations of the Portuguese ambassador. 1555.
Vol. 7, no. 449. Answer of the English merchants to the charges of the Portuguese ambassador. 1555.
Vol. 7, no. 450. Queen Mary to King John III. 1555.

S.P. 70. STATE PAPERS FOREIGN, ELIZABETH
Vol. 81, f. 168. Licence from King Philip II, permitting Gaspar Caldeira and Anton Luiz to trade to Africa. 25 Dec. 1565.
Vol. 90, f. 81 b. French ships in Guinea. 1567.
Vol. 95, ff. 242–67. Examination of witnesses in Lisbon, relating to spoils made by Englishmen on Portuguese, especially in Guinea. Sept. 1567.
Vol. 98, ff. 43–4. Letter from Portugal, written by Botolph Holder. 14 May 1568.
Vol. 99, ff. 1–49. Book of spoils made by the English privateers, Hawkins and Lovell, on the shipping and trade of the Portuguese Guinea contractors, Antonio Gonçalves de Guzman and Duarte Leo. 8 July 1568.

H.C.A. 1. HIGH COURT OF ADMIRALTY, OYER AND TERMINER
Vol. 35. (1559–65, mainly London)
13–16 Aug. 1559. Examinations of Henry Strangewyse, Thomas Wallis, Anton Luiz and others about a plan to seize Elmina castle.
1 July 1562. Examinations of John Wallett, master of the *Fleur de Lice*, William Brook and Hans M'ckson about a voyage to Guinea.
Vol. 36. (1560–65, mainly Country)
26 Dec. 1564. Examination of Thomas Fenner of Anneley (Sussex) about a voyage for Guinea.

SELECT BIBLIOGRAPHY

Vol. 37. (1565-9, mainly London)

10 Nov. 1565. Examination of James Smith of Dover reveals that Giles Cosyn was to have been employed by Mr. Winter on a voyage to Guinea.

Vol. 39. (1569-77, mainly London. Includes Instance and Prize Acts, 1558-9)

24 Feb. 1571. Examination of Richard Hamond. Tristram Maynard's intended Guinea voyage in 1570-1.

H.C.A. 13. HIGH COURT OF ADMIRALTY, EXAMINATIONS

Vol. 16. (1566-9.) This volume includes numerous scattered references to English trade with ' Barbary'. ' Barbary " was probably used to cover voyages south of Cape Verde in a few isolated cases.

8 Dec. 1568. Slaving voyage from West Africa to West Indies (?)

Vol. 17. (1569-70)

30 April, 22 June 1569. Complaints of William Garrard. Illuminating details of slave traffic between Africa and West Indies.

Vol. 18. (1570-1)

1 April 1571. Voyage of the *Castle of Comfort* " unto Caput Viride and so unto the quoast of Barbarye".

H.C.A. 24. HIGH COURT OF ADMIRALTY, LIBELS

File 39. (1567-8)

No. 16. Translated copy of an insurance policy for a French voyage from Havre de Grace to Mina and the West Indies, dated 10 Feb. 1565. Another similar policy, dated 7 May 1566.

No. 19. Policy for a voyage to Mina and the West Indies under captain Jean Bontemps, dated 29 Dec. 1565.

No. 20. Similar policy, dated 8 Jan. 1565.

No. 29. Relates to the Barbary trade.

File 59. (1591-2)

Nos. 17-26. Dispute between Prince Dom Antonio and some English merchants trading to Guinea.

(2) BRITISH MUSEUM

ADDITIONAL MSS. 5415. A. 7. Map of Guinea and Benin. 1558.
ADDITIONAL MSS. 15,760, ff. 68 b–9. Map of Henricus Martellus Germanus. c. 1489.
ADDITIONAL MSS. 26,056. B, f. 2916. Antonio Fogaca to Ruy Gomez. 16 Sept. 1572.
ADDITIONAL MSS. 34,329, ff. 1–9 b. Correspondence between Queen Elizabeth and King Sebastian. 1571–4.
ADDITIONAL MSS. 35,840, ff. 42 b–6. Correspondence between Queen Mary and the Portuguese rulers, relating to English voyages to Mina. 1555.
COTTON MSS. Nero B.1. Transcripts, relating mainly to diplomatic negotiations between England and Portugal ; ff. 240–5 include a description of the revenues of the imperial dominions of Portugal.
COTTON MSS. Galba C. IV, f. 22. Order of the Lord Admiral forbidding William Curtes and Hector (Nunez ?) to make a voyage to Guinea.
COTTON MSS. Otho E. VIII, ff. 17–41b. An account of Hawkins's third slaving voyage. Printed by J. A. Williamson in his *John Hawkins*, pp. 491–534.
HARLEIAN MSS. 167. A collection of papers relating to naval affairs ; f. 70 contains a note on the courses upon the coast of Guinea, c. 1570.
LANSDOWNE MSS. 171. Transcripts relating *inter alia* to Anglo-Portuguese diplomatic negotiations. Many references to West Africa, *e.g.* ff. 137b–9b, 142–63 ; ff. 148–9 contain the celebrated Declaration of Martin Frobisher.
ROYAL MSS. 13 B. 1. Copies of Instruments, Letters Patents, and Commissions in the sixteenth century. Letters to foreign princes from Queen Elizabeth. 1558–68. Ff. 65b, 75b, 186–8 relate to West Africa.

(3) ARCHIVO NACIONAL DA TORRE DO TOMBO, LISBON

CHANCELLARIA DE D. AFFONSO V, Livro 33, f. 147^v. Grant to Fernão Gomes on 1 June 1473. Professor E. Prestage possesses a transcript, which he kindly placed at my disposal.
LIVRO DAS ILHAS, f. 81. Grant of privileges to the islanders of São Thomé. 6 March 1500.
PARTE 1^a, maço 8, doc. f. 2, no. suc. 851. Letter from São Jorge da Mina to King Manuel. 22 Jan. 1510.

SELECT BIBLIOGRAPHY

B. PRINTED

Evidence, relating mainly to Anglo-Portuguese negotiations and interloping voyages to West Africa, may be found in the printed calendars of manuscripts, preserved at the Public Record Office, London.

Calendar of State Papers, Domestic, 1547–80. London, 1856.
Calendar of State Papers, Addenda, 1566–79. London, 1871.
Calendar of State Papers, Foreign, 1547–78. London, 1861–1901.
Calendar of State Papers, Spain, 1485–1586. London, 1862–96.
Calendar of State Papers, Venetian, 1202–1580. London, 1864–90.
Calendar of Patent Rolls, 1476–85. London, 1901.
Calendar of Ancient Deeds, vol. I. London, 1890.

The following miscellaneous collections also contain much valuable material.

Annaes Maritimos e Coloniaes. 6 vols. Lisbon, 1840–6.
BIGGAR, H. P. *A collection of documents relating to Jacques Cartier and the Sieur de Roberval.* Ottawa, 1930.
BRÉARD, C. ET P. *Documents relatifs à la marine normande aux XVIe et XVIIe siècles.* Rouen, 1889.
CLAY, J. W. *North Country Wills.* (Surtees Society, vols. CXVI and CXXI.) 2 vols. Durham, 1908 and 1912.
COELHO, J. RAMOS. *Alguns Documentos do Archivo Nacional acerca das navegacões e conquistas Portuguezes.* Lisbon, 1892.
DAVENPORT, F. G. *European treaties bearing on the history of the United States and its Dependencies.* 3 vols. Washington, 1917–34.
DONNAN, E. *Documents illustrative of the history of the slave trade to America.* 4 vols. Washington, 1930–5.
DOUAIS, L'ABBÉ. *Dépêches de M. de Fourquevaux, ambassadeur du Roi Charles IX en Espagne, 1565–72.* Paris, 1896.
FALGAIROLLE, E. *Jean Nicot, ambassadeur de France en Portugal au XVIe siècle. Sa correspondence diplomatique.* Paris, 1897.
FORD, J. D. M. *The letters of John III, King of Portugal, 1521–57.* Cambridge, Mass., 1931.
GOSSELIN, E. H. *Documents authentiques et inédits pour servir à l'histoire de la marine normande.* Rouen, 1876.
LA FERRIÈRE, (Le Comte) H. DE. *Lettres de Catherine de Medicis. (Documents inédits sur l'histoire de France.)* Paris, 1880–99.
Leys e provisões que el Rey D. Sebastião fez defois que comecou o governar. (Collecção da Legislação, Antiga e Moderna do Reino de Portugal. Pt. I, vol. 1. 9 vols. Coimbra, 1816–52.)
As Ordenações del Rey D. Manoel. 5 pts. Evora, 1521.
MARSDEN R. G. *Select pleas in the Court of Admiralty.* 2 vols. London, 1897.

230   WEST AFRICA: QUEST FOR GOD AND GOLD

PACHECO, D. J. F. and others. *Colección de documentos inéditos del Real Archivo de Indias.* 42 vols. Madrid, 1864–84.
NAVARRETE, M. FERNANDEZ DE and others. *Colección de documentos inéditos para la historia de España.* 112 vols. Madrid, 1842–95.
PARIS, L. *Negotiations, Lettres et Pièces Diverses relatives au règne de François II.* (Documents inédits sur l'histoire de France.) Paris, 1841.
Privy Council of England, Acts of the, 1542–80. London, 1890–5.
RYMER, T. *Foedera, conventiones, literae et cuiuscunque generis Acta publica.* 20 vols. London, 1704–32.
SANTAREM, (Viscount) BARROS E SOUSA. *Memorias para a historia e theoria das Cortes Geraes.* 2 pts. Lisbon, 1826 and 1828.
—— *Quadro Elementar das relações politicas e diplomaticas de Portugal com as diversas potencias do mundo.* (Continued by L. A. REBELLO DA SILVA and J. DA S. MENDES. 18 vols. Lisbon, 1842–76).
SOUSA VITERBO, F. M. DE. *Trabalhos nauticos dos Portuguezes nos seculos XVI e XVII.* 2 pts. Lisbon, 1898 and 1900.
TOMMASEO, M. N. *Relations des ambassadeurs de Venise.* (Documents inédits sur l'histoire de France.) 2 vols. Paris, 1838.
WEISS, C. *Papiers d'état du Cardinal de Granvelle, 1416–1565.* (Documents inédits sur l'histoire de France.) 9 vols. Paris, 1841–52.

II. CONTEMPORARY WORKS

ALVARES D'ALMADA, ANDRÉ. *Tratado breve dos Rios de Guiné do Cabo-Verde, desde o Rio do Sanaga até aos baixos de Sant Anna.* [c. 1594.][1] (Ed. Diogo Köpke.) Porto, 1841.
ANDRADA, FRANCISCO D'. *Chronica do rey D. João III.* 4 pts. Lisbon, 1613.
AZURARA, G. E. DE. *Chronica de Guiné.* [c. 1450.] Ed. and Englished by C. R. BEAZLEY and E. PRESTAGE for the Hakluyt Society under the title *The chronicle of the discovery and conquest of Guinea.* (Ser. I, vols. XCV and C.) 2 vols. London, 1896 and 1899.
BARLOW, R. *A briefe summe of geographie.* [c. 1541.] Ed. and printed from ROYAL MSS. 18 B. xxviii. (British Museum) by E. G. R. TAYLOR for the Hakluyt Society (Ser. II, vol. LXIX). London, 1932.
BARROS, J. DE. *Da Asia.* 10 decades. [1552–1615.] (J. B. LAVANHA edited decade IV. DIOGO DE COUTO wrote decades V–X.) A more recent edition in 24 vols. Lisbon, 1777–88.
BERNÁLDEZ, A. *Historia de los Reyes Católicos.* [c. 1510–3.] (*Biblioteca de Autores Españoles*, vol. LXX.) Madrid, 1923.

---

[1] If two dates are given, the bracketed one indicates when the work was written.

SELECT BIBLIOGRAPHY

CADAMOSTO, LUIGI DI. "Navigationi." [c. 1457.] Printed in G. B. RAMUSIO, *Navigationi et Viaggi*, vol. I. A French translation exists by C. SCHEFER, *Relation des voyages à la côte occidentale d'Afrique d'Alvise de Cà da Mosto*. Paris, 1895. There is a poor English translation in T. ASTLEY, *Voyages*, vol. I, pp. 572–96. The most recent edition is a critical one by R. CADDEO, *Le navigazioni atlantiche di Alvise da Cà da Mosto*. Milan, 1929.

FERNANDEZ ALEMA, V. ["Collection of News," c. 1508.] A summary, from the MSS. preserved in the state archives of Munich, has been published by J. A. SCHMELLER, entitled: Uber Valentim Fernandez Alema und seine Sammlung von Nachrichten über die Entdeckungen und Besitzungen der Portugiesen in Africa und Asien bis zum Yahre 1508. *Abhandlungen der philosophisch-philolog. Klasse der Königlichen Bayerischen Akademie*. Bd. IV, pp. 41–7. Munich, 1847.

FONTENEAU, J. *La Cosmographie.* [c. 1545.] Ed. J. MUSSET. Paris, 1904.

FOSSE, EUSTACHE DE LA. "Voyage." [c. 1520.] Ed. R. FOULCHÉ DELBOSC. *Revue hispanique*, 1897, vol. IV, pp. 174–201.

GOES, D. DE. *Chronica do Principe D. Joam II.* Lisbon, 1567.

—— *Chronica do felicissimo Rei D. Manoel.* 4 vols. Lisbon, 1566–7.

GOMES, DIOGO. *De prima inventione Guineae.* [c. 1460.] Printed by J. A. SCHMELLER in *Abhandlungen der philosophisch-philolog. Klasse der Königlichen Bayerischen Akademie.* Band IV, pp. 18–41. Munich, 1847. A revised text has been published by G. PEREIRA in the *Boletim da Sociedade de Geographia de Lisboa*, 1899, ser. XVII, no. 5, pp. 267–93.

GUERREIRO, (Padre) F. *Relaçaões Annuis das cousas que fizeram os padres da Companhia de Jesus.* 4 vols. Evora and Lisbon, 1603–11.

HAKLUYT, R. *The Principal Navigations, Voyages, Trafficques and Discoveries of the English Nation.* (Maclehose edn.) 12 vols. Glasgow, 1903–5.

LEO AFRICANUS. *A Geographical Historie of Africa.* [c. 1526.] Englished by J. PORY in 1600. Ed. R. BROWN for the Hakluyt Society. (Ser. I, vols. XCII–XCIV.) 3 vols. London, 1896.

MAREES, P. D. *Beschryvinge ende historische verhael van het Gout-custe van Guinea.* [1602.] Ed. S. P. L'HONORÉ NABER for the Lindschoten-Vereeniging. The Hague, 1912.

NAVARRETE, M. F. DE. *Colección de los viages y descubrimientos que hicieron por mar los Españoles.* 5 vols. Madrid, 1825–37.

NUNEZ DO LIAM, D. *Cronicas del Rey D. João I e os Reys D. Duarte e D. Affonso V.* [c. 1600.] 2 vols. Lisbon, 1780.

PACHECO PEREIRA, D. *Esmeraldo de situ orbis.* 4 books. [*c.* 1505.] Ed. E. DA SILVA DIAS. Lisbon, 1905. Earlier edition, containing documents, by R. E. DE AZEVEDO BASTO. Lisbon, 1892. A critical English translation has been published by G. H. T. KIMBLE for the Hakluyt Society, London, 1937.

PALENCIA, A. DE. *Crónica de Enrique IV.* [*c.* 1490.] 5 vols. Madrid, 1904–9.

PINA, R. DE. *Chronica do Senhor Rey Affonso V.* [*c.* 1500.] (*Colleção de livros inéditos de historia portugueza,* vol. I.) Lisbon, 1790.

—— *Chronica del Rey D. João II.* [*c.* 1500.] (*Colleção de livros inéditos de historia portugueza,* vol. I.) Lisbon, 1790.

PULGAR, H. DEL. *Chronica de los Señores Reyes Católicos Don Fernando y Dona Isabel de Castilla y de Aragon.* [*c.* 1480–92.] (*Biblioteca de Autores Españoles,* vol. LXX.) Madrid, 1923.

PURCHAS, S. *Hakluytus Posthumus, or Purchas his Pilgrimes.* [1625.] (Maclehose edn.) 20 vols. Glasgow, 1905–7.

RAMUSIO, G. B. *Navigationi et Viaggi.* 3 vols. Venice, 1554–9.

Relations des ambassadeurs Vénitiens sur Charles-Quint et Philippe II. (Ed. L. P. GACHARD.) Brussels, 1856.

RESENDE, G. DE. *Chronica que trata da vida do D. João II.* Evora, 1545.

SOUSA COUTINHO, (FREI) M. DE. *Annaes de D. João III.* [*c.* 1630.] (Ed. A. HERCULANO.) Lisbon, 1844.

STADEN, H. *The True History of his Captivity.* [1557.] (Ed. M. LETTS.) London, 1928.

III. LATER WORKS

(a) GENERAL WORKS

ALMEIDA, F. DE. *Historia de Portugal.* 5 vols. Coimbra, 1922–7.

AZEVEDO, J. L. DE. *Epocas de Portugal Económico.* Lisbon, 1929.

BENSAUDE, J. *L'astronomie nautique au Portugal à l'époque des grandes découvertes.* 2 pts. Bern, 1912 and 1917.

—— *Lacunes et surprises de l'histoire des découvertes maritimes.* Coimbra, 1930.

BETTENCOURT, E. A. DE. *Descobrimentos, guerras e conquistas dos Portuguezes em terras do ultramar nos seculos XV e XVI.* Lisbon. 1881–2.

Cambridge History of the British Empire. (Ed. J. HOLLAND ROSE, A. P. NEWTON and E. A. BENIANS.) Vol. I, chs. 2 and 6. Cambridge, 1929.

Cambridge Modern History. (Ed. A. W. WARD, G. W. PROTHERO and S. LEATHES.) Vol. I, ch. 1. Cambridge, 1907.

CARVALHO, M. E. G. DE. *D. João III e os Francezes.* Lisbon, 1909.

SELECT BIBLIOGRAPHY

CLARKE, J. S. *The progress of maritime discovery from the earliest period to the close of the eighteenth century.* 2 vols. London, 1803.
CORBETT, (Sir) J. S. *Drake and the Tudor Navy.* 2 vols. London, 1898.
CORTESÃO, J. *The national secret of the Portuguese discoveries in the fifteenth century.* Englished by W. A. BENTLEY.
DELABORD, (Le Comte) J. *Gaspard de Coligny.* 3 vols. Paris, 1879-82.
DEPPING, G. B. *Histoire du commerce entre le Levant et l'Europe depuis les Crusades jusqu' à la fondation des colonies d'Amérique,* 2 vols. Paris, 1830.
GAFFAREL, P. *Les Français au delà des Mers : Les découverts français du XIVe au XVIe siècles.* Paris, 1888.
GUÉNIN, E. *Ango et ses pilotes.* Paris, 1901.
HELPS, (Sir) A. *The Spanish conquest in America.* 4 vols. London, 1855-61.
LANNOY, C. ET VANDERLINDEN, H. *L'expansion coloniale des peuples Européens : Portugal et Espagne.* Brussels, 1907.
MARGRY, P. *Les navigations françaises et la revolution maritime du XIVe au XVIe siècles.* Paris, 1867.
MAULDE-LA-CLAVIÈRE, M. A. R. DE. *La diplomatie au temps de Machiavel.* 3 vols. Paris, 1892.
MERRIMAN, R. B. *The rise of the Spanish Empire.* 4 vols. New York, 1918-35.
NEGREIROS, A. L. DE A. *Les colonies Portugaises. Les organismes politiques indigènes.* Paris, 1910.
NYS, E. *Les origines du droit international.* Paris, 1894.
—— *Le droit international: les principes, les théories, les faits.* 3 vols. Paris, 1904-6.
PERES, D. *Historia de Portugal.* 6 vols. Barcelos, 1928- . *In progress.*
PRESCOTT, W. H. *History of the reign of Ferdinand and Isabella.* 3 vols. London, 1838.
REBELLO DA SILVA, L. A. *Historia de Portugal nos seculos XVII e XVIII.* 5 vols. Lisbon, 1860-71.
RONCIÈRE, C. B. DE LA. *Histoire de la marine française.* 6 vols. Paris, 1899.
SHILLINGTON, V. M., and CHAPMAN, A. B. W. *The commercial relations of England and Portugal.* London, 1907.
WHITEWAY, R. S. *The Portuguese expedition to Abyssinia.* (Hakluyt Society Pubn., ser. II, vol. X.) London, 1902.
WILLIAMSON, J. A. *Maritime Enterprise, 1485-1558.* Oxford, 1913.
—— *Sir John Hawkins. The Time and the Man.* Oxford, 1927.
—— *The voyages of the Cabots.* London, 1929.
WYNDHAM, (Hon.) H. A. *The Atlantic and Slavery.* London, 1935.
VIGNAUD, H. *Histoire de la grande entreprise de Christophe Colomb.* 2 vols. Paris, 1911.

(b) WORKS RELATING ESPECIALLY TO WEST AFRICA.

ANCELLE, J. *Les explorations au Senegal et dans les contrées voisines depuis l'antiquité jusqu'à nos jours.* Paris, 1886.

ANON. *Notícia corográphia e cronológica do Bispado de Cabo-Verde.* [1784]. (*Ineditos Coloniais*, série A, núm. III). Lisbon, 1937.

—— *The Golden Coast, or a description of Guinney.* London, 1665.

ASTLEY, T. *A new general collection of voyages.* 4 vols. London, 1745.

AZEVEDO COELHO, F. DE. *Descrição da Costa-de-Guiné.* [1669]. (*Ineditos Coloniais*, série A, núm I.) Lisbon, 1937.

BARBOT, J. *A description of the coasts of North and South Guinea.* London, 1732.

BEAZLEY, C. R. *Prince Henry the Navigator.* London, 1890.

BENEZET, A. *Some historical account of Guinea.* Philadelphia, 1771.

BOSMAN, W. *A new description of the coast of Guinea.* London, 1705.

DAPPER, O. *Description de l'Afrique, traduit du Flamand.* Amsterdam, 1686.

ESTANCELIN, L. *Recherches sur les voyages et découvertes des navigateurs normands en Afrique appellée Guinée.* Paris, 1832.

FARIA Y SOUSA, M. DE. *The history of Portugal from the first ages of the world to 1640.* Trans. and continued down to 1698 by captain J. STEVENS. London, 1698.

—— *The Portuguese Asia.* [c. 1666–75.] Englished by captain J. STEVENS. 3 vols. London, 1695.

KIMBLE, G. H. T. " The mapping of West Africa in the fourteenth and fifteenth centuries." (An unpublished thesis in the University of London.) London, 1931.

LABAT, J. B. *Nouvelle relation de l'Afrique occidentale.* 5 vols. Paris, 1728.

LANG, J. *The land of the golden trade.* London, 1910.

LÉMOS, F. DE. *Descrição da Costa-de-Guiné.* [1684]. (*Ineditos Coloniais* série A, núm. II). Lisbon, 1937.

LOPES DE LIMA, J. J. *Ensaios sobre a statistica das possessões Portuguezes na Africa Occidental e Oriental.* 3 bks. Lisbon, 1844.

LUCAS (Sir) C. P. *An historical geography of the British Colonies*, vol. III, *West Africa*. Oxford, 1913.

ORTIZ DE ZÚÑIGA, D. *Annales ecclesiasticos y seculares de Sevilla.* Madrid, 1677.

PINTO, M. DE R. *Historia da Ilha de S. Thomé.* [1734]. (*Ineditos Coloniais*, série B, núm. I). Lisbon, 1937.

PRESTAGE, E. *The Portuguese Pioneers.* London, 1933.

RAVENSTEIN, E. G. *The strange adventures of Andrew Battell.* (Hakluyt Society, ser. II, vol. VI.) London, 1901.

RONCIÈRE, C. B. DE LA. *La découverte de l'Afrique au Moyen Age.* 2 vols. Paris, 1924–5.

SELECT BIBLIOGRAPHY 235

Santarem, (Viscount) Barros e Sousa. *Recherches sur la priorité de la découverte des pays situés sur la côte occidentale d'Afrique au-delà du Cap Bojador.* Paris, 1842.
Senna Barcellos, C. J. de. *Subsidios para a historia de Cabo Verde e Guiné.* 7 pts. Lisbon, 1899–1900.
Villaut, N. *Relation des costes d'Afrique, appellées Guinée.* Paris, 1669.
Welman, C. W. *The native states of the Gold Coast. II. Ahanta.* London, 1930.

(c) Articles and Reprints from Periodicals

Azevedo, P. de. Defesa da navegação de Portugal contra os franceses em 1552. *Archivo Histórico Portuguez*, 1908, vol. VI, pp. 161–5.
Beaurepaire, C. de la. Presidential Address. *Bulletin de la Société de l'Histoire de Normandie*, 1887–90, pp. 255–6.
Beazley, C. R. Prince Henry of Portugal and the African crusade of the fifteenth century. *A.H.R.*, 1910, vol. XVI, pp. 11–23.
—— Prince Henry of Portugal and his political, commercial and colonising work. *A.H.R.*, 1912, vol. XVII, pp. 252–67.
Cortesão, A. Z. Subsidios para a historia do descobrimento da Guiné e Cabo Verde. A reprint from *Boletim da Agência Geral das Colonias*, no. 76. Lisbon, 1931.
Eliot, K. M. The first voyages of Martin Frobisher. *E.H.R.*, 1917, vol. XXXII, pp. 89–92.
Figueredo, F. The geographical discoveries and conquests of the Portuguese. *Hispanic American Historical Review*, 1926, vol. VI, pp. 47–70.
Fitzler, H. M. A. Überblick über die portugiesischen Uberseehandelsgesellschaften des 15–18 Jahrhunderts. *Vierteljahrschrift für Sozial-und Wirtshaftsgeschichte*, 1931, Bd. XXIV, pp. 282–98.
—— Portuguiesische Handelsgesellschaften des 15 und beginnenden 16. Yahrhunderts. *Vierteljahrschri für Sozial-und Wirtschaftsgeschichte*, 1932, Bd. XXV, pp. 209–50.
Gaffarel, P. Jean Ango. A reprint from *Bulletin de la Société normande de Géographie.* Rouen, 1889.
Kimble, G. H. T. Portuguese policy and its influence on fifteenth century cartography. *Geographical Review*, 1933, vol. XXIII, pp. 653–9.
Nys, E. La ligne de demarcation d'Alexandre VI. *Revue de droit international*, 1895, vol. XXVII, pp. 474–91.
Quinn, D. B. Edward IV and exploration. *Mariner's Mirror*, 1935, vol. XXI, pp. 275–84.
Vanderlinden, H. Alexander VI and the bulls of demarcation. *A.H.R.*, 1916, vol. XXII, pp. 1–20.

ADDITIONAL (SELECT) BIBLIOGRAPHY

AJAYI, J. F. A. and CROWDER, M. (eds.), *History of West Africa* (2 vols., London, 1971 and 1974).

BLAKE, JOHN W., *Europeans in West Africa* (2 vols., Hakluyt Society, London, 1942).

BOVILL, E. W., *The golden trade of the Moors* (2nd ed., London, 1968).

BOXER, C. R., *The Portuguese seaborne empire* (London, 1969).

BRÁSIO, A., *Monumenta missionaria Africana: Africa ocidental* (Lisbon, 1952–).

CIPOLLA, C. M., *Guns and sails* (London, 1965).

CORTESAO, A. Z. and MOTA, A. TEIXEIRA DA, *Portugaliae monumenta cartographica* (5 vols., Lisbon, 1960–62).

DAAKU, K. Y., *Trade and politics on the Gold Coast, 1600–1720* (Oxford, 1970).

DELAFOSSE, M., *Haut-Sénégal-Niger* (3 vols., Paris, 1912).

FAGE, J. D., *Ghana: a historical interpretation* (Madison, 1959).

FYFE, C., *History of Sierra Leone* (Oxford, 1962).

KUP, P., *History of Sierra Leone, 1400–1787* (London, 1961).

LAWRENCE, A. W., *Trade castles and forts of West Africa* (London, 1963).

MAGALHAES-GODINHO, V., *L'économie de l'empire portugais aux xve et xvie siècles* (Paris, 1969).

MAUNY, R., *Tableau géographique de l'ouest africain au moyen âge* (Dakar, 1961).

MAURO, F., *Le Portugal et l'Atlantique au xviie siècle, 1570–1670* (Paris, 1960).

Monumenta Henricina (12 vols., Coimbra, 1960–71).

MOTA, A. TEIXEIRA DA, *Topónimos de origem portuguesa na costa ocidental de Africa* (Bissau, 1950).

—— *Guiné portuguesa* (2 vols., Lisbon, 1954).

PARRY, J. H., *The age of reconnaissance* (London, 1963).

PENROSE, BOIES, *Travel and discovery in the renaissance, 1420–1620* (Cambridge, Mass., 1952).

Peres, D. (ed.), *Duas descrições seiscentistas da Guiné* (Lisbon, 1953).
Rodney, W., *History of the Upper Guinea Coast, 1545-1800* (Oxford, 1970).
Ryder, A. C. F., *Benin and the Europeans, 1485-1897* (London, 1969).
—— *Materials for West African History in Portuguese archives* (London, 1965).

The following recent editions of standard contemporary works may be mentioned:

D'Almada, André Alvares, *Tratado breve dos rios de Guiné* (ed. Luis Silveira) (Lisbon, 1946). A Brásio has published an even more recent edition (Lisbon, 1964).
Cadamosto, Alvise, *Voyages* (ed. G. R. Crone) Hakluyt Society, ser. II, vol. LXXX (London, 1937). Crone included in this volume an edited translation of the *Voyages* of Diogo Gomes. See also the edition by D. Peres, which included the voyage of Pero de Cintra (Lisbon, 1948).
Fernandes, Valentim, *Description de las Côte Occidentale d'Afrique (Sénégal au Cap de Monte)* (ed. T. Monod, A. Texeira da Mota and R. Mauny) (Bissau, 1951).
Guerreiro, F., *Relaçaões Annuis* (ed. A. Viegas) (3 vols., Lisbon and Coimbra, 1930-42).

INDEX

ACCRA, 101, 140, 157, 180, 182–3; description of, 102; negroes burn, 177, 191
Admiralty, English High Court of, 92; examinations in, 167, 170, 182, 191
Affonso, João, 112, 136; Guinea voyage of, 116–18
Africa, Islands of, 131
—, North, 1, 2, 4, 19, 26, 43, 45, 56, 192; *see also* Barbary, Morocco
Albirouni, Arab geographer, 4
Albuquerque, Lope de, Count of Penamacor, 63, 71
Albuquerque, Manoel d', 129
Alcacer, 76
Alcaçovas, Treaty of, 52–3, 65, 66, 67, 72, 78
Alcantara, 52
Alcatrazes, 93
Aldaye, James, 167
Alexander VI, Pope, 67, 68, 70; and bull *Inter Caetera* (June 1493), 67; and bull *Dudum Siquidem* (26 Sept. 1493), 68
Alfonso V of Portugal, chs. I–IV, 67; laws of, relating to Guinea trade, 29–35, 39, 54, 72, 75–7, 83–4; invades Castile, 43; seeks French support, 52; abandons claim to Canaries, 53; sends MSS. to King of Naples, 64; death of, 73
Algarve, chief magistrate of, 117
Aljubarrota, battle of, 1
Almada, André Alvares d', captain, 92, 139–40, 181
Alvarez, Fernão d', 125
Alvide, Braz d', 144, 145
Amber, 6, 91, 191
Ambergris, 17, 105
America, discovery of, 65; slave trade to, 87
—, South, scheme for English plantation in, 171
Amtas, João Pereira d', 146, 159, 187
Andalusia, chs. I and III; fleet of, 17, 21, 50; merchants of, 59, 65; fishermen of, 65; French trade in, 190

Andalusians, 2, 6; exploits in Guinea of, 38–40, chs. I and III
Andrada, Francisco de, 123, 132
Anglo-Portuguese negotiations, 143–4, 145, 147–51, 158–9, 164, 172, 187–9
— — treaty, 189
Ango, Jean, 107, 108, 109, 132, 136, 147, 186; letter of marque of, 110, 111; sends ships to Guinea, 115, 121
Angola, 6; slaves from, 86, 88, 95, 96; trade of, 97, 104
Angolares, 86; revolt of, 140, 177
Annobon, 7, 28, 92, 96
Antão Island, 94
Antwerp, 73, 84, 96, 143, 151; Portuguese factor in, 78, 85; trade of, 115, 144, 183
Arabs, 4, 7, 16
Aragon, 1, 2, 43
Aranjo, Emanuel d', 168
Arguin, 97, 131, 172; fort of, 6, 16, 124, 140; fishing near, 17, 90; trade at, 27, 28, 30; contract of, 31, 33; Prince John receives trade of, 72–3; original centre of slave trade, 86
Arras, Bishop of, 159
—, Congress of, 70
Artero, Lorenzo, 64
Ashurst, Thomas, 71
Asiento, The, 88
Ataide, Antonio d', Count of Castanheyra, 108, 110, 111, 115, 116, 120, 124–5, 126, 129
Aveiro, João Affonso de, 84
Avila, Alonso de, 55
Aviz, House of, 1, 2, 56, 176
Axem, 10, 28, 80; fort of, 101–2, 140, 155, 192
Azambuja, Diogo d', 98–9
Azenegues, The, 7, 17, 44, 50, 51, 90
Azevedo, Lucio de, 87
—, Ruy Gomes d', 178
Azores, Islands of, 52, 67, 71, 117, 127, 131, 132, 136, 148, 162, 186, 189
Azurara, Gomes de, 5, 16, 35; his *Chronica de Guiné*, 64

INDEX

BARBA, Fernão Rodrigues, 122–3
Barbacini, The, 8
Barbary, 17, 44, 51, 185; Arabs of, 7, 16; fisheries of, 58, 65, 66, 68, 89–90, 186; English trade to, 61, 143, 167, 189; Pinteado at, 123; French trade in, 190; voyages to, 191
Barbot, Jean, 3, 11, 41, 90, 102, 103; his *Description of Guinea*, 41
Barcelona, 68
Barker, Andrew, 189
Barlowe, Roger, 142
Barros, João de, 20, 21, 28, 32, 81, 99, 101, 102, 103; his *Da Asia*, 28, 79, 143
Barros, Tomas de, 125
Bayão, Bartholomew, 139, 170–1, 176, 189
Bayonne, Conference of, 133
Beafares, The, 8
Beatrice, Princess of Portugal, 52
Beiçudos, The, 10
Bemoij, Prince of Senegal, 102–3
Benin, 11–12, 136, 150, 186; Bight of, 12; trade of, 40, 74, 93, 96, 103, 150; pepper of, 64 84–5, 151; slaves of, 86, 87, 95, 192; ivory of, 89; negro wars in, 97; Wyndham's voyage to, 123, 143, 144; Sumbas invade, 138; Portuguese influence in, 140–1; King of, 140, 156; French voyages to, 163, 165, 190
Benincasa, Gratiosus, 65
Bermudes, João, 139
Bernáldez, Andrés, 42, 43, 53, 100
Beziguiche, 13, 92, 191
Biafra, Bight of, 12
Bianco, Andrea, 65
"Bilad Ghana", tales of, 4, 6
Bland, captain, 166
Blundell, Denis, 152
Boavista Island, 94
Boileau, Michel, 156, 165
Bolulão, King of Malagueta, 139
Bontemps, Jean, 163, 166
Bordeaux, 121
Boudomel, King, 8, 191
—, King Noghor of, 92
Bouloees, The, 8, 9, 10, 80
Bourbon, Antoine de, King of Navarre, 156
—, Henry de, King of Navarre, 184
Bourel de la Roncière, Charles, 3, 134
Boviage, Martin Annes, 34, 89
Braganza, Fernando de, 3rd Duke of, 63
Brava island, 94

Brazil, 97, 103, 124, 128, 130–1, 150, 185; slave trade to, 86, 88, 104, 110–11; French traffic to, 108, 109, 118, 121, 133, 134, 147, 150, 167; William Hawkins and, 114, 120; Pinteado visits, 123; planters of S. Thomé go to, 177
Bristol, 61; merchants of, 71
Brittany, 108, 109; ports of, 107, 110; merchants of, 112, 115, 116, 133, 145
Bruges, 58, 59

CABO DAS REDES, 80
Cabo da Verga, 8, 92
Cabot, John, 71
Cacheo, 91–2, 141; burnt, 182
Cadamosto, Alvise, 8, 17, 87
Cadiz, 2, 17, 18, 19, 23, 44, 51, 58, 65; province of, 24
Calais, staple at, 60
Calixtus III, Pope, 22, 23
Camden, William, 144
Caminha, Alvaro de, 104,
Canary Islands, 13, 56, 58, 62; Castile and, 18, 19, 41, 43–5, 64; lands beyond the, 52–3, 54, 182; Portuguese try to reoccupy, 76, 98; French at, 117, 130, 166, 190
Cancer, Tropic of, 160
Cantino, Alberto, 65; map of, 65, 82
Cantor, Land of, 5, 8
Cão, Diogo, 59, 75, 98
Cape Barbas, 58
Cape Bojador, 5, 106, 165; lands beyond, 20–1, 29, 53, 56, 58, 67, 78; licences for voyages beyond, 31, 62; fishing near, 65, 66, 89
Cape Lopo Gonçalves, 65
Cape Nam, 22, 67
Cape of Good Hope, 7, 104, 108
Cape of Santa Maria, 65
Cape of Saint Anna, 10; gold at, 80; slaves at, 86
Cape Palmas, 9, 10, 13, 84, 89, 172
Cape St. Catherine, 7, 12, 28, 29, 86, 97
Cape Threepoints, 10, 13, 37, 59, 80, 101, 141, 151, 152; French at, 121, 135, 146
Cape Verde, 2, 13, 14, 65, 124, 131, 181, 189; discovery of, 17; trade of, 18, 23, 74; Flemish ship wrecked near, 58–9; slave trade at, 86–7; soap manufactured at, 91; French at, 92, 135, 150, 166, 170, 190; English at, 169, 171, 182, 191

INDEX

Cape Verde Islands, 7, 38, 50, 51, 52, 185, 186; trade of, 6, 27, 36, 93–4, 97; discovery of, 17, 26, 40; privileges of islanders of, 31–3; demarcation from, 67–8; fisheries of, 90, 187; forts in, 102–3; piracy in, 108, 128, 136, 150; French at, 109, 113, 114, 120, 121, 166; English at, 169, 189
Caramansa, King of Mina, 99
Cardoso, Ayres, 174
Carlet, David, 169
Carreiro, Diogo, 142, 182; letter to King Sebastian, 181
Carthaginians, The, 5
Castile, 12, 17, 26, 35, 37, 38, 72, 94, 148, 162; colonial rivalry with Portugal of, 6, 14, 15, 19–25, 57, 62, 66–8, 90, 98, 106, merchants of, 18–19, 36, 44, 59, 63, 64, 65–6; activity in Guinea of, 40–56, 61; fishermen of, 58, 66; chroniclers of, 80, 81; ships at S. Thomé of, 96
Castlyn, Edward, 148, 163
Catalans, The, 2
Cateau-Cambrésis, Treaty of, 160, 165
Catherine of Portugal, wife of John III, 29, 187; as regent, 158–9, 176
Cavalli, Marino, 118
Cecil, Sir William, 164, 167, 175–6, 188
Cercamp, 159
Cerda, Luis de la, Admiral of France, 69
Ceuta, 1, 2, 3, 5, 47
Chabot, Philippe de, Admiral of France, 112, 116; bribing of, 120, 132–4, 136
Charles V, Emperor, 111, 115, 131–2, 133, 136, 147; council of, 135
Charles IX of France, 163, 187
Chateaubriand, M. de, 109
Chester, Sir William, 163
Cintra, Pero de, 26, 65
Civet, 17, 27, 34, 90, 191
Clement V, Pope, 70
Clement VI, Pope, 69
Cloth, 9, 45, 80, 93, 142, 153
Coelho, Duarte, 117–19, 123, 124; commands Mina fleet, 122; sent to fortify Malagueta, 126–7
Coligny, Gaspard de, 161, 162–3, 165
Columbus, Christopher, 9, 66–7
Comani, The, 11, 99, 176, 184
Condé, Prince of, 184
Congo, slaves from, 88
Contractors of Guinea trade, 73, 76, 82, 96, 113, 124, 179–80, 182–3, 192; privileges of, 74–5; see also Gomes, Fernão; Torres, Affonso de; Gonçalves de Guzman, Antonio
Convoy system for Guinea fleets, 116, 122, 128–32, 136, 137, 158, 162, 184–5
Cook, Edward, 186
Copper, 9, 93, 142
Coronado, Gonçalo, 46
Correa, João Rodrigues, 148, 149
—, Jorge, 52
Cortes, Portuguese, 36, 37, 61, 62, 77, 98
Costa, Soeiro da, 28
Counter-Reformation, The, 161–2
Covides, Pedro de, 52
Crespy, Treaty of, 134–5
Cunha, Pero Vaz da, 102–3
—, Simao da, 97
Curtis, William, 188

D'Agincourt, M., 116
Das Povoas, Antonio Fernandes, 36
Dassell, Thomas, 74
De Haro Christobal, 73, 74
—, Diego, 73
De la Motte, M., 109
De Lugo, João, 36, 38, 39
—, Pedro, 36, 38
Denmark, Prince of, 184
De Prado, interloper, 23–4, 30, 38, 75
De Sousa Coutinho, M., 122, 126, 144
D'Este, Hercule, Duke of Ferrara, 65
Diaz, Diego, 55
—, Bartholomew, 82
—, Juan, 51–2
Dieppe, 3, 92, 107, 121, 150, 166
Donation of Constantine, 69
Duckett, Guinea trader, 175

Eannes, Gil, 5
East Indies, The, 4, 5, 29, 103, 104, 108, 118, 124, 131, 134–5; ambassadors to Portugal from, 82; pepper of, 84; trade of, 97, 105; Parmentier visits, 109; fleets of, 117, 118, 119, 127, 132, 185
Edrisi, Aran geographer, 4
Edward IV of England, 60, 62; letter to Pope Sixtus IV, 61; attitude towards Portuguese claim to Guinea, 71
Elizabeth of England, 69, 161, 167–8; favours English traffic to Guinea, 164, 173; and Portuguese complaints, 187–9
Elliott, Hugh, 71
Elmina, see S. Jorge da Mina
— " Note", 99

INDEX

England, 14, 15, 63, 77, 78, 98; ports of, 57, 60, 148, 168; merchants of, 57; government of, 69, 106, 152, 163, 165; crown of, 71; fleets equipped in, 110, chs. VII, VIII; privy council of, 147, 149, 189; protestants in, 161-2, 192; Portuguese quarrel with, 188

English merchants, privateers and interlopers interested in Guinea, 9, 13, 24, 50, 51, 55, 58, 60-2, 75, 89, 105, 106, 107, 114, 121, chs. VII and VIII; collaborate with French, 109-10; plan to build forts in Guinea, 155, 163, 173-6

Equatorial current, 14, 38
Escolar, Pero de, 27, 98
Esteves, Alvaro, 27-8
Estuñiga, Gonzalo de, 44
Eugenius IV, Pope, 47, 70
Evora, 52, 63

FABIAN, John, 60-1
—, Thomas, 60-1
—, William, 50, 60-2, 78
Faim, Jean, 108
Fenner, George, 169-70, 172, 182
—, Thomas, 186
Ferdinand, King of Aragon and Spain, 2, 20, 41, 43, 50, 57, 66; encourages Guinea traffic, 44, 46-7, 49; claims Guinea, 45, 53; council of, 51; admits Portuguese ownership of Guinea, 52, 54, 56; letter to Alfonso V, 55; forbids fishing near Cape Bojador, 65; appeals to Alexander VI, 67; negotiates with John II, 68, 70
Fernandes, Martin, 27
—, Ruy, 111, 133
Fernando, Prince of Portugal, 31, 36, 38
Fernando Po, 7, 28, 66, 95, 96
Fernão do Po, 28, 59
Ferreiro, Gonçalo, 23
Ferreyra, Jeronimo, 123
Fetu, 11, 99, 176, 184
Fish, 17, 79, 100; Portuguese impose tolls for right to, 17, 90, 102
Fishing Trade, 89-90
Flanders, 63, 84, 115; ship at Mina of, 37, 39, 40, 58-9; merchants of, 57, 59, 61; trade with Guinea, 60, 184; annual spice fleets to, 133
Fleury, Jean, 107
Florentine merchants, 57, 62
Fogo Island, 94, 128, 170
Fonte Nables, 110, 112
Fonteneau, Jean, 143

Fosse, Eustache de la, 9, 65, 82, 98, 145; sails to Guinea, 54, 58-60
Foulos, The, 139
Fourquevaux, Raimond, baron de, 179
France, 14, 15, 78; spurious claim to prior discovery of Guinea, 2, 3, 42, 48; government of, 69, 106, 136, 163; crown of, 71; at war with Spain, 159; huguenots in, 156, 161-3, 164, 165, 166, 167, 187, 190, 192
Francis I of France, 108, 110, 132, 145, 163; champions freedom of seas, 111-12; forbids Guinea voyages, 133-4, 150, 164, 187
Franco-Portuguese negotiations, 108, 110, 112, 115-16, 132-5, 136, 146-7, 158-60, 164, 187-8
French, traders in Guinea, 85, 96, 105, chs. VI, VII and VIII; corsairs, 13, 51, 55, 66, 78, 83, 90, 92, 101-2, chs. VI-VIII; raid S. Thomé, 104; first visit Guinea, 108-9; plan to build forts in Guinea, 155-6
— West African Company, 41
Frobisher, Martin, 101, 102, 167; imprisoned in S. Jorge castle, 142; plans a raid in Guinea, 175

GABUN, 12, 40, 74
Gama, Vasco da, 82, 84
Gambia river, 7, 8, 23, 24, 105, 136; king of land round, 44; gold near, 80; French traffic at, 92, 182; mulattoes near, 179
Garrard, Sir William, 163
Garratt, John, 188, 191
Gató, 12, 93, 103, 140, 151; factory at, 84, 86
Genoese in Guinea, 17, 37, 40, 57, 62, 96
Gibraltar, Straits of, 2
Goes, Damião de, 31, 42, 43
Gold of Guinea, *passim*; cause of colonial rivalry of Portugal and Castile, 53; mine of, 53, 55, 58, 68; tales of, 4, 5, 61
— Trade, 57, 65, 79-83, 142-3, 179
— Coast, 3, 7, 9, 58, 141-2, 151; see also Mina, Axem, Accra, Cape Threepoints, S. Jorge da Mina, Samma
Gomes, Diogo, 5, 23, 24, 30, 31, 35, 150
—, Fernão, da Mina, 30-7, 89; terms of 1469 grant to, 26-7, 33; renewed grant to, 27, 33; relinquishes

Guinea privileges, 49; discoveries of, 26–9, 65, 80
Gonçalves, Antam, 5, 85
—, Luis, 51
— de Guzman, Antonio, 74
Gonneville, 146
Gonson, Benjamin, 163
Gosselin, captain, of Dieppe, 182
—, Edouard, 149
Gouvea, Francisco de, 183
Grain Coast, 3, 9, 154; *see also* Malagueta
Granada, siege of, 1, 2
Great Fante, 11
Guerreiro, Fernão, Padre, 139
Guinea, charts and maps of, 3, 64–5, 66, 77, 82; discovery of, 3–6; trade of, 6, 7, 9, 16–17, 29, 31–5, 72, ch. V, 113–14, 141–3, 154; white enterprise confined to coast of, 7, 12; Gulf of, 7, 28, 86, 93, 95–6, 121, 156; interior unknown, 8–9, 11–12; physical and climatic features of, 12–14; piracy in, 51, 66; "Isles" of, 55; Ordinances of, 75–7; House of, 75; Judge of, 75, 76; crews drowned in, 118, 128; armed Portuguese fleets in, 118–20, 121–4, 128, 136, 137, 157–8; trade rivalry in, 150–5; fortification of, 98–104, 124–7, 154–6, 157, 163, 173–6, 181–3
— Current, 13, 14, 27
"Guinea of Cape Verde", 6, 7–9, 19, 26, 33
"Guinea Portugalexe", 65
Guinea "Season", 61
Gum, 6, 17, 34, 36, 76, 121, 191
Guoguoliis, The, 8, 9
Guzman, Henry de, 2nd Duke of Medina Sidonia, 50–1, 60, 62
—, Juan de, 19

HABAAN, King of, 155, 173, 175
Hakluyt, Richard, 60, 144–5, 149, 172; his *Principal Navigations*, 60, 92, 101, 143
Hallé, Laurent, 190
Hallé-Le Seigneur Company, The, 190
Hansa, The, 61
Hapsburg, House of, 133; empire of, 146
Harfleur, 110, 112, 113, 118, 146
Harmattan, The, 14
Harwich, 189
Havre, 150, 166, 167
— de Grace, 145

Hawkins, John, 64, 166, 174–5, 184, 186, 188, 189; and slave trade, 168, 170–2; burns Cacheo, 182
—, William, 109–10, 114, 120, 138, 144
Henry II of England, 69
— of France, 145, 146–7
Henry III of France, 190
Henry IV of Castile, 19, 20, 43, 46
Henry VII of England, 63, 71–2
Henry, Cardinal, Regent of Portugal, 176
—, Prince, the Navigator, 2, 16, 17, 20, 22, 24, 26, 30, 31, 40, 72, 78; at Ceuta, 3; motives for seeking Guinea, 4, 5; Guinea monopoly of, 21; as grandmaster of Order of Christ, 23
Hickman, Anthony, 163
Hides, 17, 36, 91, 105, 109, 128, 184, 191
Hispaniola, 171
Holder, Botolph, 174
Holland, 14; traders of, 89, 90, 140, 141, 191; takes fort S. Jorge, 100; subjects of, exploit "Gift" system in Guinea, 114; zealots of, 192
Homem, André, 175
Honguière, Jean, 166
Huelva, 51
Huet, Rouen merchant, 116

IBN SAID, Arab geographer, 4
Iceland, Fisheries of, 61
Ireland, 69
Isabella of Castile and Spain, 2, 20, 43, 46, 48, 51, 52, 56, 63, 66
Islam, 1
Italy, 70
Ivory, 9, 10, 28, 33, 34, 36, 47, 76, 79, 89, 91, 105, 109, 115, 128, 138, 146, 150, 154, 165, 172, 179, 184, 191
— Coast, 10, 36, 89, 154
— Trade, 89

JAALUNGUAS, The, 9
Jalofo, Kingdom of, 8, 97
Jalofos, The, 7, 191
Jenni, 8, 9
Jerez, 51
Jews in Guinea, 95
Joanna, Princess of Castile, *la Beltraneja*, 43, 50
John I of Portugal, 2
John II of Portugal, 55, 63, 66, 67, 80, 96; receives, as prince, the Guinea trade, 28, 29, 30, 34–5, 49, 72; sends armada to Guinea, 52

INDEX

instructions to Guinea captains, 54, 75; embassy to Edward IV, 60, 62, 98; negotiates with Henry VII, 63; sends pepper to Flanders, 64; negotiates with King Ferdinand, 68, 70; accession, 73; and Canary Islands, 76, 98; builds S. Jorge castle, 98-9; plans to fortify Senegal and Sierra Leone, 102-3, 181
John II of Castile, 19, 20, 22, 23, 24, 45, 47
John III of Portugal, 9, 29, 69, 78, 81, 85, 88, 93, 94, 101, 139, 140, 143, 144, 159, 161, 177, 181; correspondence of, 79, 82, 83; death of, 96, 158; embassies to France, 107, 108; champions monopoly, 111; negotiates with Francis I, 110, 112, 115, 132-6; tries to expel French from Guinea, 116-20, 121-8, 145; organises convoys, 128-32; negotiates with Henry II, 146-7; embassies to England, 147-51
John, Prince of Mina, 141
Jos, The, 12
Julius II, Pope, 68

LACERDA, Antonio Vaz de, 116-17
La Ferrol, 156
Lagos, 6, 16, 17, 19, 41, 64
— Company, 6, 16, 24, 26, 28, 30, 40
Lambert, Francis, 167
Lançerote Island, 69
La Rochelle, 121, 150; a nest of pirates, 186, 190
Lateran Council, The, 70
League, Catholic, The, 190
Leo, Duarte, 74
Leo Africanus, Arab geographer, 6, 8
Le Seigneur, Adrien, 190
—, Alfonse, 190
—, Jacques, 190
Letters of marque, 76, 111, 115, 145, 146-7; granted to Jean Ango, 108-9, 132, 136; granted to William Winter, 188
Licensees of Guinea, 75, 76, 113
"Lines of Amity", 160, 162, 189
Lisbon, *passim*; archives of, 79, 101; government at, 83; reports sent to, 185-6; French trade at, 190
Little Fante, 11
— Sabou, 11
Lloyd, John, 61
Loanda, 86, 192
Lodge, Sir Thomas, 163

Lok, John, 101, 156, 167, 173; Guinea voyage of, 147, 148, 155
London, 60, 65, 146, 150, 158, 166, 168, 187; Tower of, 63; merchants of, 143, 147-8, 161, 188; lord mayor of, 148; Guinea syndicate in, 169, 173; Spanish ambassador in, 174
Lopes de Lima, J. J., 33
Lopez de Burgos, Fernandes, Dr., 19
Lorraine, Cardinal of, 151, 156, 167
Louis XIV of France, 3
Lovell, John, 170, 172
Lower Guinea, 14, 29, 30, 123; *see also* Malagueta, Mina, Slave Coast
Luiz, Antonio, 175
Lyons, Treaty of, 133

MACHADO, Francisco, 123
Madeira Islands, 52, 189, 190; inhabitants of, 144; raided, 175
Maio Island, 94, 170
Malagueta Coast, 6, 9-10, 30, 40, 59, 120, 134-6, 144, 150, 152, 154; Flemish ships at, 37-8, 58; Genoese at, 62; pepper of, 83-4; plans to fortify, 103, 104, 122, 125-7; French on, 109-18, 121, 143; Portuguese armadas off, 118-19, 121-4; annual fleets to, 128-32, 135, 158; Sumbas pass behind, 138-9
Mandiguas, The, 8
Mandimansa, King, 7
Manes, *see* Sumbas
Manicongo, 6, 73, 95
Manuel of Portugal, the Fortunate, 66, 72, 73, 137, 180; Ordinances of, 75, 76-7, 82, 90, 92; forbids importation of Benin pepper, 84; regulates Senegambia trade, 87-8
Marees, Pieter, 101, 102, 176
Marguerite, Duchess of Valois, sister of Henry II, 187
Martin V, Pope, 20, 21, 47
Mary of England, 143, 147, 150, 159, 161, 163, 167; marriage of, 148; council of, 149
Mary Stuart, Queen of Scots, 188
Maynard, Tristram, 184-5
Medici, Catherine de, 163, 165
Melchior, captain, 167-8
Melli, empire of, 8, 9, 17
Mello, Fernão de, 95
Mesquita, Ruy Mendes de, 122-3
Mina Coast, *passim*; discovery of, 27-8, 36, 40; Flemings on, 37, 45, 58-60; annual fleet to, 49, 50-1, 66, 82, 83, 117, 128-32, 158, 185; contract of, 73-5, 82; meaning

of the name, 80–1 ; trade of, 97, 189 ; " Commonwealth " of, 100; fortification on, 98–102, 104, 155, 173–6 ; Portuguese armadas on, 119–20, 121–4 ; Casa da Mina, 125 ; Sumbas pass behind, 138 ; Simão Pires visits, 144 ; trade rivalry on, 151–5
Mina blacks, 11, 99–100, 141–2, 157
Monluc, Pierre de, 175
Montaroio, Fernando de, 81
Moors, 1, 2, 4, 17, 23, 24, 34, 51, 86, 192
Morales, Alonso de, 64–6
Morocco, 17
Mulattoes in Guinea, 95, 179

NALUNS, The, 8
Nantes, 120
Naples, King of, 64
Navarre, 1, 2
Navarre, M. de, 109
Navarrete, F. de, 42, 43
Negroes, 4, 62, 66 ; Portuguese skirmishes with, 97, 140–2, 176–7, 180 ; wars among, 97–8, 138–9 ; attack Axem, 101 ; burn Accra, 102, 177 ; besiege S. Jorge, 176
Netherlanders, 13, 55
Newhaven (Havre ?),'92, 162, 165, 166
Nicholas V, Pope, 22
Nicot, Jean, 151, 156 ; embassy to Lisbon, 159, 163, 187
Nieto, Anton Martin, 51
Niger, 4, 6, 12
Nile, 4, 6, 8, 9
Noli, Antonio da, 17
Normandy, ports of, 107, 149 ; shipowners and merchants of, 108, 112, 115, 116, 133, 145
Northern Earls, The, 188
Nunez, Hector, 188
—, Paulo, 140

OFFICIALS, Royal, in Guinea, 75, 95, 96 ; corruption among, 177–9
Ogané, The, 12
O Principe Island, 7, 28, 92, 142

PACHECO PEREIRA, Duarte, 5, 6, 10, 38, 59, 80, 83, 85, 87, 93, 97, 101, 102 ; *Esmeraldo de Situ Orbis* of, 8–9, 11, 12, 37, 42, 77, 79, 89
Palencia, Alonso de, 19, 20, 42, 43, 44, 48, 49, 50, 53
Palenço, captain, 18
Palha, Meni, 52
Palos, 2, 17, 23, 51 ; fishermen of, 44
Papacy, 69–71

Papal Bulls, *Dudum cum* (31 July 1436), 47 ; *Romanus Pontifex* (8 Jan. 1455), 22, 47, 69, 78 ; *Inter Caetera* (13 March 1456), 22, 47, 69, 78 ; *Aeterni Regis* (21 June 1481), 67 ; *Inter Caetera* (4 May 1493), 67, 68, 69, 70, 71 ; *Dudum siquidem* (26 Sept. 1493), 68, 69, 70, 71 ; *Ea quae* (24 Jan. 1506), 68, 70
Paris, 112, 146, 147, 158–9 ; Portuguese agent in, 116, 187 ; Spanish ambassador in, 174
Parmentier, Jean, 107, 109
—, Raoul, 107, 109
Pepper, 9, 47, 76, 80, 89, 105, 115, 128, 144, 154, 165, 172, 179
— of Malagueta, 9, 27, 34, 58, 62, 79, 109, 121 ; carried to Antwerp, 115 ; trade of, 122, 129, 143, 146
— of Benin, 64, 84, 143, 151
— Trade, 83–5, 88–9
Perestrello, Manuel de Mesquita, 178
Perrot, Thomas, 58
Philip II of Spain, 161, 167, 188, 192; as prince, 135 ; marriage of, 148 ; supports Portuguese complaints against English corsairs, 149, 159 ; service of, 171 ; reports English Guinea schemes, 174
Picardy, 112
Pina, Ruy de, 20, 21, 42, 43, 103 ; *Chronicle of John II* of, 60
Pinteado, Antonio Anes, 123, 143, 144
Pires, Simão, 144
Pisans, 69
Pius V, Pope, 188
Plymouth, 138, 150–1, 161, 170, 185
Pole, Reginald, Cardinal, 159
Pollard, Prof. A. F., 188
Ponce de León, Rodrigo, Marquis of Cadiz, 48–50
Porto d'Ali, 86
Portsmouth, 143, 151, 165
Portugal, *passim* ; renegades of, 18, 51, 64, 66, 87, 136, 150, 170, 173, 179 ; spies of, 62, 77–8, 116–18, 128, 185–6 ; and Castile, 18–25, 43–55, 62, 66–8, 90 ; national secrecy of, 38, 63, 64–5, 77, 162 ; laws of, relating to West Africa, 29–35, 72, 75–7, 82–3, 87–8, 91 ; Guinea monopoly of, 78 ; Guinea empire (*c.* 1553) of, 138–43 ; finances of, 176, 179 ; treaty between England and, 189 ; Spanish annexation of, 189, 192
Portuguese, *passim* ; contact with African interior, 8 ; achievement in Guinea of, 14, 106 ; impose

INDEX

fishing tolls in Guinea, 17, 90, 102, 192 ; schemes to exclude Guinea interlopers, 156-7 ; fear Spanish invasion, 176 ; Guinea company of, 183
— Order of Christ, 22, 23
Povoasan, port of S. Thomé, 96, 104
Prado, 24
Praia, 128
Prester John, 4, 12
Pulgar, Hernando del, 42, 43, 45, 53

QUADRA, Alvaro de la, Bishop, 174

RAINOLDS, Richard, 74, 92
Rangel, Alvaro, 63
Regnal, Gomes, 88
Resende, Garcia de, 60
Ribeira Grande, 35, 93-4, 122 ; forts in, 103, 181 ; captain of, 128
Rio da Furna, 92
Rio de Casamansa, 86
Rio de Case, 80, 86, 89
Rio de Nuno, 89, 139
Rio de S. Domingo, 74, 92, 141, 182, 184, 191
Rio de São Vicente, 84
Rio de Soiera, 28
Rio do Ouro, 58, 65, 89-90
Rio dos Camarões, 12, 90
Rio dos Escravos, 11, 59
Rio dos Sestos, 2, 3, 109, 114, 120, 125, 151, 152, 154, 157, 182 ; gold of, 80 ; pepper of, 85 ; slaves at, 86
Rio Fresco, 2, 3
Rio Grande, 8, 16, 80, 191
Rio Real, 12, 95
Rodrigues, Francisco, 144
Rodriguez, Sebastian, 51
— de Lillo, Anton, 46
Rome, 22
Rouen, 3, 107, 109, 110, 115, 121, 163, 165, 166, 190, 191
Rutter, William, 168

S. GERMAIN, 134
S. Jorge da Mina, castle of, *passim* ; officials at, 75, 177-9 ; description of, 98-101 ; upkeep of, 124-5 ; convicts in, 126 ; French prisoners in, 158, 163 ; negroes attack, 176-7 ; Dondou town at, 183 ; galleys at, 184
S. Martha, fort, 103
S. Nicolão Island, 94
S. Philip Island, 31
S. Thomé Island, *passim* ; contract of, 73-5 ; trade of, 86, 88, 92, 93, 97, 144 ; description of, 95-6; fortification in, 102, 103-4, 183; armada of, 121-2 ; native discontent in, 140, 177 ; sugar of, 142 ; French raid, 175, 183 ; decline of, 192 ; *see also* Povoasan
Sal Island, 90, 94
Salema, Diogo, 183
Salme, Sebastian de, 121, 128
Salt, 17, 90, 94
Samma, 11, 27, 28, 59, 80, 140, 192 ; description of, 101-2 ; fight at, 147 ; English burn, 157 ; King of, 180
San Juan de Ulua, 171, 172
— Lucar, 17, 51
Santa Luzia Island, 94
Santarem, João de, 27, 98
—, 2nd Viscount de, 3, 42
Santiago Island, *passim* ; piracy in, 38, 170 ; Seville fleet visits, 50 ; trade with Upper Guinea, 73, 75, 87, 91-2, 93, 184, 191 ; forts in, 103, 157, 181-2 ; rendezvous for convoys, 185 ; *see also* Alcatrazes, Praia, Riberia Grande
Sapes, The, 139, 170
Saracens, 69, 70
Sardinia, 69
Sarmiento, Luis, 121, 127
Scilly Isles, 184
Sebastian of Portugal, 15, 69, 78, 161, 164 ; leases Mina traffic, 74, 179-80 ; reorganises convoys, 131, 158, 185 ; embassies to England, 168, 187-9 ; as a minor, 176, 181-3 ; spies of, 185-6 ; strengthens forts in Guinea, 181-3 ; proposed match with Marguerite of Valois, 187 ; and siege of La Rochelle, 190 ; expedition against Moors, 192
Senegal river, 2, 4, 6, 7, 8, 9, 19, 33, 102-3, 104 ; gold at, 80 ; slaves from, 86, 171, 172, 189 ; French at, 92 ; trade with Sierra Leone of, 93 ; mulattoes of, 179 ; explored by Diogo Carreiro, 181
Senegambia, 7, 10, 14, 16, 18, 23, 30, 35, 38, 44, 45, 47, 51, 87, 94, 97 ; slave-raiding in, 86 ; trade with Santiago Island, 92, 184 ; forts in, 102-3, 181 ; decay of profits in, 85, 88, 91, 113 ; settlements in, 141-2 ; French traffic to, 190, 191
Sequeira, Ruy de, 28
Serreri, The, 8
Setuku, 8, 80
Seville, 2, 17, 18, 19, 41, 44, 46, 48, 49, 50, 51, 58, 59, 171

Ships, *la Bolandra, la Toca*, 55; *Pantafa*, 82; *Marie*, 108; *Paul*, 109; *la Michelle, l'Alouette, la Muselle*, 115; *Trinidade*, 120,129, 130; *la Grande-Martine*, 121; *São João*, 122, 129; *la Bonne Aventure*, 135, 150; *Retenta*, 136; *São João*, 136; *Primrose, Lion, Moon*, 143; *Lamulle*, 146; *Trinity, Green Dragon*, 166; *Greyhound*, 166; *Minion, Mary Fortune*, 169; *Flower de Luce, l'Auge*, 182; *Castle of Comfort*, 189
Sierra Leone, *passim*; fort in, 102, 103–5, 125; Sapes of, 139, 170–1; Portuguese settlements in, 141, 182
Silk, 9, 91
Silva, Bento Corrêa da, 141
Silveira, João da, 107
Sixtus IV, Pope, 61, 98
Slave Coast, 11, 161
— Trade, 85–9, 95, 105, 139–40, 142, 179; Hawkins and, 168, 170–2
Slaves, 5, 6, 9, 11, 16–17, 45, 74, 76, 80, 89, 136, 184; Andalusians seize, 44, 65; of Benin, 93; discontent of, in S. Thomé, 96
Soarez, Belchior, 125
Sores, Jacques de, 165, 166
Souris, *see* Sores
Sousa, Diogo Lopes de, 147, 148
—, Faria y, 41, 42
—, Lopo de, 81, 125
Southampton, 60, 186
Souza, Antonio Correa de, 128
Souzos, The, 9, 139
Spain, 54, 58, 69, 88, 105, 107, 152, 159, 161, 164, 165, 176, 192
Spes, Guerau de, 171
Stockbridge, Richard, 148
Strangewyse, Henry, 167, 168, 174, 183, 186
Sugar, 9, 79, 95–6, 121, 128, 140, 142, 145
Sumbas, Invasion of the, 138–40, 142, 176

Tavora, Bernadim de, 116, 132
Teymenes, The, 8, 89
Thomas, John, 71
Throckmorton, Sir Nicholas, 164, 168, 188
Timbuktu, 4, 5, 6, 8, 9, 17, 102–3; Diogo Carreiro visits, 142, 181
Tintam, John, 50, 60–2, 78

Toledo, Treaty of, 52–3, 54
Tooth Coast, *see* Ivory Coast
Tordesillas, Treaty of, 58, 68–9, 70, 78, 111
Toro, battle of, 47, 52
Torres, Affonso de, 73–4
Tournai, 58
Towerson, William, 148–50, 151–5, 157, 159
Trastamara, House of, 2
Travache, Eustache, 190

Upper Guinea, *passim*; contract of, 73–5; trade of, 86, 87, 89, 90–1, 93; Souzos over-run, 139; Portuguese settlements in, 141; *see also* "Guinea of Cape Verde"
Usodimare, Antoniotto, 17

Valera, Carlos de, 46, 50–1
Valladolid, 20, 46, 55
Valois, House of, 133
Vander Linden, Prof. H., 70
Vaz, Dr. Gaspar, 108, 110, 111, 113, 114, 115, 117, 118
—, João, 132
—, Simão, 82
Velho, Gonçalo, 5
Venice, galleys of, 60; Guinea chart drawn by native of, 65; government of, 70; ambassadors of, 118, 133, 135, 143, 146; doge of, 143, 146
Verrazano, Giovanni da, 107
Village of Two Parts, 59, 80, 99
Villaut, Nicolas, 2, 90
Villegagnon, Nicolas Durand de, 165, 166

Wallet, John, 182
War of Succession between Castile and Portugal, 24, 28, 43–52, 57
Ward, Richard, 71
Wax, 17, 36, 79, 91, 121, 184, 191
West Indies, slaves for, 87, 88, 96, 134, 189; Spanish empire in, 105; privateers in, 131, 166, 167, 170–2, 190; trade in, 159
Williamson, Dr. J. A., 109, 168, 171
Winter, William, 163, 169, 171–2, 175, 188
Wyndham, Thomas, 14, 146, 184; visit to Benin of, 140–1, 143–5,151

Zúñiga, Ortiz de, 20, 23; *Annales de Sevilha* of, 42

For Product Safety Concerns and Information please contact our EU representative GPSR@taylorandfrancis.com
Taylor & Francis Verlag GmbH, Kaufingerstraße 24, 80331 München, Germany

www.ingramcontent.com/pod-product-compliance
Lightning Source LLC
Chambersburg PA
CBHW061436300426
44114CB00014B/1714